Globalization and Families

Bahira Sherif Trask

Globalization and Families

Accelerated Systemic Social Change

 Springer

Bahira Sherif Trask
Department of Human Development and Family Studies
University of Delaware
Newark, DE
USA
bstrask@udel.edu

ISBN 978-0-387-88284-0   e-ISBN 978-0-387-88285-7
DOI 10.1007/978-0-387-88285-7
Springer New York Dordrecht Heidelberg London

Library of Congress Control Number: 2009939432

Springer is part of Springer Science+Business Media (www.springer.com)

Preface

This work is the outgrowth of my realization that globalization and families are interrelated in a manner that has not been adequately explored in conventional approaches. Most analyses of globalization focus on its economic nature and the implications of this process for markets and nation-states. Other aspects of globalization have been virtually ignored, except for some contentious and significant, yet often marginalized debates about the relationships between globalization, poverty, and inequality. Nevertheless, there are substantial, complex social aspects associated with globalization. Economic conditions and the actions of nation-states have direct impacts on family lives. Conversely, the decisions that are arrived at in families ultimately contribute to the success or failure of economic agendas and nation-state programs and policies. The relationship between globalization and families, however, is even more profound and complex than economic or political perspectives reveal. Globalization is the critical driving force that is fundamentally restructuring the social order around the world, and families are the center of this change. In every society, traditional notions about family life, work, identity, and the relationships of individuals and groups to one another are being transformed due to globalizing forces. It is this critically important and little understood social dynamic that is the focus of this book.

In order to explore the nature of contemporary social change, globalization needs to be examined by highlighting the complex dynamic relationship between families, economies, nation-states, and transnational institutions. Globalization has been accompanied by unprecedented rapid transformation at every level of social life. As the flow of capital, goods, people, and ideas continues to accelerate, these processes have altered fundamental concepts about family forms, roles and relationships, gender norms, and identity formation. A focus on globalizing processes reveals that the restructuring of economies and the changing role of nation-states, the mass migration of individuals from developing countries to the industrialized world, and the widespread entrance of women into the formal and informal labor force are interrelated with significant changes for families around the globe.

Globalization is associated with the spread of specific ideologies that are realized and negotiated in the intimate sphere of the family. Families are integrated into the global economy through formal and informal work, through production and consumption, and through their relationship with nation-states. Moreover, constantly evolving communication and information technologies allow families and individuals to have access to others in an unprecedented manner. These relationships are accompanied by new conceptualizations of appropriate lifestyles, identities, and ideologies even among those who may never be able to access them. In the West we are witnessing an increasing emphasis on individualism, a democratization of family life, the decreasing authority of men, the growing acceptance of alternative lifestyles such as cohabitation, divorce, and same-sex couples, and more varied life course trajectories. These depictions of family life have also spread to the developing world. However, due to a complex set of interrelated factors, the acceptance of varied family forms has not taken hold in the same manner. Instead, developing countries have been faced with their own unique challenges with respect to family life. In particular, economic concerns such as labor force participation, rising inequalities within and between countries, and fears about 'Westernization' have elicited, in some cases, nationalistic responses. Globalization is closely related to all of these social phenomena.

Globalization is a complex phenomenon: one the one hand, it has brought about a restructuring of economies that has opened up different venues for work and social relationships. However, on the other hand, a vital aspect of globalization centers around the proliferation and spread of new images and ideologies to the farthest reaches of the world. Moreover, globalization occurs on multiple levels simultaneously. It is realized on local, national, and transnational levels, and is accompanied by a compression of time. As information spreads ever more quickly, the impact of globalization can be felt immediately. When a crisis occurs in one area, it can have immediate repercussions in other places. This realization has been brought home by recent economic developments. As markets react to an economic downturn in one country, there are immediate aftershocks felt in multiple other areas around the globe. Families are not immune from these processes. In fact, it is within families that all of these forces come to bear. As we move into an increasingly interconnected, accelerating, globalized world, it is imperative to understand the dynamic nature of globalization by examining the transformations of the social order and how these changes are related to the linkages between globalization and families.

This study is the outgrowth of my own scholarly trajectory in cultural anthropology, political science, and family studies. Through immersion in these different disciplines, I have come to realize the importance of examining different phenomena from macro- and micro-level approaches, and to recognize the limitations of disciplinary orientations. I have also become aware that, in order to truly understand social phenomena, we need to take a multi-pronged approach that takes into consideration cultural, political, and economic factors. It is only through greater holistic perspectives that we can arrive at a more comprehensive understanding of the processes and impacts of globalization.

My immersion in this research on the linkages between globalization and families has led me to understand that we are in the midst of a change that is more profound than is realized by more casual observers of these processes. We are experiencing a fundamental global restructuring of social life, unlike anything that we have witnessed since the Industrial Revolution in the West. One of the fascinating and dissimilar aspects of this process, however, is that unlike the Industrial Revolution, this transformation is global and is rapidly affecting every part of the world, albeit differentially. Problematic for most analyses, however, is the fact that this transformation is highly complex and nuanced. No single approach and no topic area in isolation can capture the enormity of the change. Thus, what is required is an holistic examination of multiple spheres and their points of intersection. This book approaches this complicated issue by focusing on families as the arena where macro- and micro-forces come together. An investigation of the linkages between families and globalization allows us to understand how individuals and broader social forces intersect, and to gain greater insight into the fluidity and rapid social change that are an inherent feature of globalization.

In order to delve into the significance of global forces in the lives of families the world over, a progression of topics are examined systematically in this analysis. As a foundation, and in order to familiarize the reader with the significant arguments in various social science disciplines, multiple perspectives and controversies around globalization and the current state of knowledge about families are initially considered. This overview reveals that, despite a prolific literature on each subject, neither globalization nor the state of families are clearly understood and actually suffer from many of the same conceptual problems. Both globalization and families are each distinctly politicized phenomena that lack definitional clarity and incite contentious discourse despite a dearth of empirical data to support many of such claims. Moreover, they are ephemeral phenomena changing constantly depending on context and time, thus provoking debate about their makeup and processes. Compounding this complexity is that, while most analyses purport to be interdisciplinary, they usually draw just from one primary disciplinary orientation, and focus on Western perspectives. These inherent biases skew analyses and conclusions, and distort most attempts at universal generalizations. They also thwart the creation of policies that could potentially harness some of the forces of globalization for the well-being of families and societies.

The discussion then turns to the multifaceted subject of globalization and gender. A critical but marginalized perspective suggests that every aspect of globalization is distinctly gendered. This standpoint highlights the fact that globalization does not just impact gender discourses and relationships, but the phenomenon itself is affected by gendered responses and challenges. Specifically, the relationship between gender and economics emphasizes that globalization has had unequal effects on men and women, particularly in the developing world. With the major restructuring of economies beginning in the late 1960s, and the growth of multinational corporations, certain parts of the labor market have become 'feminized' as women increasingly take on part-time, low-paid, and, at times, risky jobs. Moreover, in industrialized and developing countries, women struggle to balance participation in the formal and informal workforce with caregiving in their families. In the industrialized world, middle and upper class women are coping with this dilemma by increasingly employing women from developing countries to assist with child and elder care responsibilities. In the developing world, many of these tasks are being relegated to extended family, husbands, siblings, and poorer women who are willing to perform this labor for minimal wages. Complicating this issue is that this form of work, also referred to as reproductive labor, is often unacknowledged in mainstream discussions. A gendered analysis of globalization reveals that this phenomenon has implications for the construction of femininities and masculinities on a global level, and that the process of globalization itself is a gendered one.

The focus of the book then shifts to some of the tangible linkages between globalization and families, and examines the changing nature of global migration. As our world becomes increasingly interconnected, migration from the developing to the industrialized world is playing an increasingly important role. While the United States, Canada, Australia, and Israel have always been 'immigration' societies, contemporary receiving countries such as Japan, and certain countries in Europe and the Middle East, are struggling with incorporating large numbers of noncitizens into their societies. In part, as a reaction to the magnitude of the migration, governments have responded by tightening laws and services to immigrants. Even in countries with a long history of immigration, such as the US, the rapid increase of immigrants has been met with resistance. Consequentially, immigrants are increasingly marginalized and, especially, low-skilled immigrants have been excluded from the mainstream. This movement and marginalization has led to new forms of transnational families, as migrants retain ties in their home societies, while also forging new relationships abroad. Of significance in this trend is the gendered nature of contemporary migration patterns. Increasingly, women from the developing world are leaving their families and communities behind, as they seek new opportunities in other regions of their own societies or in other countries, sometimes very distant from their homes.

From an overview of the importance of contemporary migration, the discussion moves to the changing nature of the relationship between the work and family spheres. While there is a burgeoning scholarship on work and family, this topic is dominated specifically by a US perspective on the issues faced by middle-class, white families. This approach emphasizes dual-earner couples, unequal gender roles in marriage, occupational stress, and work–family spillover. However, work/family issues are much more complex than many of these perspectives indicate. Care labor, ideologies about family roles and responsibilities, and the restructuring of work and businesses are all intertwined with family economies and ideologies. For example, among some of the poorest families in developing countries, children perform the majority of caregiving and economic assistance in their families. However, this significant aspect of the work/family interface is usually not acknowledged in mainstream discourse. Economic concerns, coupled with the issue of care, highlight the importance of expanding policies that allow families in industrialized and developing countries to balance their work/family responsibilities.

While mainstream approaches acknowledge the global spread of ideologies pertaining to women's empowerment, recognition of the worldwide expansion of conceptualizations of children, childhood, and children's rights has been more limited. As globalization leads to increasing interconnectedness, images and ideologies pertaining to children are spreading around the world. Most of these depictions stem from a Western perspective about 'what' children need in order to 'develop' in a healthy manner. This point of view, however, does not account for children's extremely varied living conditions. Not all children are able to attend school for a set number of years and to grow up in conditions that encourage play and a responsibility-free childhood. Instead, for millions of children, poverty plays a pivotal role in their lives, forcing them, under certain conditions, to become primary breadwinners in their families. These same economic conditions also dispute popular assumptions that children the world over are being transformed into a homogenous group of consumers, increasingly assuming the same tastes and fads as communication and information technologies proliferate. In fact, growing inequalities between children within and between societies translate into varying amounts of risk for them. Also problematic is the un-gendered nature of conventional approaches to children and childhood. Depending on location, the concerns and challenges that girls face may be quite dissimilar from those of boys. For example, in certain cultural contexts, it is primarily girls who are pulled out of school to care for other family members, thereby limiting their future opportunities. This raises complex questions about the universal utility of laws pertaining to children's rights and the applicability of the Convention on the Rights of the Child in an undiscriminating manner.

Globalization is also closely interconnected with aging and the elderly. While there is general acknowledgment in the West that the aging of the population portends difficulties for societies in the near future, there is less recognition that, within a relatively short time frame, the largest number of elderly individuals will actually reside in the developing world. Currently, most of these societies do not have programs and policies in place for the elderly, due to cultural norms that usually relegated care to females in families. However, as women are increasingly incorporated into the labor force, the elder care that they performed in the invisible sphere of the family is becoming a growing and, at times, impossible burden on them, their families, and their societies. Simultaneously, this transformation is occurring as many states are cutting provisions in services to families. The arena of aging and the elderly provides, however, also a sphere where globalization can be deployed in a positive manner. For example, by raising awareness of the impending issues surrounding the aging of the global population, the inequalities within and between societies with respect to the elderly, the increasing multicultural nature of an older cohort, and the demands of care work, globalizing forces can be used to mobilize and disseminate solutions for these issues.

Concern over family-related issues such as gender roles and work, the socialization and care of children, and the well-being of the elderly also entails an examination of the contemporary role of nation-states. Today's nation-states need to be understood as engaged in a global framework that is in a consistently dynamic relationship with its inhabitants, as well as with transnational institutions. Globalization is raising questions about basic issues such as the role of territory and the rights of citizens versus non-citizens. Increased migration coupled with accelerated information and communication technologies is bringing individuals from very varied locales and cultures into contact together. New communities and identities are created that are often divorced from territorial belonging. Contemporary nation-states are also part of a new social fabric that places them in direct purview of transnational institutions that attempt to regulate a range of issues from economic activities to environmental concerns. While these concerns are primarily realized on a local level, nation-states function as an intermediary between the global arena and the local sphere. From this perspective, nation-states are not losing their functionality, but through globalization, are reformulating their activities. This reformulation has direct impacts on families and individuals, with respect to policies and the provision of services.

Nation-states and transnational institutions are also closely tied to the conditions that are leading to increased inequalities within and between societies. While the relationship between poverty and globalization is a contentious issue, few dispute that, under current conditions, some individuals, groups, and countries have become wealthier, and others are increasingly poorer. Even though it is unclear which specific factors contribute to conditions of progress through globalization, and which contribute to decline, it is generally acknowledged that globalization is an uneven process that interacts with local conditions. All of these transformations have repercussions for families as they navigate economic and social fluctuations.

Global transformations have significant implications not just for the material side of life, but they are intertwined with ideologies about the rights and roles of individuals. These shifting conceptualizations are accompanied with profound implications for families. As families are increasingly integrated into the global economy, and simultaneously exposed to new and varied representations of lifestyles and choices, they are forced to adjust to changed conditions and representations. This process, however, is not occurring in a uniform manner. Within various societies, and in a number of regions of the world, new images and ways of life have been met with opposition, resistance, and the growth of fundamentalist and nationalistic sentiments. Thus, what we find is that globalization is a highly uneven process. Globalization may be a transnational economic, political, and social process, but it is primarily realized in local contexts.

As material foundations of life, concepts of space and time, and identities are increasingly redefined and transformed, globalizing forces are reaching into the very core of contemporary social life. In this new world, individuals are able to adopt multiple identities, form new sorts of families, and claim membership in a variety of communities, many of them not bound by place or region. As identities are increasingly in flux, new affiliations, and ethnicities are created and sustained through ties with other places and people across far away spaces. This has given rise to new unimagined types of issues and problems. We are faced with new forms of inclusion and exclusion, with increasing economic inequalities and shrinking conceptions of boundaries and space. Proliferating communication and information technologies allow for instantaneous communication and transmission. In our time, our lives have become more fluid, our beliefs and concepts, once believed to be natural and immutable, are in greater states of flux. With this transformation have come challenges, in every culture, to assumptions about family life, the life course, and the role of the individual. There exists greater variability with respect to images of children, youth, adulthood, aging, marriage, gender roles, and power relationships in families, in communities, in societies, and between nation-states.

These transformations portend a deep-rooted restructuring of the social fabric of our world, our societies and our families.

This book is not meant as a treatise on either the benefits or challenges of globalization, nor does it take a stance on the role of families in society. Instead, I would like to initiate a dialogue about the transformative processes of which all of us are a part today. This includes the naturalness of so much that we take for granted with respect to gender, to intergenerational and familial relationships, and our relationships to others, both whom we know, but also our fellow world citizens whom we do not know. I would like for us to think about the future and to see if we can build a better and more just world; one that harnesses some of the forces of globalization for the benefit of mankind, instead of perpetuating and ignoring gross inequalities and the despair of so many. There are many topics that are touched upon in this book, but there are also many others that are open to investigation and discourse.

Newark, DE   Bahira Sherif Trask

Acknowledgements

I would like to thank a number of individuals who played a pivotal role in ensuring that this work came to fruition. First and foremost, I would like to express my gratitude to my editor at Springer, Teresa Krauss for encouraging me to develop this project. In the fall of 2005, I brought together my colleagues Raeann Hamon, Mark Hutter, and Seongeun Kim to address issues around globalization and families at a symposium at NCFR (the National Council on Family Relations). That initial dialogue led to my formulating some of the basic concepts that are explored in this book. Teresa Krauss had the foresight to understand the significance of this topic and encouraged me to develop the book proposal and manuscript, which she cheerfully shepherded through reviews, revisions, and publication. Her assistant Katie Chabalko was also consistently helpful, providing me with the technical competence that is needed with an ambitious venture such as this.

Several of my colleagues also played a significant role in the development of this book – specifically for their intellectual input and encouragement along the way. Foremost, Michael Ferrari understood the importance of this work and was consistently available for discussion, analyses, and support. He recognized the complexity of the project and some of the intellectual challenges I faced as I delved into, for me, some previously unexplored scholarly arenas such as feminist economics and the contentious, complex debates on poverty and inequality. Donald Unger offered kind and encouraging words throughout the process, Michael Gamel-McCormick provided intellectual and material support, and Rob Palkovitz has always been available to me for patient and thoughtful counsel. Ruben Viramontez Anguiano's enthusiasm for this project inspired me to pursue this topic from new perspectives. He read various segments of the book and provided useful observations. Mark Miller, who luckily for me, is at the University of Delaware, was consistently accessible for clearing up some ambiguities in the scholarship on migration. My colleagues Monika Shafi and Margaret Wilder also understood the amount of work, patience and fortitude that it takes to complete a work such as this, and encouraged me throughout the process. Moreover, I would like to thank Nancy Gonzales for reading a draft of this manuscript and providing me with some very useful editorial suggestions. She is truly a resource and friend.

Many of the ideas that I explore in this book stem from interactions I have had with several key scholars over the years. In particular, as a young undergraduate at Yale,

Robert Dahl and David Apter played an important role in shaping my future academic orientation. They introduced me to the importance of understanding the role of the state in individual's lives, and the complexity of analyzing the interaction between macro and micro level politics from an international perspective. Later on in my doctoral studies, Sandra Barnes and Peggy Sanday, at the University of Pennsylvania, mentored me in my cross-cultural research on family and gender issues. It was at that point that I began to realize that the social sciences needed to take a more holistic, interdisciplinary approach to the analyses of social phenomena.

Also pivotal to the development of many of the concepts explored throughout this work, are discussions I have had with my graduate students in various seminars that I teach. In particular, in the course of the last several years, Laura Thompson Brady, Julie Koivunen, Ilka Riddle, Tara Woolfolk, Melina McConatha Rosle, Bethany Willis Hepp, Wei Qui, and Dorit Radnai-Griffin have consistently challenged me to refine my observations. I thank them for their friendship and support!

Much appreciation and thanks also go to my parents and my brother. They understood the significance of bringing together the dialogues on globalization and families, and constantly engaged me in conversations on this topic. In particular, my father, who is a scientist, recognized the potential contribution of this work to the greater academic world. He, thus, consistently challenged me to make my ideas and concepts clearer and more concise, in order to increase their accessibility to a broader audience.

My greatest gratitude goes to my husband Richard. He understood how important this project was to me, and he truly facilitated complicated personal circumstances in order to provide me the necessary space to complete this work. He encouraged me, took an interest in each of the topics that was preoccupying me at various times, and took care of some of our family tasks in order that I would have the time to write. I would like for him to know how truly appreciative I am!

Lastly, I would like to thank my beautiful children, Ian and Julia. They are too young to understand the demands of a book – but they dealt with the circumstances with good humor, expressing great excitement for when I was able to be with them. Ian and Julia are the ones who will truly grow up in a new and different globalized world. They will never completely realize how varied their life experiences are from those, which we who are just a couple of generations older, experienced. This book is dedicated to them and the other children of this world. May globalization provide them with the tools to finally create a world of greater equality, social justice, and peace.

Contents

Part I
Theoretical Perspectives and Paradigms

Chapter 1
Globalization as a Dynamic Force in Contemporary Societies

> What difference it would make to our understanding if we
> looked at the world as a whole, a totality, a system, instead of
> as a sum of self-contained societies and cultures; if we under-
> stood better how this totality developed over time; if we took
> seriously the admonition to think of human aggregates as
> 'inextricably involved with other aggregates, near and far, in
> weblike, netlike, connections.'
>
> Eric Wolf (1982). Europe and the people without history.
> Berkeley: University of California Press.

Globalization is bringing about profound changes. The farthest reaches of the world
are becoming accessible, in ways that most of us were unable to imagine even just
20 years ago. Accelerating advances in communication and information technologies are changing the ways in which we connect, access information, and interact
with each other. For some, these changes have opened up new venues and opportunities: distant places are increasingly accessible, new relationships can be forged, and
work and learning can occur from any location that has an Internet connection. For
others, these same changes have been associated with loss: the loss of traditions, or
jobs, or significant relationships. But whatever form these changes take, few realize
the magnitude, intensity, and long-term implications of these transformations.
Fundamental widespread beliefs and naturalized relationships are being questioned,
negotiated, and, at times, dissolved. These changes are not just restricted to the West
or the industrialized world. Instead, extreme transformation is rapidly becoming a
global experience. While societies, communities, families, and individuals in all
regions of the world, live under a multitude of conditions, they are not immune to
the increasingly accelerated, profound, deeply rooted changes that we are witnessing. These changes, however, are not distributed equally between or within societies.
Instead, in some areas we are witnessing extremely rapid societal transformation,
and in other places only certain groups or regions are affected.

Even though globalization is a hotly contested phenomenon, there is some agreement
that globalization entails a new form of bridging geographic and cultural distances,
and that these developments are the product of constantly evolving transportation,
communication and information technologies. From mid-1990 onward, there has been

B.S. Trask, *Globalization and Families: Accelerated Systemic Social Change,*
DOI 10.1007/978-0-387-88285-7_1, © Springer Science+Business Media, LLC 2010

an increased awareness on the part of economists and political scientists on the impact of globalization.[1] Of particular interest has been the movement of capital, the changing role of the nation-state, the increased transnational migration of individuals, and the growth and expansion of multinational corporations and transnational organizations. Despite the fact that individuals and families are affected by these phenomena, there has been remarkably little attention focused on the social side of globalization. This omission has occurred, in spite of a general realization that in a global context the meaning of the very categories that are a part of globalization have been altered: the nation-state, economies, communities, social class, gender, ethnicity, and families (Baars et al. 2006). Thus, it is remarkable that we do not have more extensive dialogue and critical analyses that examine the transformative nature of these processes from more societal and local levels. In particular, the implications and effects of globalization on families is a striking oversight.

Currently, the analyses of globalization continue to focus almost exclusively on the political and economic arenas. In fact, for many, globalization primarily describes basic changes in the world economy – the growing mobility of international capital and labor, and changes in production brought on through economic restructuring, coupled with advances in communications and information technologies. These transformations are understood to have brought economies together, and have led to the realization that we are becoming an increasingly interdependent global economy. Mainstream approaches to globalization do not delve into the effects of this phenomenon on cultures, on societies, on families, and on individuals. Globalization is perceived as an autonomous force, removed from social interactions. Critics of this approach, however, point out that globalization itself is a construction of a particular version of global space and interaction, and that incorporating individuals, families, communities and societies, with understandings of national and transnational economies and politics, gives us greater insight into the dynamics and effects of the phenomenon. In other words, globalization is not just an economic, political or social force. Instead, globalization is socially constructed; a dynamic phenomenon that is itself constantly under transformation, in part through human activity. This perspective allows us to understand globalization as multifaceted, and not just as an inevitable material process (Nagar et al. 2002).

Globalization debates have remained distinctly separate from discourses on families and family change. This is remarkable, given that individuals and families are directly, and indirectly, affected by globalizing processes all over the world. While family arrangements vary, depending on place and time, some form of bonded intimate human relationships characterizes all societies.[2] As we increasingly become integrated into new complex systems, individuals and their relationships, necessarily, are implicated in the process.[3] An individual's ideational and

---

[1] See, for example, Rodrik (1997), Prakash and Hart (2000), Guillen (2001), Stiglitz (2002), Glatzer and Rueschemeyer (2005) and Dehesa (2007).

[2] In the following chapter, the debate on family definitions is reviewed.

[3] Individuals are bound to each other either through emotional, legal or kinship ties. In the West, as in many other parts of the world, we characterize these relationships as family.

material worlds are transformed, strengthened or even lost.[4] Globalization is accompanied by new transnational concepts about productivity, gender, work, nationalism, identity, familial relationships, and women's and children's rights. In some cases, individuals are empowered to change their lives, and in other cases, they are forced into situations that are disadvantageous and destructive.

Nowhere are social transformations more evident, than in the rapid changes that characterize contemporary Western families. Over the last several decades, new types of publicly accepted relationships and living arrangements have become increasingly prevalent. For example, most industrialized countries have witnessed a rapid rise in cohabitation, divorce rates, single-parent households, same-sex partnerships and new forms of extended families that include kin and nonkin. Concurrently, a growing number of women are now in the paid labor force, affecting issues as diverse as child bearing, elder care, relationship formation and the desirability of marriage. The result of some of these trends is also that fertility rates are falling to below population replacement levels, particularly in Europe and Japan.

These social changes, however, are not confined just to the West as many presume. In fact, many societies in other parts of the world are also witnessing significant societal transformations. Divorce is on the rise in places as diverse as Korea, China, Jordan and Brazil. Meanwhile, the number of female-headed households is rapidly growing as women increasingly choose, or are forced, to raise children on their own due to personal choice, economic conditions, the consequence of wars, HIV/AIDS, and other tragedies. Around the world, women are working outside the home in increasingly greater numbers, while men in many places are losing their once taken-for-granted role as the primary or only breadwinner in the family. All of these changes are intimately connected to globalizing processes that are restructuring work and family life, while also introducing, at times, very new and radical ideas about social life.

Approaches to globalization, which focus exclusively on economic and political dimensions, do not capture the dynamism or the human consequences that are an inherent feature of this phenomenon. Conversely, mainstream perspectives and analyses of families have not incorporated globalization into their discourse.[5] This has led to an incomplete understanding of these profound influences on individual and family life. What we find is a situation where both our insights into globalization, and families, are impoverished and deficient through this omission.

Linking globalization with the family dimension opens up new avenues of understanding interpersonal relationships, household economies, gender concerns, societal changes and relations between groups. It leads to greater insight into the dynamics of inequalities, of power relations, and of the importance of scale and locale. Relating globalization and families, however, is not equivalent to studying "global families." Instead, integrating globalization and families highlights the complex and dynamic relationships between economics, the nation-state, transnational

---

[4] See Parkin and Stone (2004) for the anthropological perspective on kinship and family discussions.

[5] As of the writing of this book, one article on this topic (Edgar 2004) had been published.

institutions, the flow of information, and new conceptualizations of self, identity, family, territory, and space. Examining these linkages requires a holistic analysis that illustrates how processes at one level or in one society or group, can have, at times, unexpected and unintended consequences on other aspects of the human experience.

1.1   The Debates on Globalization

Globalization evokes vehement disagreement on virtually every level of analysis. Mainstream as well as academic approaches to globalization do not agree on its definition, on its processes, effects, or even on its historical origins. An inherent problem with many of these debates and discussions is that they are presented as sweeping generalizations and in sound bites. Globalization is described as dangerous, as beneficial, or, as too complex to be useful as an analytical tool. Many of these arguments are not based on empirical evidence, and often selectively utilize specific data or phenomena as "proof." For example, dominant discourses on globalization that focus on its economic nature are primarily disengaged from local circumstances, from socio-historical moments and from cultural contexts. Grew (2005) suggests that "by positing common influences and pressures across countries, it invites comparison and stimulates generalization" (p. 853). He points out that certain assumptions about globalization are themselves the product of the process. An examination of the arguments around the allegedly homogenizing effects of globalization, or its influence on purportedly undermining family relationships, reveals dissimilar conversations where participants are using the same language, albeit with very different meanings. These difficulties are further exacerbated by detractors who argue that globalization is an overused term with little meaning or utility and, thus, should be discarded.

The intensity and magnitude of deliberation around globalization, itself, indicates its significance. There may not be any agreement on what globalization is, or how to define it, but the sheer volume of mainstream and scholarly discourse, books, articles, conferences and projects that concern themselves with this phenomenon negates those critics who write globalization off as just another product of academic debates.[6] The immense dispute surrounding this term implies that globalization is a formidable force that needs to be investigated and understood. Scholte (2000) argues that the: "current knowledge of globalization may be largely confused and contradictory, but that is no reason to abandon the topic as a vacuous buzzword. On the contrary, when key issues of security, justice and democracy are so prominently in play, social responsibility demands that researchers give globalization serious attention." (p. 40). It is only through further discourse and multilevel investigation, that globalization and its impacts can be more thoroughly understood.

---

[6]The world catalogue currently lists over 61,000 publications dealing with various aspects of globalization.

1.2 Definition

To many, globalization has become both a catchphrase and an overused, misunderstood term that refers to the political and economic implications of an increasingly inter-connected world. The term globalization is relatively new, and did not enter common usage vocabulary until the mid-1980s. Before that, global processes were referred to primarily as international relations rather than global relations (Mittleman, 2002).[7] The usage of this new term, itself, suggests an emergent realization that globalization is not just another form of modernization and internationalization; instead, globalization is associated with other aspects of material, social, and ideational life (Guillen 2001).

Social scientists, particularly in economics and political science have expended a great deal of energy arguing about the exact meaning and usage of this term.[8] In general terms, globalization can be categorized as having five somewhat differentiated meanings: internationalization, liberalization, universalization, westernization, and deterritorialization (Scholte 2000).[9] The most popular usage of globalization is to describe a form of internationalization. Basically, this definition refers to an increase in the flow between international trade and capital exchanges and their corresponding interdependence. This growing interdependence is thought to negate the importance of national economies and, instead, to create a larger economic entity characterized by processes and transactions across borders.

Closely related is the concept of globalization as liberalization. From this perspective, globalization removes restrictions on movements between countries, creating an "open," "borderless" world economy (Scholte 2000). This argument is particularly popular with those analysts who advocate the removal of regulatory trade barriers.

Globalization is sometimes also used as a synonym for universalization. This usage equates the concept of globalization with a worldwide distribution of ideals, values, and material culture. For example, the spread of Internet and communication media such as television and radio and the images and messages that they convey, are understood by some as a form of globalization.

From a somewhat different perspective, globalization has also been associated with Westernization or even a type of "Americanization." Sometimes, this is even referred to as the "McDonaldization" of the world – this perspective suggests that as Western concepts such as democracy, individualism or rationalism are spreading around the world, they destroy in their wake traditional values and collectivist ways of life.

In the last several years, globalization has also become equated with deterritorialization. From this perspective, globalization refers to a reconfiguration of social

---

[7] Interestingly, globalization has entered into the vocabulary of other languages also.

[8] The varying meanings accorded to globalization have been concisely discussed by J. Scholte in *Globalization. A critical introduction* (2000).

[9] There is a great deal of controversy about which of these depictions of globalization accurately delineate the term

spaces, whereby geography becomes less important and social relations become ever more closely linked with locales, both close and far away. According to this perspective, knowledge transcends boundaries and links individuals to one another, even across physically distant lands. This can be understood as "*trans*border exchanges *without* distance" (Scholte 2000, p. 49). Such exchanges and relations are becoming more significant as communication and production increasingly occur without regard to geographic constraints, as transborder organizations of many kinds proliferate, and an increasing number of individuals become aware of the holistic nature of global relations. Deterritorialization is understood as adding complexity to all levels of social relationships. Anthony Giddens, one of the major proponents of this viewpoint, has famously stated that "the emergence of global-ized orders means that the world we live 'in' is different from that of previous ages" (1991, p. 225).

1.3   Globalization and Causation

Besides definitional confusion, we are also faced with a related complex chrono-logical issue: is globalization a new development or basically an old phenomenon? There are those scholars (see for example, Scholte 2000; Dehesa 2007) who argue that globalization has characterized world history: there has always been a move-ment of ideas and individuals from one society or one geographical location to another with corresponding impacts. Others claim that globalization can be traced back to colonization and the spread of Western civilization to remote parts of the globe, beginning approximately 500 years ago. And there are those that argue that globalization really began with the introduction of airplanes and computers (Drucker 1993). From this perspective, we are in a constantly changing, global-izing world, and there is fundamentally nothing new about the processes that are taking place.

Chronological arguments are obscured by definitional problems, as well as disagreements on causation. Most commonly, explanations of globalization begin with technological innovation as the foundation and driving force behind this phe-nomenon. Other arguments suggest that changes and transformations in economic regulatory frameworks have facilitated and strengthened globalization. Capitalism, cultural politics and changing knowledge structures have also been cited as potential sources of globalization. However, limiting our understanding of the ori-gins, spread, and intensity of globalization to single-factor explanations is too simplistic, given the complexity of the phenomenon. By reducing globalization to a one-dimensional concept or variable, its impacts are shortchanged, while the enormity of the phenomenon is diminished. Moreover, globalization itself is sub-ject to rapid transformation due to its accelerated nature. Thus, the phenomenon that we are trying to capture today may actually have looked somewhat different 5 years ago and will exhibit new and potentially unexpected characteristics in just a short while from now.[10] There are complex interconnections at work of which we only see some of the surface. It is this acceleration of linkages between time, space and consequences that makes globalization a unique phenomenon, different from occurrences in previous periods of time.

Embedded in approaches to causation and globalization, is the question of social structure and agency. To what extent do social phenomena come about as a result of existing structures such as capitalism or patriarchy, and what is the role of individual actors who, through their constant interactions with social systems, transform them and are in turn affected by them? The arguments in this book are based on the dynamic perspective that the interaction of individual agency (albeit, limited at times), with ideational, cultural, and material frameworks, produces social relations and social phenomena. These frameworks provide choices for individual actors to choose from and to modify, at times with free will, and at times based on constraints. Concurrently, material, cultural and ideational frameworks and structures depend on *individuals*, on people, for their creation, continuation, and transformation (Scholte 2000). From this perspective, the social order can be intrinsically transformed during times of flux or change. As individuals are caught in conflicting or opposing forces, be they ideational or material, they react. Their reactions, in turn, result in either incremental or transformative change to the forces themselves. This argument lends credence to the observation that globalization has occurred under a specific set of circumstances that allowed for its fruition, and that it is closely linked to social change. It also provides a rationale for examining the role of families and individuals in this process. This line of thought will be pursued later on, specifically with reference to the widespread changes in the roles played by women, men, children, and the elderly, which have become an important part of globalization.

Grew (2005) gives us a useful distinction by delineating globalization from global history. He suggests that globalization "indicates a process of change and places it in time" (2005, p. 849). Thus, the definition of globalization is dependent on the specific temporal period, the social circumstances, and the cultural context with which it is associated. He also points out that much of the preoccupation with globalization concentrates, as was noted before, on economics. But globalization is actually a force concerned with future developments rather than current circumstances. He advocates that other factors such as ideology, technology, economics, culture, and political circumstances also be taken into account in analyses of globalization, which help us to conceptualize the fact that these phenomena do not necessarily work towards a common end or result in the same form of all-around change. Instead, from this perspective, an intrinsic feature of globalization is its unequal impacts on individuals, on families, on regions, on nation-states, on economies, and even on transnational processes.

---

[10] An interesting example is the current popularity of social networking sites that link individuals across the globe. These networks are now being harnessed into certain social movements – a phenomenon in this form was unimaginable even just 2 or 3 years ago.

At a fundamental level, the globalization debate can be simplified to basically representing two opposing viewpoints. There are the "optimists" who enthuse that globalization, defined through the lens of information dissemination, is bringing individuals closer together, promoting social integration, introducing democracy to nondemocratic places, and taking our world on a path to greater global stability. On the other side of the spectrum are the "detractors" or critics, who disseminate dire warnings about the dangers of globalization and its inherent inequities and abuses, which they see as being promoted through multinational corporations and transnational institutions such as the International Monetary Fund (IMF). From their perspective, globalization undermines basic values such as security and equality, and democratic principles (Lieber and Weisberg 2002).[11] Underlying these disputes is again the fundamental conceptual problem that globalization often means different things to those who expound both its virtues and its shortcomings. Depending on their standpoint, some analysts may be basing their arguments by actually referring to the economic aspects of globalization, while others are basing their view points on an understanding of globalization that is related to the spread of ideational convictions or values.

Complicating these arguments, on both sides, are issues such as scale, social change, and historical developments (Scholte 2000). Basically, there coexist four areas of debate about the relationship between globalization and causation. There are those (the majority of analysts, in fact) who argue that the key to understanding globalization is found in examining the nature of economic activities. From this point of view, production has changed what is produced and how it is produced, and this is reflected in the visions, transportation, communication, data processing, behavior of companies, and the like (Grew 2005). These changes in production have led some to label the global economy as "an informational, knowledge-based, postindustrial or service economy" (Scholte, 2000, p. 20). An opposing opinion is that there is a certain continuity underlying globalizing forces. Manufacturing remains central to economic behavior, and in fact, continues to be the primary source for capitalism. From this perspective, what has changed is the manner in which surplus accumulation is occurring. Globalization has brought with it world division of labor, greater accumulation of wealth through consumerism and finance, and concentration of production in large corporations. However, capitalism has remained central to human pursuits.

A different, less vocal group argues that the basic changes wrought through globalization converge around issues of governance. From their perspective, the future of the nation-state is at stake. They argue that global relationships are undermining the role of the nation-state, while multinational corporations are gaining in strength and power. Again, there are those who oppose this hypothesis and suggest, instead, that globalization has strengthened some nation-states due to the fact that

---

[11] This is also the perspective that leads to the mass demonstrations every year against meetings of the G8 and the World Trade Organization.

states remain in the position to govern global economic activities and to control boundaries, and, that nation-states, thus, remain powerful (Rudra 2008).

A third arena of dispute centers on the relationship between cultures and globalization. The question under debate is if globalization entails a homogenization of cultures or does globalization allow for the continued existence of traditional local ways of life? Proponents of globalization as homogenization point out that we are moving to a unified world culture that centers around the English language, American pop culture, consumerism and mass media (Scholte, 200). They argue that globalization has homogenized individuals, communities and cultures, and that as a result, traditional ways of life are being abdicated. Meanwhile, opponents argue that while there is no arguing about the exportation of Western (often American) ideas, values, and products, this flow is often adapted to local niches (Ritzer 2003). From this perspective, global social forms and movements take different forms and make different impacts based on local interpretation. This adaptation is sometimes referred to as "glocalization" (Ritzer 2003). "Glocalization" occurs because individuals turn to local traditions and beliefs when exposed to new, different, or opposing values and beliefs. Instead of unification, what we are seeing is new social forms created through contact, blending, and hybridization.

Lastly, a small but vocal minority, represented most prominently by Anthony Giddens argues that globalization has moved us past modernity into an age of postmodernity (Giddens 1990). Giddens argues that modernity is inherently globalizing, and that the consequences of this process have taken us into a new world that we currently do not understand very well. He states, "In the modern era, the level of time-space distanciation is much higher than in any previous period, and the relations between local and distant social forms and events become correspondingly 'stretched.' Globalization refers essentially to that stretching process, as the modes of connection between different social contexts or regions become networked across the earth's surfaces as a whole." (p. 64).

1.4   What Is "New" About Globalization

An intrinsic question in the disputes on globalization concerns what is inherently new in this process. As we have seen, there are those who argue that globalization is just another phase of human exploration and movement, not unlike the first voyages around the world. However, there are those who disagree with this analysis. For example, Scholte, in agreement with Giddens, argues that what is "new" about globalization is that it is a "reconfiguration of social space" (2000, p. 46). For instance, Scholte argues that geography, i.e., the physical surroundings of a social group is directly related to its culture, economy, and politics.[12] This has certainly

---

[12] This ecological argument is found in a multitude of writings juxtaposing the Northern hemisphere with the Southern hemisphere, and arguing that the North is industrialized, while the South is "developing."

been the case historically. Until relatively recently, regional economies have been constrained by their territories and access to resources. Even today, the lives of Eskimos, nomadic Bedouins, hunter and gathering tribes, and other such groups are strongly influenced by the physical environment that they inhabit. Over the last several thousand years, much of contemporary civilization has been characterized by the ability of humans to modify their environments to such an extent as to separate themselves from complete dependency on environmental conditions.[13] Until quite recently, "home" for most people's has always been associated with a certain territory (even for groups such as the Bedouin, who roam in a larger and yet bounded terrain.) Geography or territory has exercised a profound influence on various aspects of people's lives: their sense of identity (I am from …/I am a …), their sense of nationalism and citizenship (I belong to this group, place/community/ country), and their ability to interact with others, both in terms of frequency and importance. Historically, individuals have interacted primarily with others who inhabit the same space they do, be it neighborhood, workplace, recreational facilities, community, and/or nation. Much of this interaction was also bounded by socio-economic, cultural and religious affiliations. Migration was associated with leaving most of these associations and relationships behind.

Globalization, however, has altered human being's relationship with the physical environment, and transformed social interactions between various inhabitants of the globe. These changes have profound implications for social institutions such as economies, nation-states, and families – and they are happening at an increasingly rapid pace. As Giddens (1990) points out, we are in a fundamentally different world where the trajectory for transformation is accelerating at unimagined speeds. This form of globalization can also be termed as a form of global connectivity (Kelly 2001).

This phenomenon of global connectivity can be described as encompassing three interrelated aspects. One aspect pertains to the mixing of social and spatial ties on a global scale. A second aspect points to shortened social and spatial distances beyond local areas. And a third aspect concerns the increase in social interaction among individuals. Each of these factors brings to the table a new aspect of globalization. For example, the intersection of social and spatial ties that span geographical boundaries, now occurs virtually instantaneously. It can also refer to individuals who migrate but retain strong ties to their home societies (Kelly 2001). These ties range from regular contact, to visitation, to remittances and cultural and political relationships.

Global connectivity has both material and cultural consequences. For example, currently, many of the processes that are associated with manufacturing are tied to multiple places: a country of origin, a country/or countries of production, and also destination countries. Global commodities that are produced in multiple places serve to create complex linkages between locations. For example, the shoes that

---

[13] One of the most dramatic modern day examples can be found in the United Arab Emirates where the world's largest man-made islands have been constructed on water (The Palm Dubai and The Palms) and desert conditions have even been modified to include an indoor skiing arena.

used to be made in the United States from the hide of cows that were raised in the Midwest, now may have various places of origin. The cows to be used for the leather may be raised in one country, the design of the shoes will be executed in another, and the actual production of the shoes can occur in a third country. All of this happens before these shoes are ever even marketed in the United States. Of course, production processes can be much more complicated than this – but this example illustrates that business and production have changed radically conjoining often vastly disparate locations.

Local cultures are also implicated in the process of global connectivity: responses can range from a retreat from foreign influences to an embracing of new and sometimes radically different ways of thinking, acting, and doing. This process is not unidirectional nor is it constant. Instead, it may speed up under certain conditions, slow down under others, and affect various individuals and groups differentially. More often than not, older theoretical social scientific models that attempt to predict the nature of change do not adequately capture the nature of this differential transformation. It is basically a moving target that adds a highly heterogeneous element to the distribution of values, images, practices and the like. Different places receive, process, and put into practice information in varying ways, depending on local conditions and sociohistorical context.

Viewing relations between individuals, entities, and nation-states from this interlinked perspective is not meant to imply that territory has become insignificant, on the contrary, it remains of great consequence in our world. However, territory, today, is imbued with a somewhat different meaning than it has had in the recent past. Territory, or physical location is still one of a number of identifiers for individuals. Conversely, nation-states still retain power to decide over various activities that are defined as falling within their purview, for example, issues of citizenship. In fact, as movement between regions has become more common, some nation-states have tightened their boundaries and the laws that are applicable to their citizens. A primary contemporary change is that territory and nation-state boundaries are much more porous today than they have been in the past. New information and communication technologies are allowing individuals to interact with one another across every manner of boundary. Territorial boundaries often do not retain any kind of real significance in these interactions. Thus, we find that new relationships are formed that are not based on territoriality, and other relationships are maintained and even strengthened despite territorial distances. Moreover, these interactions are occurring in an instantaneous multilevel global arena that includes monetary, material, environmental, ideational and social components. This implies that distance or boundaries do not necessarily present an impediment or constraint to relationships anymore.[14]

Today's world is characterized by a compression of experiences and interactions. Communication technologies allow for the dissemination of information virtually instantaneously to multiple locales. We see this with the broadcasting of

---

[14]Obviously this is not true for all individuals nor all relationships – however, it is present to a much greater extent than was imagined even just a couple of decades ago.

news, for example. As soon as a crisis occurs, words and images spread immediately around the globe, eliciting multiple responses depending on audience and region. Brands, media, celebrity status, and fads can be spread within seconds with complete disregard to boundaries. Individuals and phenomena can be instantaneously united. In our new world, space-time relations have been forever altered. Our way of viewing the earth, and how we relate to individuals around us, as well as those quite distant from us, is changing more rapidly than we can, at times, comprehend. Some of the change is material. For example, as was discussed above, virtually every consumer good today is the product of multiple places and processes. Furthermore, most individuals are inundated with images of catastrophes such as tsunamis, wars, and diseases from other parts of the world. The distant nature of many of these events is subsumed due to the speed with which the images are conveyed, making individuals often feel as if they are part of the disaster. This can result in a renewed empathy for fellow human beings who are being subjected to the ravages of the experience. At other times, the spread of imagery is used to create disturbing portraits of other individuals, groups, or regions, emphasizing ill feelings, hatred, and disgust.

The instantaneous, unbounded spread of information is also often associated with the dissemination of Western, often American values. As depictions of lifestyles, fads and consumer goods expand around the globe, so do questions about their effects on those who may be disadvantaged or who share very different life philosophies. Levitt (1991) suggests that the interconnection of global markets is creating an international homogenization of preference; that international marketing, the migration of large numbers of people and the influence of the Internet allow for people to be exposed to similar messages and consumer products. Companies respond to this global accessibility by coordinating business strategies, advertising in local languages and gaining brand recognition. While this may be the case for certain types of consumer goods, there is little evidence that we are truly moving towards a homogenous world. In fact, there is a great deal of speculation about how the movement of images and messages, specifically from the West are understood and internalized at local levels (Ritzer 2003). In many areas of the world, exposure to certain goods or messages does not necessarily entail their acceptance or their utility. While urban areas, for example, are much more susceptible to these forms of globalizing processes, rural areas still remain relatively immune to them. What we find is that globalization is characterized by a contradictory process that involves a growing concurrent propensity towards certain types of emergent global cultural uniformity, accompanied by increased cultural differentiation and fragmentation.

It may be instructive to examine an example of these processes in the contemporary context. In a recent study, Sun (2005) found that in the expanding city of Shanghai, the perceptions of an increasing number of well-to-do inhabitants of local communities are greatly influenced by globalization. As more upscale residents move into new residential areas, they employ a global framework with respect to what they desire in their physical environment and in the provisions of a range of services. These demands seem to be fueled primarily by exposure to foreign influences either through media, travel or encounters with foreigners. However, Sun (2005) suggests that while Shanghai has been strongly influenced by the global economy, Western norms have not made significant inroads into Chinese culture. The more affluent residents of Shanghai may make certain material demands on their environment, but their value system – with regard to their personal and familial relations – have remained intact. Building on the work of Appadurai (1990) Sun argues that what we are seeing are "complex, overlapping disjunctive orders" that "can no longer be understood in terms of existing center-periphery models" (2005, p. 186). Sun's work indicates that globalization is not eradicating cultural differences, but instead, is leading to more hybrid value orientations. Sun's study also illustrates that individuals' orientation and behaviors are "informed and formed by global socialization to differing degrees" (p. 190). While modernization theory, which was popular in certain circles particularly in the 1960s and into the 1970s, predicted social change to be linear, evolutionary, and internally driven, contemporary evidence disputes this notion. In particular, the modern/traditional dichotomy that still characterizes certain approaches, is increasingly an inaccurate analytical tool.

From another perspective, historical case studies illustrate that social transformations are seldom uniform in their effects, and that, instead, almost invariably, as one change takes place, it involves a form of substitution rather than clearly defined gains or losses (Coontz 2000). Thus, as messages and images spread from one region of the world to another, they may be adopted, rejected, or modified in the local context (Cvetkovich and Kellner 1997). It is important to note here that these processes do not just link the local with the global in a vertical interaction, but instead also involve a horizontal process that links local worlds (Stephens 1994). For example, as images of childhood are exported from one arena to other areas, they are not uniformly applied in local settings. Instead, aspects of these messages are adopted and negotiated depending on context. Rosenau (1997) explains this process as,

"Localizing dynamics derive from people's need for psychic comforts of close-at-hand, reliable support – or the family and neighborhood, for local cultural practices, for a sense of 'us' that is distinguished from 'them'" (p. 363). New ideas and practices may be introduced and be transmitted more easily than in the past, but individuals still cling to their local contexts, be it their families or other intimate relationships and at least some part of their belief systems, in order to maintain some stability in what is perceived as a constantly shifting and rapidly transforming environment.

1.5 Ideational Approaches to Understanding Globalization and Families

A central tenet of this book is that globalization and families are interrelated in a critical manner that has not been adequately explored in conventional approaches. This point will be elaborated on in subsequent chapters. At this juncture, I would like to suggest that part of the problem may stem from the underlying epistemology that is used to understand globalizing processes. Analyses of social phenomena continue to be conceptualized as bounded by territorial and chronological demarcations (Appadurai 1999). Phenomena are understood to occur in "clearly" delineated societies, within certain groups, and at specific socio-historical points in time.[15] What is lost in these analyses is variability, movement, and the complexity of social relations and the transmittance of ideas and ideologies across time. Social dynamics are more complex than simplistic categorizations are able to capture.[16] They are the product of interrelated macro factors and micro characteristics. Globalization further complicates this relationship, due to the fact that the speed of interaction between multiple levels and various factors is continually accelerating. When it comes to the study of families, we need to acknowledge that conceptions of space and time are in the process of transformation and that this influences our understanding of family processes. That is not to imply that territory and chronology do not remain an important aspect of social life, and as part of the study of social phenomena. However, it is important to recognize that the very nature of understanding has changed primarily due to our ability to supercede certain boundaries and the compression of time. As Appadurai explains,

> There is a growing disjuncture between the globalization of knowledge and the knowledge of globalization. The second is that there is an inherent temporal lag between the processes of globalization and our efforts to contain them conceptually. The third is that globalization as an uneven economic process creates a fragmented and uneven distribution of those resources for learning, teaching and cultural criticism which are most vital for the formation of democratic research communities which could produce a global view of globalization. (1999, p. 229)

Globalization changes the inherent process of knowledge accumulation – how knowledge is produced, where it is distributed and how it is received and interpreted. This is true for understandings of globalization itself, as well as the phenomena with which it intersects. Raising this issue is imperative with respect to

---

[15] For example, when it comes to the study of families, books on global families are virtually all organized by country. As an illustration, "French families" will be contrasted to "Chinese families" and Latinos are compared to Asians. In a globalized context, these demarcations have little significance and do not offer us useful insights.

[16] For example, immigrant families to the United States today may, on the surface, look like immigrant families at the turn of the twentieth century. The small nuclear family leaves the larger extended family behind as it resettles in the United States (this is just one example – the multiple types of immigrant families will be discussed in a later chapter). However, today's immigrant family will differ in tangible and intangible ways. One hundred years ago, immigrants were limited in their communications with their home societies. Re-settlement meant a loss of cultural ties with family, friends, and all that represented their lives. This also implied assimilation to the host society – we see this in language acquisition, the socialization of children, and even often name changes. Today's immigrant, and/or immigrant family enters on a new trajectory once it decides to make the radical shift. They may move to a new society but the ties with the old one need not be broken. Communication technologies allow individuals to remain in constant contact with family and friends, mass transportation allow for relatively easy access to home again should that need arise, and a growing pride in ethnicity allows individuals to retain the vestiges of their backgrounds be they language, customs, names, etc.

investigating the relationship between family dynamics and other intimate relationships and their intersection with globalizing processes.[17] On another level, it is important to understand not just what is happening in families but also how these internal processes are reflected in the larger culture. As Hareven (2000), points out, how a family initiates and adapts to changes and how it interprets the impact of larger structural changes into its own operations, is one of the most promising areas of research. Underlying this perspective is the understanding that families are active agents in the dynamic interplay between societal institutions and societal change. Families do not just react in response to societal stimuli. Instead, families are active players that plan, initiate and at times reject change. It is these interactions that need to be captured in order to better understand social processes and the dynamic nature of families in society.

It is useful at this point to provide a quick overview of the relevance of ideology in this work. Ideology focuses on the way ideas serve to structure relations of power and inequality (Geertz 1973). Ideology is also commonly defined in an encompassing sense as the worldview or the common-sense set of assumptions with which people think about their lives. It is the framework or paradigm within which attitudes and actions are shaped, decisions made, and questions raised. Drawing on Gramsci's reformulation of the concept of ideology, ideology can be thought of as an overarching arena for both thought and behavior, a discourse that shapes the way people tend to think about and act on opportunities for change. Such a concept supersedes the old concept of duality, of the world of ideas versus the world of objective institutions, a superstructure of ideas versus people's lives. Instead, according to Gramsci, ideologies serve to integrate these disparate elements into a "relational whole" or "historical bloc" of both ideas and institutions (Gramsci 1985, p. 65).

From a Gramscian perspective, ideologies are "articulating principles" that organize beliefs, behavior, social structures, and social relations within a certain perspective of the world, into a "hegemonic formation" (p. 67). Among today's global citizens, multiple and rapidly changing ideologies of family, gender, citizenship, rights and economic relationships emerge as critical in shaping individuals' perceptions and consequent actions. Traditional ideologies become increasingly subject to revision and questioning as in the contemporary environment, a growing number of individuals are constantly exposed to new, and at times, conflicting ideas that they must navigate, negotiate, and either reject or adapt. While change is an

---

[17] We continue to be faced with complex unanswered questions: Under what conditions do we move to greater egalitarian relations between men and women in the intimate sphere of the family? If so, under what socio-economic and cultural conditions? Do families socialize their children in increasingly similar ways due to the spread of certain types of knowledge? Do the structural changes that have affected so many people around the globe (women working outside the home in unprecedented numbers, later ages at marriage and childbearing) influence families in varying ways? Does the local still take precedence over the global? How do we categorize people in a census, a research study, a society – according to class? Religion? National affiliation? And we need to pose newer questions about the role of technology in social relationships within families and outside of families? Are we moving to new social forms that will eventually replace families as we know them? How does transnationalism affect family processes?

inherent aspect of the human experience, the rapidity and profusion of a widely ranging set of values and norms makes contemporary analyses of social life increasingly complex and even inaccurate. It is difficult to pinpoint with certitude which aspects of a society's ideology is truly providing the framework from which individuals draw their values and norms. In this discussion, it is important to recognize that individuals are active agents who are neither the victims of dominant ideologies, nor autonomous representatives of self. They have the potential to resist or restate conflicting representations that may result in alternative constructions to previously existing, dominant discourses. As Weedon (1987) clearly states:

> In the battle of subjectivity and the supremacy of particular versions of meaning of which it is a part, the individual is not merely the passive site of discursive struggle. The individual who has a memory and an already discursively constituted sense of identity may resist particular interpretations or produce new versions of meaning from the conflicts and contradictions between existing discourses. Knowledge of more than one discourse and the recognition that meaning is plural allows for a measure of choice on the part of the individual and even where choice is not available, resistance is still possible. (p. 106)

Weedon's articulation of agency allows for a more comprehensive understanding of globalizing processes as they articulate with individual's and families' lives. Global communications allow individuals to have immediate contact with each other around the world. They introduce new ideas, ways of behaving, and lifestyles. But how these messages are received is dependent on the local context and on the actors themselves. From this perspective, one cannot speak about a homogenous experience or response to globalization. Instead, each situation requires analysis which can then be integrated into more complex patterns of understandings.

1.6   Comprehensive, Holistic Approaches to Globalization

Perspectives on globalization approach this phenomenon primarily as a large-scale economic and political process. Most significant work in this area repeatedly focuses on state and market mechanisms, and, at times, on how these may interact with new technologies. For example, there is significant interest in the relationship between new information technologies and regulatory laws concerned with the movement of capital around the globe. Further, multiple perspectives examine how these transformations have assisted in shifting models of production from localized loci of control to shifting, flexible sites. Concurrently, other approaches have dichotomized "the global" and "the local" viewing them in a constant power play with one another (Cole and Durham, 2006).

In this book, globalization and its interrelationship with families is presented from a somewhat different standpoint; not purely from the analysis of an outer global actuality and its interaction with localized beliefs. Instead, the focus is on the dynamic interface of negotiations and transformations that take place on the familial level with respect to globalization. These negotiations and transformations are understood to play a vital role in social change: on familial, community, societal, and transnational levels. From this perspective, globalization plays a fundamental role in every family's matrix of choices, decisions, and negotiations, and conversely, that which happens at the familial level is a critical aspect of globalization.

A dynamic perspective such as this, assumes that as individuals struggle to carve out an existence for themselves and their families, they make choices based on opportunities, challenges and needs. This occurs primarily in a local context. However, globalization introduces new factors and contexts into the mix. In a globalized environment, individuals and their families, may, in certain cases, have more fruitful, and at other times, more constricted choices. For example, in many parts of the world, the work arena has changed dramatically. But, depending on context, ability level, and a whole wide array of factors, individuals will have varied experiences with respect to the kind of work they can access, retain and be successful at. The same type of work may be defined and compensated very differentially between places or even in the same society. The factors that influence an individual's relationship to the world of work will also be closely interrelated with personal roles and relationships. As decisions are arrived at in a familial context, values, norms, and relationships that may have traditionally been accepted and followed, may be modified or more dramatically redefined. Eventually, repetitive patterns lead to intensified social change. In a globalized context, it is the speed of this transformation that is one of the most remarkable features of the globalization phenomenon.

A more comprehensive, holistic and dynamic approach to the relationship between globalization and families, allows insight into power relations and the underlying causes for social transformations. As Ong (1999) warns models "that analytically define[s] the global as political-economic and the local as cultural do[es] not quite capture the horizontal and relational nature of the contemporary economic, social, and cultural processes that stream across spaces" (p. 4). In order to begin to understand globalizing processes we need to consistently acknowledge the fluid relationships between individuals, institutions, and contexts.

Throughout this analysis, globalization will be examined from this perspective of global connectivity, deterritorialization, the acceleration of change, and the concomitant meanings of these changes for families. In agreement with Giddens (1991), it is argued that we do live in a "different" world and that this new globalized order *has* changed individuals' and families' lives, on an ideological level, and with respect to live experiences. For example, the patriarchal family that has characterized so much of Western history seems to be slowing dissipating (Castells 2000). However, transformative changes within families are even more profound than is captured in narrowly focused analyses of patriarchy. The changes occurring in families portend to radically transform the world social order in new and not yet completely understood ways.

Globalization is playing a significant role in several major social trends. For example, the massive global movement of women into the formal and informal labor force is radically reshaping family dynamics. Labor force participation has been accompanied in certain places, with empowerment and self-actualization for some women, and even children, and on the other hand, with the increasing poverty of women, children and men in other places. Other issues such as migration, fertility, aging and citizenship are interacting with globalizing phenomena, effecting unexpected social changes for which most individuals, families, communities, and nation-states are not prepared. Furthermore, globalization does not just affect some families, i.e., families who live in developing countries or those families that migrate from one area to another across regions or countries. In today's world, all families and their members are touched by globalization in a multitude of ways and as was pointed out before, globalization itself is transformed through these interactions.

It is important to note that one cannot empirically make the argument that globalization is either "good" or "bad" for families. Nor can one assume that globalization will lead to uniform behaviors within or between families. For instance, there are those who argue that the traditional importance of the nation-state has given way to a focus on the family, neighbors and the marketplace, and that this process will engender an increasing concern with family and other fundamental social units (Lieber and Weisberg 2002). This perspective assumes that as individuals are inundated with a multitude of images, beliefs and ideas, their impulse will be to retreat to that which is known and familiar – their kin and fictive kin (Berger 2002). [18] Meanwhile, other voices contend that as individuals are able to construct new identities for themselves based on relationships across distances and in virtual worlds, families in all parts of the world will transform themselves and play very different roles than in the past (Giddens 2003). As will be seen further on, transnational families today may maintain, extend, or transform relationships with those left behind in their home regions in a manner that was virtually impossible even 20 or 30 years ago. Concurrently, families that may never have interacted with anyone beyond a certain geographical distance are now able to communicate with others half way around the world around shared projects, such as adoption. Thus, globalization has brought on unforeseen and unimagined changes. As we move forward, it is imperative to keep in mind Bourdieu's insight that domestic life is not insulated from the wider social sphere (1977). Changes in meanings, values and categorical relations are part of our accelerating world. In order to gain greater insight into these transformations, we need to consider how these changes are reflected and realized on the familial level.

---

[18] Fictive kin refers to those individuals who someone may feel emotional and/or economic ties to without a biological, adoptive, or marital relationship.

Chapter 2
Approaches to Understanding Families

Mainstream approaches to globalization primarily focus on its economic and political manifestations. However, it is within families that globalization is realized. Ideological and material changes in the national and transnational arena intersect with personal decisions that are arrived at in family contexts. As globalization accelerates, so do the choices, dilemmas, opportunities, and outcomes that are accompanied by this dynamic process. Given the volatility of markets, the speed of communication, and the intersection of labor force demands with transnational forces, it is becoming increasingly difficult to predict familial responses to fluctuating economies and policies, as well new representations of alternative lifestyles and roles. The traditional blueprints, that so many individuals rely on in their societies, are increasingly challenged, negotiated, and revised.

Specific phases of the life course, crossgenerational and intergenerational relationships, and accepted forms of private living arrangements are in the process of transformation. As women and men negotiate breadwinning and domestic labor, and as children, youth, and the elderly increasingly occupy new ideological and productive roles, family arrangements are modified and reconceptualized. These transformations, however, are not happening in an equivalent or sequential manner. In the West, differences exist between and within countries in attitudes toward varied lifestyles such as single parenthood, same sex couples, and cohabitation. However, more stark are the differences between the West and the developing world. While representations, ideologies, and even practices, pertaining to different family forms and lifestyles are spreading globally, in some areas, they have been met with nationalistic and fundamentalist responses. This has resulted in a worldwide focus on the intimate arrangements of individuals in the family arena.

Around the globe, virtually, every Western and non-Western society identifies some form of family as part of its basic foundation. Crossculturally, members of contemporary families are engaged with each other in various forms of material, economic, emotional, and ideational exchange. Families also function as the primary site for the early socialization of children, and as a source of identification for adults. Despite ethnographic documentation about the wide variety of family arrangements found in different parts of the world, almost every society privileges certain family forms over others. In fact, as Coontz (2000) explains,

B.S. Trask, *Globalization and Families*: *Accelerated Systemic Social Change*, DOI 10.1007/978-0-387-88285-7_2, © Springer Science+Business Media, LLC 2010

Almost every known society has had a legally, economically, and culturally privileged family form that confers significant advantages on those who live within it, even if those advantages are not evenly distributed or are accompanied by high costs for certain family members. Individuals, who cannot or will not participate in the favored family form, face powerful stigmas and handicaps. History provides no support for the notion that all families are created equal in any specific time and place. Rather, history highlights the social construction of family forms and the privileges that particular kinds of families confer. (p. 286)

The concept of family is imbued with symbolic meaning and lived experiences. And whatever its form, families provide the earliest types of nurturance, protection, and socialization for its members. Families provide the initial foundation for entering into community and societal relations, and they reflect meanings, trends, and conflicts in specific cultures. As we become increasingly interconnected through globalizing forces, family issues and relationships remain of consistent, universal interest and concern to most individuals. In fact, in many places, family issues are often elevated into the public arena and are thought to symbolize the basic health of the larger society.

In some areas of the world, fears about societal change have resulted in large scale movements toward "maintaining" or "restoring' family values", while in other places, the recognition of a plurality of family forms and relationships has become valorized as reflective of an ever increasing and enriching form of diversity.[1] Families have also been the site for significant feminist critiques, who have questioned the "naturalness" of traditional family arrangements and have highlighted the tie between the ideology of a monolithic family form and the oppression of women. These critiques have elicited widespread, intense cultural disputes, above all, around men's authority in families, and women's responsibilities for nurturance (Thorne 1982).

Despite controversy around family forms and functions, kinship and family organization form the basis for much of human existence. Many of the earliest philosophical and ethical writings reflect a preoccupation with family life. For example, Confucius wrote that "happiness and prosperity would prevail if everyone would behave 'correctly' as a family member" (in Goode 1982). The microcosm of the family, while perceived as of utmost importance, was also thought to symbolize relations in the larger society. Thus, behaving correctly as a family member also meant fulfilling one's obligations to the group or society. This same notion of the importance of familial and community relationships is reflected in the Old and New Testaments, the Torah, the Qur'an, and in some of the earliest codified literature in India, the Rig-Veda and the Law of Manu. All emphasize kin relationships and the role of the individual in fulfilling his or her responsibilities to others. Even in distant and historical tribal societies, kinship relations play a crucial role in social structure. From an anthropological perspective, these relationships and accompanying obligatory responsibilities are part of the social fabric that joins individuals together and forms the basis for what we call society.

---

[1] Nowhere is this more evident than in the U.S. where opposing movements juxtapose "traditional family values" against "new" family forms such as same-sex couples.

In contrast, in contemporary Western and non-Western societies, kinship relations are just one out of a multiple set of affiliations. Today, for many individuals, families are constructed and maintained through social bonds and support networks instead of biological ties. Individuals are forming "families of choice" to whom they turn for emotional, financial, and physical assistance. Global communications such as the Internet, e-mail, and satellite linkups are facilitating these relationships over space and time. While in the past, locale mattered, today social relationships are maintained over great distances with ease. This leads us to a new perspective on families, one that is less mired in the static nature of a family's form and structure, and, instead, focuses on its dynamic nature. Carrington (2001) suggests that in today's globalized environment, families need to be recast as open, nebulous systems. "Conceptualizing family as a fluid and dynamic sociospace removes its status as a foundational and enduring social structure. It places emphasis on the activities and shared symbolic systems of people and clearly articulates a vision of individuals moving across various sociospaces in the course of a day or a lifetime." (p. 193).

More dynamic conceptualizations of families allow us to understand that individuals and their families are actively engaged in constant dialectical negotiations with larger forces that shape their interactions from within, and also with external entities. In contrast to more historical perspectives on families as a unified interest group, today, we recognize that individuals are active agents within families who are engaged in a constant production and redistribution of resources. From this perspective, the family "is a location where people with different activities and interests in these processes often come into conflict with one another" (Hartmann 1981, p. 368). In a globalized context, there is growing uncertainty about which choices will primarily benefit the individual versus those that are of advantage to the familial group, and it is increasingly more difficult to determine whose interests should dominate. Interestingly, however, with all the choices and variations with respect to families that we recognize and acknowledge in our contemporary world, even in the West, individuals still continue to segregate themselves into separate family groups, living in close dwellings (Carrington 2001). In order to understand why the phenomenon of family life persists as a critical aspect of the human experience and the current changes within and around family life, it is instructive to examine some of the debates surrounding who and what are families.

2.1 Defining Families

Despite agreement about the pervasiveness and continuity of some form of familial relationships throughout human history, in the current context, there is no single uniform agreed upon definition of what a family is. The revolution in social thought with respect to family issues in the West that had its origins in the upheaval of the 1960s has continued to exert influence on contemporary discussions on families by breaking down unified concepts of "the family." Despite this conceptual problem, social scientists and policy makers continue to debate which individuals constitute family and why that should matter.

One of the earliest social scientists to be concerned with identifying the structure and processes of families, Emile Durkheim, emphasized in his work that families took on many forms and yet, formed a core social institution (Lamanna 2002). This concept was elaborated by George Murdock (1949) whose classic crosscultural treatise on families dominated the social sciences from the middle of the twentieth century onward. Using data from both Western and non-Western societies as his basis, Murdock concluded that every society was characterized by family units that are organized around economic cooperation, sexual reproduction, and common residence. His definition, while still in use by some, has been widely criticized due to its functionalist nature. Contemporary theorists point out that the concept of family is really an ideological construct with moral implications (Collier et al. 1992).

Conceptualizations about the form, function, and utility of families change over time and result out of a unique interplay of historical, political, economic, and social forces. We can see this process at work in the current discourse on families. For example, contemporary discussions range from structural definitions of "nuclear" families as composed of men, women, and children to representations of families as emotionally bonded social groups. Different groups emphasize different definitions of families based on a wide range of factors. In surveys, most Americans define family as individuals living together who share close emotional ties and who identify with this group in significant ways. However, Americans are also quite divided on the issue of equating same sex couples with a "legitimate" family form. In contrast, in contemporary Europe, standard understandings of families include gay and lesbian couples. While sentimental and open ended definitions of family, such as in the American case, evoke poignant images, the lack of uniform agreement on family definitions has resulted in much controversy in the social sciences about using family as an analytic category. These debates have also spilled over into the realm of policy formation, with some sides arguing for individual rights instead of family rights, and others standing firm that only certain types of families should be considered as recipients of social benefits. In a more conciliatory fashion, Bogenschneider and Corbett (2004) suggest that "no single definition of family may be possible". Existing definitions of family might be categorized in two ways: (a) structural definitions that specify family membership according to certain characteristics such a blood relationship, legal ties, or residence; and (b) functional definitions that specify behaviors that family members perform, such as sharing economic resources and caring for the young, elderly, sick, and disabled." (p. 453).

In the United States, the Census Bureau defines family as two or more people living together who are related by birth, marriage, or adoption. In agreement, most Americans indicate that for demographic and policy purposes, families should be defined as a unit made up of two or more people related by blood, marriage, or adoption, who live together to form an economic unit, and raise children (Bogenschneider and Corbett 2004). However, these definitions are at odds with contemporary manifestations of families. Narrow definitions of family exclude relationship units such as cohabiting couples, homosexual and lesbian couples, foster parents, and grandparents raising children, just to name a few.[2] The debate and controversy around family definitions has taken on political connotations in the United States, with many conservatives advocating the "traditional" family as defined by the census (or even the breadwinner-homemaker form), and most liberals supporting the notion of multiple family forms.

Apart from political debates, a working definition of family is deemed necessary by many, both from a policy as well as a lay perspective. Currently, places of employment, government programs, and other institutions in the United States issue benefits based on a clearly delineated definition of family. However, as we have moved away demographically speaking from the post World War II breadwinner/homemaker family type, that pervades so much of the public consciousness, it has become increasingly difficult to determine who should be the beneficiary of family based benefits. For example, many employers now offer same sex partner benefits, suggesting that when a couple has lived together for a certain period of time, the partner of the employee is entitled to retirement benefits, educational credits, health insurance, etc. The debate about who actually constitutes family is reflected in the variation between employers as to how these benefits are allocated, and who the beneficiaries are. Still, the most prevalent assumption, underlying work, school, and social benefits, presumes a male in the household who acts as its head, and the presence of children (Smith 1993).[3] Current statistics, however, indicate that it is highly problematic to create policies based on outdated notions of family forms. Today in the U.S., fewer than 25% of households are married couples with children, and of these only 7% represent families were the parents have not been divorced, the father works outside of the home and the mother takes care of the children. In order not to get mired in this issue, some analysts suggest that it may be more useful to define families in a manner that reinforces the goals of specific programs or policies (Moen and Schorr 1987).

In a later chapter, we will examine the radically different perspective on the relationship between policies and families underlying the Scandinavian welfare state system. In the Scandinavian model, the rights of individuals, rather than families or "groups" are understood as the fundamental unit for allocating social programs and welfare benefits. While this is an approach that is not particularly popular in the United States, it serves to move the debate away from definitional issues and, instead, focuses attention on the basic needs and rights of all individuals. In order to understand the nature of the debates around families, it is useful to turn briefly to a historical overview of the scholarly study of families.

---

[2] In a symbolic gesture, that acknowledges the multiplicity of family types, the flagship journal on the study of families changed its name from *The Journal of Marriage and the Family* to *The Journal of Marriage and Family* in 2001.

[3] See Smith (1993) for a pivotal article on SNAF – the Standard North American Family and its ubiquitous presence in school and benefits policies.

2.2   The Formal Study of Families

The formal study of families commenced in the United States in the period between 1880 and 1920, during the same period of time that home economics and sociology were becoming formal disciplines. While a wide variety of scholars and professionals were concerned with the study of families, the formative period of studying families was most closely intertwined with the development of North American sociology (Boss et al. 1993).This era was characterized by significant interest and concern about social issues that had come about through urbanization and industrialization. Families were viewed as fragile, and subject to social pressures that could, potentially, destroy them. Of particular interest was the problem of community disintegration, which was seen as coupled with vulnerability of family. A landmark work (Thomas and Znaniecki 1918–1920) published during this period suggested that family goals needed to be realigned with individual ambitions in order to strengthen the role of the institution of families in all societies around the globe. Emile Durkheim writing shortly before the development of these suggestions had also argued that families, as they had been conceptualized through the Middle Ages in the Western world, were moving to new configurations that worked less to serve the group and, instead, increasingly only benefited the individual (Lamanna 2002). Social scientific treatises on the family began to focus on to the socialization aspects of families and how families could be harnessed in such a manner as to produce solid, committed citizens that would uphold the values of society. These arguments, now over one hundred years old, are important to reflect upon in current analyses of families. While superficially, contemporary arguments may seem similar (that families are disintegrating, and individuals are increasingly governed purely by loyalties to themselves and not the collectivity), it is important to note that the social context within which these disputes are taking place has changed quite dramatically.

While early family scholars were concerned with the sociology of Western families, in the field of anthropology, ethnographers became increasingly interested in the varied family forms that they encountered in far away corners of the world. However, a preoccupation with matrilineality vs. patrilineality, kinship, descent, and marriage forms in non-Western settings led to relatively separate discourses on families. Nonetheless, Bronislaw Malinowski, concerned with the nuclear family, introduced the functionalist notion, later adopted by most family scientists, that family was the basic unit of all societies, historically and crossculturally, and served to fulfill individuals', especially childrens' basic needs (Parkin et al. 2004).

The 1920s and 1930s saw the emergence of the study of families that set the stage for our current context. During this period, an increasing interest in the "personal" and the "private" developed. The discipline of psychology flourished, and public attention focused on the self, the unconscious, and that which was "unseen." Concurrently, family scholars turned toward understanding internal family dynamics as a means of explaining why some families seemed to be stronger than others, what factors could be used to understand the stability and instability of marriages, how to prevent divorce, and the implications of family life for personal well-being. In 1926, Ernest W. Burgess published his pivotal article, in which he termed the family as "a unity of interacting personalities" and, thus, set the contemporary parameters for studying families from a psycho-social perspective. His work influenced other family scholars as they became increasingly preoccupied with marital adjustment, and how individuals could attain satisfaction from their membership in families (Boss et al. 1993).

World War II and the ensuing period saw a slight shift among scholars concerned with family issues. The topic of national security became paramount, and strong families were seen as the key to a strong nation. Families were the institution that could produce loyal, committed citizens. Replete with a strong ideology that advocated early marriage and traditional gender roles as crucial components for the foundation of families, family scholars emphasized the need for "normalcy" and complete assimilation to the "American way of life." One of the most dominant voices of that time, the sociologist Talcott Parsons, impacted the study and theorizing about families with his analysis of the role of nuclear (or conjugal) families. From his perspective, nuclear families were of utmost importance in industrial societies due to their small size and lack of obligations to kin which allowed for greater mobility. Importantly, Parsons focused on the conjugal tie between husband and wife, suggesting that this had become the central family relationship in the Western world (Parsons 1943). Simultaneously, he intimated that the bond between parents and children would decrease in significance, resulting in the erosion of kinship ties. In Parson's version of the contemporary nuclear family, a strong division of labor was the key; thus, the breadwinner/ homemaker couple represented a critical differentiation of sex roles. He postulated that competition between spouses for occupational status would, otherwise, negatively impact the solidarity of the marital relationship (Parsons 1949). In his description of sex roles he depicted, the man as the "instrumental leader" of the family and the woman as the "expressive leader." In accordance with the popular notions of his time, sex roles resulted from the "natural" biological bond between mothers and their children. Arguing from a social structural and functionalist perspective, Parsons indicated that the contemporary family would be imbued with only two remaining functions: the socialization of children and the "personality stabilization" of adults. His perspectives, while criticized and refuted today, still permeate certain sectors of the family literature.

The 1950s are often described as the "golden age" of family; media and scholarly images of families depicted a situation where families were "stable," and characterized by low divorce rates, few single-parents raising children, and a limited number of children born out of wedlock (Mintz and Kellogg 1988). "Psychologists, educators, and journalists frequently repeated the idea that marriage was necessary for personal well-being. Individuals who deviated from this norm were inevitably described as unhappy or emotionally disturbed" (Mintz and Kellogg 1988, p. 181). The traditional perspectives from this period continue to exert a surprisingly strong influence even in contemporary scholarship. While not overt, these beliefs and ideals are often embedded into family related research questions and analyses that mask the inherent value orientations of the researchers (Smith 1993). The significance of these value laden ideologies extends far beyond Western borders, as scholarly and lay publications now reach every part of the globe, perpetuating a unique brand of family life and concurrent acceptable behaviors (Ambert 1994).

More contemporary scholarly approaches, however, have negated the depiction of the "ideal" breadwinner/homemaker, stable white family of the 1950s. Coontz (1992, 1997) has persuasively argued that this so-called 1950s family which today is contrasted with the "deteriorating" twenty-first century family does not take into account the millions of families of that period who did not fit this uniform representation: the poor and those with low-incomes, African-Americans, immigrants, single-parents, and widows and widowers, just to name a few. Coontz has also noted that despite a great deal of evidence to the contrary, families of that period which did not fit this uniform depiction were perceived as dysfunctional at that time. The ideal nuclear family that formed the core of significant scholarship and media portrayals, continued to be conceptualized as a father who worked outside of the home for pay and a homemaker mother whose primary responsibilities were to her husband and children.

These portrayals of families became popular during the post World War II period in the midst of a major demographic shift that encouraged white middle class families to relocate to the suburbs. Simultaneously, their homes in urban areas became occupied by African American families moving north. The ideal of ethnic kin networks that had characterized depictions of urban life, became replaced by the "non ethnic," suburban family (Boss et al. 1993). Now, "other" types of families were suspect and perceived as deviant or pathological. Of particular concern were "ethnics" and immigrants, who brought diverse family traditions with them that were at odds with the ideals being advocated by scholars and the popular media. Assimilation to the American way of life was advocated as the key to successful integration – and this integration was to be achieved, at least in part, by socializing families into the middle class ideal characterized by a nuclear family with a breadwinning father and homemaking mother.

The 1960s introduced new social perspectives that had their roots in the civil rights movement, the expansion of sexual behavior outside of marriage, the Vietnam War, the revival of feminism and a general antiauthoritarian stance. The divorce rate started to climb to unprecedented rates and women with children flocked into the work force. While statistics indicate an increase in the percentage of two-parent families during the decades of the 1950s, 1960s, and 1970s (Seward 1978), Masnick and Bane (1980) point out that it was only in the late 1970s that the number of nuclear families affected by divorce began to exceed those disrupted by death. As the prevalence of divorce, and mothers with children under age 18 entering the work force increased, American families began to deviate from the 1950s and 1960s concept of the "typical" family. Other notable family trends also accompanied ideological changes: fertility decreased while cohabitation increased, and "other" forms of families such as step-families, female-headed households, and gay and lesbian families became increasingly common.

By the mid-1970s, the theoretical convergence that resonated through much of the research and writing on families collapsed. The societal changes that were impacting every aspect of American life also became reflected in the academic focus on families. The postwar consensus on "ideal" families broke down and, instead, scholars started to criticize the patriarchal hierarchical model that had been the unexamined basis of virtually all perspectives on families. Interdisciplinary foci on families became more common with fields as diverse as psychology, home economics, communication, and history concentrating new efforts on understanding family life and composition. For example, historical scholarship on families introduced a new analytical dimension: families needed to be differentiated from households. This was an important step forward in family research since it directed the focus away from relationships based on biological ties, and redirected it to an emphasis onto domestic groups (households) which could contain nonrelatives as well (Seward 1978).[4] Conversely, families were now understood as also encompassing members that extended beyond the household (Goody 1972; Hareven 1974, 2000). Reconceptualizing families and separating them from households allowed scholars to focus on macro-processes such as urbanization and migration and their effects on family life (Hareven 2000).

In more recent decades, feminists and minority group scholars have teamed together to criticize the white middle-class breadwinner/homemaker family model that had dominated the study of families. The "traditional" Parsonian family became a hotbed for discussions by Marxist feminists who argued that this family type is the most fundamental site of women's oppression. They also ascertained that the cohesive system of fixed sex roles that had been promoted by social scientists, benefited men while oppressing the talents and rights for self-expression of women.

This deconstruction of the "traditional" family and "natural" sex roles introduced a new dialog about families, gender roles, and the place of patriarchy in society. Feminist analysis highlighted the gendered experience of family life and brought to the forefront the experiences of marginalized and oppressed groups (Osmond and Thorne 1993). By emphasizing a postpositivist philosophy of science, they also suggested that a researcher's values and culture could color research, analysis, and the dissemination of findings.

Throughout the late 1970s and in the 1980s, gender, patriarchy, and inequality became widely recognized aspects of family scholarship. However, American scholars of color and feminist researchers from non-Western societies increasingly argued that universal analysis of families and the subjugation of women obscured and misinterpreted the experiences of marginalized groups. Instead, they proposed that in certain contexts family life provided a safe haven for women; a place where they could be protected from the inequalities and persecution they faced in the outside world (Baca Zinn 2000). These scholars suggested that it was precisely through the relationships with men in their families, that women were empowered

---

[4] In the field of anthropology the study of family has continued to be tied to "kinship" studies and social organization. See Parkin et al. (2004) for a detailed overview of kinship and family studies from the nineteenth century onwards. Thus, there is little intersection today between the fields even though both could benefit from much more cross fertilization.

to resist social, political, and economic pressures. They highlighted the perspective that, for marginalized men and women, gender was not of the same import as it was for white middle class women. Gay and lesbian feminists added their view to these approaches, illustrating that heterosexuality dominated family scholarship and that even feminist discourses were normative and value-laden (Baca Zinn 2000).

More recently, multi-cultural feminists have introduced the concept of the "matrix of domination" (Collins 1990). This analytical tool allows us to conceptualize families as part of a multiplicity of forces that include race, ethnicity, class, gender and sexuality, each intersecting and functioning, as determinants of lived experiences. Utilizing this perspective of a "matrix of domination" allows for an insight into the varied experiences of individuals and families, despite occupying the same socio-historical timeframe. This analytical tool introduces the concept of social positioning. Social positioning is related to issues such as the access to power, social class, discrimination, and cultural values. All of these factors affect every aspect of family life from marital relations to parenting, to the division of labor. Yet, despite the theoretical contributions of feminist scholars, contemporary writings on families continue to be critiqued, because of a persistent lack of focus on the interrelationship between families and macro forces. Daly (2003) depicts the state of current empirical research on families as if "…they are suspended in time, space, and culture" (Daly 2003, p. 774).

Currently, in other parts of the world, the study of families tends to be an underdeveloped field and, as Segalen phrases it, "under the influence of a consciously empirical American sociology….without precise references to its social and cultural environment and not as a domestic group undergoing change within a specific historical framework" (1986, p. 3). "Family" is approached as a natural unit, not to be pursued as an object of study and in need of analysis.[5] Family related research in much of Europe, the Middle East, South Asia, and China concentrates on the demographic impacts of fertility, mortality, and labor force participation of men and women. Generally speaking, most of this research never makes it into the dominant scholarly discourse on families.[6] The exception to this trend is the work that has originated in Northern Europe focusing on the study of the history of the family.[7] While stemming initially from historical demographers such as Louis Henry and the *Annales* group, working out of the Institut National des Etudes Demographiques, this research has been expanded by the Cambridge Group for the History of Population and Social Structure, established in 1964 under the leadership of Peter Laslett. The focus on households has probably garnered the most interest in terms of a more transnational approach to research on families and domestic groups

---

[5] I first became aware of this fact in graduate school. I was very interested in pursuing the study of non-Western families but was discouraged by conversations with scholars from various parts of the world who told me that "there was no new knowledge to gained from pursuing this topic."

[6] In fact there is a growing hegemony of thought stemming from the U.S. This will be seen later on in the chapter on children and childhood.

[7] On a personal note, this body of scholarship provided the impetus for all of my future research on non-Western, and consequently Western families.

(Comacchio 2003). While today there is some intellectual crossfertilization especially with scholars from English speaking countries, most current scholarship on families continues to be dominated by research based in the United States.[8] We shall return to this issue of dominant hegemonic discourses that flow from Western parts of the world to non-Western regions, and the ensuing consequences, in later chapters.

2.3   The Current Situation

The current segmentation in the West of "the family" into varied family forms has superseded the unified concept of the family that dominated through the 1980s. Recognition of multiple family configurations has broken down the notion of a monolithic "natural" family form. This trend has been accompanied by the slow deterioration of the patriarchal foundation of the Western family, defined as a unit under the care and responsibility of the father who is accorded primary decision-making rights. In the formerly traditional model of the family, the homemaker/breadwinner model can be imagined as a pyramidal power structure where decision-making flowed from the father to the mother and the children. The family unit could be conceptualized as a "centralized hierarchy of relationships" (Oswald 2003, p. 311). According to some scholars, today's family can be imagined as a "decentralized network of relationships where decision making tends to flow in all directions" (Oswald 2003, p. 311). Allegiances are not focused just on the well-being of the family but are, instead, interspersed with pertinent generational affiliations and specialized interest groups. In other words, young people may identify with the "Millennial Generation," the "Generation X," or the "Generation Y," while older people may be "Baby Boomers," or "Traditionalists."[9] In this model, individual allegiance is not necessarily just bound to familial relationships but, instead, is interspersed among multiple groups.

As scholarly perceptions of families have multiplied, so have their more mainstream depictions. As has been noted, throughout the 1950s and the 1960s, scholarship and the popular media celebrated a particular version of family. This family was white, married, lived in the suburbs, had children and was characterized by a clear, gendered division of labor. Families that deviated from this dominant model

---

[8] There are many reasons for this issue including the inability of most English speakers to read other languages and the domination of journals published in the English language. Even when books and articles on family issues are published in other countries, they are rarely included in bibliographies, book reviews and the like.

[9] There is a great deal of debate about the usage of terms like Millennials or Generation X'ers. The question centers around stereotyping of generalizing about large groups of individuals who are characterized by differences of social class, race, religion, education and other variables. Nevertheless, a life course perspective suggests that individuals born in the same cohort do experience and internalize certain world events such as wars, technological change and other such phenomena with a somewhat similar effect. See Elder (1999), for example.

– families that were characterized by divorce, race and ethnicity, sexual preference, or any other type of difference – were not part of the popular representation. This ideal of a strong unit characterized by a clear hierarchy and division of labor that was to be either included or excluded from the mainstream, has in the contemporary Western social landscape, been replaced by a recognition of plurality (Oswald 2003). Today, particularly in the West, there is a much greater acceptance of a multitude of family forms that range from single-parent, to same sex to cohabiting families, among others. Some even attribute this pluralism in families to an emerging paradigm of culture that includes ever more subcultures (Talbot 2000). This phenomenon also pertains to other forms of social life in the West. For example, today, many places of employment emphasize multiple team projects and shared responsibility, instead of a top down hierarchical model of work. The movement of corporations from urban centers to suburban locations is also perceived as part of this larger social movement. In fact, some argue that we are witnessing a decentralization of power, with urban areas not exercising the same amount of political and social power as in the past (Thomas 1998).

From a global perspective, a similar phenomenon is, in the process, of taking place. As corporations shift their activities from the West to other parts of the world, power relations are being rearranged. Economic and political power is no longer just concentrated in one or two areas in the world. Instead, power is increasingly synonymous with multiple locations, and even with shifts between locations. In other words, power has become decentralized and may be fluid and diffused to different places, individuals, groups, or entities. This makes any analytical discussion that primarily focuses on bounded units of analysis, such as "the family," "the nation-state," or "the corporation" in isolation, obsolete. Instead, in order to understand contemporary phenomena such as globalization, we need to examine interactions between entities, between micro and macro levels, and the multiplicity of changes that may result from these interfaces.

2.4   Crosscultural Perspectives on Families

Families continue to exert a strong cultural presence world-wide. Some form of kin relationships including parents and children, grandparents, aunts, uncles, cousins constitute varying forms of acknowledged families.[10] In many North European countries and Canada, family conceptualizations now include same sex marriage which became legal, beginning with Denmark's officially enacted registered partnership law in 1989, followed by the extension of legal rights to registered same-sex couples in Norway (1993), Sweden (1994), the Netherlands (2001), Belgium (2003), Spain (2005), Britain (2005), and Canada (2005). Moreover, an extensive anthropological literature has documented domestic groups and families that differ radically

---

[10]When using the term "kin relationships" I am not implying just blood lines. I include all types of relationships including adoption, foster children, and other bonded units.

from Western conceptions of families.[11] However, for the purposes of this discussion, the focus is on families as they are most commonly defined in both Western and non-Western societies; by traditional kinship, legal, and/or emotional ties.

In order to gain a broader perspective on the relationship between globalization and families, it is instructive to examine conceptualization of family in non-Western societies. In many non-Western societies, the reference group for an individual today, continues to be his or her kin, relationships that extend far beyond the ties of the nuclear family that form the norm for so many in the United States and Europe (Sherif-Trask 2006).[12] In these societies, families are often drawn into the decision-making process that influence individual lives on issues that would be considered, in the West, an individual "private matter." However, in many non-Western places obligation to kin is of utmost importance, and any deviation from caring for the collective group can ruin the reputation of an individual. For example, in many African and Middle Eastern societies, there is both cultural and religious pressure for men to take care of their large extended families, no matter what their financial situation may be. Family responsibilities are taken extremely seriously and despite economic, social, and political changes, some form of the extended family remains central to individual's lives (Sherif-Trask 2006).

This situation challenges earlier proponents of modernization theory such as William Goode, whose classic writings in the 1960s proposed that the introduction of industrialization to less developed areas of the world would eventually render the extended family obsolete. According to this popular framework at the time, modernization was accompanied by the evolution of extended family forms to more flexible nuclear families. Scholarships, both from the fields of the sociology of the family, as well as history of the family, have disputed this prediction. Specifically, historical studies illustrate that in the West, from preindustrial times onward, extended families did not devolve into nuclear families. Instead, the Western nuclear family has continually played an important role in society and is part of a particular constellation of ideologies and legalities peculiar to this part of the world (Goody 1972). Conversely, extended forms of families are not disappearing, as is so often suggested by scholars and mainstream perspectives, but instead are changing through their articulation with contemporary factors. For example, communication technologies can facilitate regular interactions between family members in a manner that could not have been predicted even just 20 years ago.[13]

---

[11] Anthropology is replete with examples of marriage and families that differ quite radically from contemporary family forms, such as ghost marriage among the Nuer (Evans-Pritchard 1940) and a specific culturally sanctioned type of adult-child marriage among a northern Russian tribe (Levi-Strauss 1956). Most anthropological readers have many such fascinating examples, indicating the cultural nature of relationship formation.

[12] A significant issue in many countries in Europe and in the US, Canada, and Australia is the infusion of immigrants from societies with very different notions of who is and who is not "family." This issue promises to grow in the future with continued mass migrations.

[13] The popularity of free Internet services such as Skype allow individuals to video conference with one another creating new linkages to far away places.

2.5   Fertility

A major shift in family life, primarily in the West and also increasingly in
non-Western regions of the world, is related to fertility. Fertility is dropping at
unprecedented rates, especially in Europe. In fact, there is ever increasing concern
throughout European societies that extremely low fertility rates could bring about
unintended consequences such as a dwindling labor supply and the lack of care for
the elderly. According to recent statistics, in the Western world, family size has
decreased to 2.8 individuals per household, while in the non-Western world household size has decreased to 5.7 in the Middle East and North Africa, 4.9 in Southeast
Asia, 4.1 in the Caribbean and 3.7 in East Asia (United Nations Programme on the
Family 2003). It is important to note that national fertility rates subsume variations
between and within countries, and also between urban and rural areas. Nevertheless,
from a global perspective, fertility has decreased significantly and at a faster pace
than demographers have predicted (Bulato 2001).[14]

The significance of a rapidly dropping fertility rate revolves around the major
changes that this phenomenon implies with respect to the family and the role of
women. This point is poignantly made by R.M. Timus (1966) in Easterlin (2000, p.
39) in his description of working class women in England.

> The typical working class mother of the 1890s married in her teens or early twenties and
> experiencing ten pregnancies, spent about 15 years in a state of pregnancy and in nursing
> a child for the first years of its life. She was tied, for this period of time, to the wheel of
> childbearing. Today, for the typical mother, the time so spent would be about 4 years. A
> reduction of such magnitude in only two generations in the time devoted to childbearing
> represents nothing less than a revolutionary enlargement of freedom for women.

The intentional limitation of family size in the West is one of the most significant
changes affecting contemporary families and gender roles. Throughout the twentieth
century, fertility control has been accomplished primarily through the use of
contraception or abortion. In contrast to the past and even today, to other parts of
the non-Western world, most people in the West no longer attempt to have as many
children as they are able to. Instead, they deliberately limit the size of their families
by using technologies or practices that were non-existent 50 years ago.

This radical shift in women's roles in the family, which has occurred in a
relatively brief period of time, historically speaking, has not come under much
scrutiny or debate in the family or gender literature. Instead, an overwhelming
focus continues to emphasize the division of labor, gender roles, and women's
working outside of the home. Nonetheless, it is important to remember that there
are still regions of the world, where, despite the introduction of a variety of birth
control methods and a general decline in fertility rates, women are bound primarily
by their childbearing roles. Specifically, in rural areas in the developing world,
many young women spend virtually their whole youth and far into mid-life,

---

[14] In Chap. 8 we examine the link between women's fertility, employment and nation-state policies
more closely.

pregnant, nursing, and caring for children. This impedes their opportunities for furthering their lives through education, training, and participation in their communities (Trask and Hendriks, 2009).

2.6 Gender Role Trends

The worldwide trend of very high numbers of women working outside of the home has set the stage for an unprecedented degree of debate about the appropriate distribution of roles in families. From a historical perspective, in the United States, until the early 1960s, most women who sought employment outside the home were poor and women of color. White women only participated in the labor force in their early twenties, stepping out once they married and had children. A short deviation from this pattern occurred during World War II when women were needed in the labor force because of a shortage of men. However, with the return of large numbers of GI's, women were encouraged to once again take up their domestic roles. Beginning in the late 1960s, a new trend emerged: women entered into the labor force and remained through their child bearing years (Bianchi et al. 2007).

In the United States, the debate about women's and men's roles has taken on strong political connotations. It is primarily referred to as the "family values" debate even though, in reality, it focuses on women's paid employment and the resultant changes in family life. For example, one prominent scholar has suggested that "families have lost functions, power, and authority; that familism as a cultural value has diminished, and that people have become less willing to invest time, money, and energy in family life, turning instead to investments in themselves" (Popenoe 1993, p. 527). This particular scholar has gone on to perpetuate the argument that the institution of family is in decline. In order to strengthen families, he suggests that we need to return to a traditional model of one partner being a wage earner, and the other caring for the children and other dependent family members. What this model of family life does not adequately address is the concern that one family member will, thus, be economically vulnerable, and that many households both in the United States, and worldwide, are either dependent on multiple incomes, or are composed of only one head of household (McGraw and Walker 2004). Embedded in this suggestion is the notion that women are at fault for the "decay" of societies, as their appropriate role should be as primary caretakers of the home and family.

In the West, opponents of a traditional distribution of roles in families advocate a family institution that is less hierarchically organized, that allows for greater personal growth for its members, and that allows women to pursue educational and employment opportunities which benefit both individuals and society as a whole. From this perspective, societies need to be restructured to provide greater social benefits such as adequate child care, universal health insurance, and flexible work schedules in order to accommodate care giving and formal labor force participation.

Some of the trends with respect to gender roles that we see in the United States are mirrored in both industrialized and developing nations around the globe. In most regions of the world, women increasingly constitute a significant percentage of the labor force. For example, between 1960 and 2000 the labor force participation of women jumped from 31 to 46% in the North American continent, from 32 to 41% in Western European countries, from 26 to 38% in much of the Caribbean, from 16 to 33% in Central America, from 17 to 25% in the Middle East, from 27 to 43% in the countries of Oceania and from 21 to 35% in South America (Heymann 2006). It is striking that even in North Africa and western Asia, areas where historically women did not work outside home due to cultural and religious norms, participation in the labor force has risen to over 20% (United Nations 2000). One implication of this movement of women into the paid labor force is that children are increasingly being raised in households where both parents are now working in the paid labor force (if there are two parents present). This phenomenon, which will be explored in greater depth in a subsequent chapter, is one of the most pivotal social changes that has taken place in the late twentieth century.

Through increased educational opportunities, and by participating in the formal and informal labor force, certain groups of women acquire the necessary economic resources to postpone marriage, gain greater power vis a vis their spouse in marriage, and are able to leave abusive and exploitive marriages. However, for many women, particularly those at the lower end of the socio-economic scale in Western countries and the developing world, participating in the formal and informal labor force has not led to self empowerment and autonomy. Instead, their employment outside home or away from traditional means of subsistence has translated into low-paying and, at times, risky jobs. For example, in certain areas of Africa, where women remain primarily employed in agriculture or tend to pursue the option of beginning small-scale businesses such as selling food supplies in open air markets, becoming involved in export production has worsened their lives. In order to provide for themselves and their families, these women now have to take on multiple forms of employment in order to make ends meet. For other women, their economic engagement has come at a high personal cost. Men socialized into "traditional" social roles may become embittered and downright abusive, due to feelings of inadequacy about not fulfilling their provider role. This phenomenon occurs in both Western and non-Western societies but is downplayed due to a dominant emphasis on women's empowerment through work.

Increasingly, women are also the likely heads of household, and potentially, even the primary breadwinners. This phenomenon can be attributed to a multiplicity of reasons including widowhood caused through wars, HIV/AIDS, or disease, the longevity of women as a result of longer lifespans, and rising rates of divorce. Out of wedlock childbearing is also becoming increasingly common in Western societies and some, but not all developing nations.[15] As women and men adjust through a wide

---

[15] In fact, a recent New York Times article detailed how a growing number of American women are choosing to have two children on their own, through new reproductive techniques, in the quest for the "perfect" family.

variety of responses to these new possibilities and representations about appropriate roles in families and societies, national and transnational policies have not been able to keep up with these transformations. In fact, some scholars have termed the current global situation with respect to family arrangements as a worldwide crisis (Mattingly 2001). This pattern of labor force participation has taken hold not only in the United States, but also Europe and Australia. The large number of working women has spurred similar worldwide debates revolving around parenting issues, social policies to support working parents, and the issue of "appropriate" gender roles. However, the cultural, political, and economic contexts within which these debates are held differ widely, eliciting at times very diverse responses. In shifting complex environments, individuals tend to draw on both time-honored values and present-day contexts in order to create innovative, negotiated identities for themselves.[16] These findings alert us that we need to be careful about making universal assumptions about how individuals and families will react to shifting circumstances and conditions.

2.7 Changes in Families

While globalization continues to draw together individuals into new types of relationships, communities, and social groups, not dreamed of even just one or two decades ago, we actually know little about how individuals are experiencing these changes. There continue to be many unexplored aspects of family life both in the West and in the other areas of the world (Daly 2003). For example, in order to extend scholarly frameworks and understandings of family dynamics, it is necessary to delve into the actual crosscultural experiences of marriage, parenthood, singlehood, aging, intergenerational relationships, same sex couples, and childhood, in order to begin to understand how these social processes interact with globalizing forces. Little is understood about the role that communication technologies play in the lives of families and, in particular, in the lives of transnational families. Moreover, research needs to be directed to understanding the relationship between economics, markets, and family life. What propels individuals in and out of the labor force at different stages in life? How does the family economy influence the market economy and vice versa? How is fertility in the industrialized world related to fertility in the developing world in the context of migration matters? Also, of interest should be the role of multiculturalism in the family realm. As societies become, more diverse, new concepts about families, gender roles, childhood and aging are introduced and debated. Simultaneously, as individuals from different groups interact, they may form new associations based on shared interests, proximity, and the like. We need to know how this growing diversity is absorbed, interpreted and acted on, in the family realm. In the United States, the growth of home schooling is a direct reflection of the values of certain religious families who do not wish for their children to be exposed to what they consider, "deleterious" or

---

[16] This phenomenon will be described in greater detail in Chap. 3.

"dangerous" values. These types of behaviors indicate that there is an immediate and close connection between value systems, transformations, and behavior.

To further gain insight into the relationship between globalization and family life, we also need to highlight the association between women's participation in the formal and informal labor force in *both* the industrialized and developing world. The current dominant Western social scientific focus does not allow us to understand the multiplicity of conditions under which families negotiate and come to terms with changing economic, political, and cultural conditions (Edgar 2004). Moreover, the unprecedented large number of women working outside home worldwide is only one of a number of factors affecting significant family change. Issues of migration, the aging of the global population and changing intergenerational relationships are also important components of these transformations. Moreover, family change varies, depending on a multitude of factors influenced in part, but not only, on region, religiosity, culture, social class and access to opportunity structures.

Ethnographic and crosscultural examples illustrate that we need to be cautious in hypothesizing and investigating that which is deemed to predict or constitute "family change." Until relatively recently, most explanations of family change focused mainly on structural influences such as innovations in technology, the movement of individuals from rural to urban areas, and declines in mortality and disease. However, an increasing number of researchers are now accounting for family change by focusing on international networks, interpersonal relationships, and ideational factors (Jayakody et al. 2008). As Daly (2003) explains, "Examination of families as a cultural form is all about understanding families as they change. It is also about understanding families as they perform in relation to perceived collective codes and beliefs. Family members draw on the rituals, practices, and expectations that are available in the cultural toolkit, and in the process they create themselves as a cultural form that expresses systemic beliefs and ideals. They draw meaning from the cultural matrix of which they are a part and express meanings about the kind of family they wish to appear as, all in the service of creating a definition of who they are as a family." (p. 774).

As broad norms and values such as an emphasis on freedom, equality, and individualism continue to spread through globalizing forces, they translate into new ideas about the place and role of individuals in relation to their families and larger communities. These new concepts are integrated into new perspectives on marriage, the roles of women and men, the relationship between generations and the role of children in families. As we begin to examine the relationship between globalization and families it should be noted that historians of the family have carefully proven that despite stereotypical depictions of the decline of family life, the modern nuclear family has remained dominant in the West. These scholars have highlighted the fact that kinship patterns have not necessarily lessened in value, despite social change, and that the process of industrialization, while impacting family life, was itself impacted by families (Hareven 2000). We can, thus, learn from historical patterns and assume that as globalization and its concomitant forces play an ever greater role in family lives, the phenomenon of globalization itself will also be impacted by families, however they may be defined.

Chapter 3
Gendered Analyses of Globalization

Insight into the relationship between globalization and gender remains limited, despite the fact that globalization is a widely recognized and disputed phenomenon. Mainstream approaches to globalization frame it as a gender-neutral occurrence that is characterized by transnational economic, political, and social flows and processes between and within societies. This omission is particularly profound in the light of a marginalized but insightful scholarship that has critically documented the role of gender in globalizing processes. Globalization is experienced by women and men around the world in a very different manner, depending on regional location, race, ethnicity, and socio-economic class. By not incorporating gender into mainstream analyses, the internal mechanisms and the external manifestations of globalization are not adequately captured. As a result, policies and programs meant to aid or circumvent potentially negative consequences that may arise as a response to globalizing processes, often have limited, if any, utility. As Chow (2003) states,

> Current debates on neoliberal and universalistic globalization pay little attention to gender and under-represent the experiences of diverse women in specific societal contexts, especially those in the developing world. This oversight has serious implications for theorizing about the powerful dynamics and vital consequences of globalization, for developing policy and practice, and for engaging in collective empowerment for effective social change that will reduce inequalities, human insecurity, and global injustice. (p. 444)

The relationship between globalization and gender has several significant dimensions. In particular, this connection is related to both economic and social justice agendas. As an increasing number of women in the industrialized world have entered into the paid labor force, socio-political changes in both the industrialized and the developing world have also encouraged, and at times, forced, women in the developing world to seek paid employment. The massive foray of women into the paid labor force in the West can be traced back to the convergence of economic restructuring that started to take place in the late 1960s, with the ideological and social movement that is today an international women's rights agenda. Economic restructuring, in both the industrialized and developing world over the last several decades, is primarily related to a complex, interrelated series of corporate, transnational and government initiatives, whose primary goals consisted of moving toward

B.S. Trask, *Globalization and Families*: *Accelerated Systemic Social Change*, DOI 10.1007/978-0-387-88285-7_3, © Springer Science+Business Media, LLC 2010 export production and greater incorporation into global markets.[1] These economic initiatives, which were enacted during the same period as the women's rights movement with its emphasis on empowering women by increasing their economic prospects, gained power and began to spread around the globe. Some economists have even termed this as an increase in the "supply" factor that was, concurrently, accompanied by a "demand" factor (Beneria 2003). As evidence for this shift they point toward a new penchant in certain sectors of economies around the world, specifically for women's labor participation and skills.

The complex relationship between globalization and gender is not limited to the worldwide entrance of women into the formal and informal labor force, sometimes also dubbed the "feminization of the labor force." Instead, we are witnessing some new unexpected phenomena arising through this conjoining of economic restructuring with the spread of specific ideological trends. Most politically controversial has been the shift of manufacturing and lately, even technological, banking and some types of managerial work, from the industrialized to the developing world, where low-wage earning women, in particular, are plentiful and have filled these jobs. Simultaneously, women's lives in industrialized and developing countries have become intertwined over the global landscape. The move of middle class women in industrialized countries into the work force has opened up the sphere of reproductive labor as an arena to be serviced out.[2] In response, a massive migration of women from the developing world has sought to fill jobs as domestic workers and caretakers (Pyle 2005). This phenomenon has been termed as a unique form of a transnational division of labor that links women across nation-states, and is tied to the production of transnational families (Pyle 2005).

Globalization not only impacts women, but has gendered effects for both sexes: as women's roles change, conversely, so do those of men. As Chow (2003) writes,

> Moreover, globalization presents a junction where global and local masculinities and femininities are constructed, existing gender regimes are challenged in different geopolitical locations, and gendered effects are registered beyond the border of a single country. (p. 447)

Globalization does not just impact gender discourses and relationships, but the phenomenon itself is affected by gendered responses and challenges. Globalization joins men and women, citizens and non-citizens, and individuals in industrialized and developing countries in various relationships with each other. These relationships are characterized by power differentials and varying access to systems of prestige, status, and resources. But the process itself is affected by the players – and since the players are engaged in gendered relationships, globalization, too, becomes a gendered phenomenon, a crucial point that cannot and should not be ignored.

---

[1] The actual details of economic restructuring will be more closely discussed further on in Chap. 8 detailing the relationship between nation–states and globalization. For an example of the highly controversial nature of these trends, see Eisenstein (2005).

[2] Interestingly, predictions in the 1970s and 1980s assumed that the service sector would lessen due to greater automation in the future. However, the service sector has actually expanded beyond most people's estimations.

3.1 Hegemonic Gender Discourses

Globalization affects a specific set of economic, political and social processes with often unintended implications and outcomes. Women and men are incorporated, and participate, in globalized activities on both an ideological, representational level as well as in a very practical applied manner. This makes any insight into understanding gender roles and relationships in various societies and their linkages to globalization complex. It becomes necessary to distinguish between ideologies of gender and the actual practices that may belie them (e.g., Macleod 1993; Bernal 1994). This problem is compounded by a continuing tendency for many social scientific writings, particularly with respect to globalization, to privilege dominant or hegemonic representations of gender (Ortner 1990). Dominant representations of gender refer to those models that support the claims of a particular group of people to superior status and power (for example, until recently in the West, men). These models are most likely to be invoked in formal discourse, and are often accorded a dominant position with respect to potentially competing models. [3] Ideologies, particularly the clearly articulated gender ideologies that people tend instantly to refer to, often take precedence, even when competing models are available. This occurs even though these representations may not exhaust the complete range of cultural discourses or social practices. As a result, dominant discourses emphasize certain, generally male-focused gender ideologies, while paying little attention to less systematically articulated conceptions of gender, especially those that are voiced more often by women themselves. Brenner (1995) suggests that "no single configuration of gender relations be considered absolutely "correct" or total because constructions of gender invariably encode conflicting and ambivalent meanings that can never be fully reconciled." (p. 22).

Since women's and men's interpretations of gender guide and give meaning to their social actions, they both call for examination. The key is not to emphasize one set of interpretations in lieu of others, just because they are not voiced as formally or as insistently. For example, Flax (1990) advocates a rapprochement between feminist and postmodernist theoretical approaches. She also suggests that the problem may stem from the perception that "Perhaps reality can have 'a' structure only from the falsely universalizing perspective of the dominant group. Perhaps only to the extent that one person or group can dominate the whole can 'reality' appear to be governed by one set of rules, be constituted by one privileged set of social relations, or be told by one 'story'" (p. 28).

The "rules" that are often invoked for a certain society only represent "reality" as it exists within the limited framework of a particular ideological system: one that grants superior status to men and their domains of activity and that delegates women to a subordinate female sphere. Nonetheless, we find that "reality" is changing as women and men negotiate and struggle with the tensions brought on through increasingly divergent, competing, and dominant ideologies.

---

[3] Claims for patriarchy have been challenged throughout American history by the experiences, particularly of women of color and immigrants who were not able to live by these "idealized" norms.

This chapter considers the relationship between constructions of gender and the material forces that shape families, communities, and the negotiation of everyday life in a global context. It presents some of the findings, particularly from feminist economists that reveal that this intersection produces and reproduces "an intricate web of inequalities between and among men and women" (Marchand and Runyan 2000, p. 8).

Gender is now understood as a form of socially learned behavior and expectations, and, thus, culturally and time specific and can be conceptualized as operating on three inter-connected levels: One, gender is an ideology with respect to social processes and practices; two, gender impacts all social relationships; and three, gender has a physical impact through the social construction of male and female bodies (Marchand and Runyan 2000). In this chapter, the construction and praxis of gender in a globalizing environment is examined on an ideological, as well as on a material level. It is understood as a negotiated phenomenon that is also constantly evolving – often with unintended consequences. This viewpoint suggests that cultural constructions of gender are best understood when viewed as inextricably enmeshed, both with global structures of production and exchange, and with the more encompassing systems of prestige to which these structures are tied (Ong and Peletz 1995). Through their integration into the global economy, women and men are forced to re-negotiate and re-define their position in their families and in society. These negotiations are closely tied to often conflicting ideological representations of men's and women's roles.

When one looks beyond gender symbolism to the praxis of gender, one finds that men's and women's contribution to the international, national, local, household and family economies are creating new forms of male and female autonomy and social power. However, as Ong and Peletz (1995) point out, gender politics are rarely just about gender. Instead, these conflicts represent and crystallize a nation-wide, and, at times, transnational struggle over a crisis of cultural identity, class formation, and ideological change. The contradictions between official and practical depictions of power become highlighted and illustrate that representations and interpretations of gender must be situated in ever-shifting and interrelated historical, social, and economic conditions.

3.2   Framing the Relationship Between Globalization and Gender

Despite the significant contributions to understanding globalization by social scientists, explicit ties between globalization and gender remain distinctively marginalized. Freeman (2001) points out that most analyses of globalization fall into one of two categories: either they are concerned with macro analyses of the history, structure and growth of economic forms of globalization, (and are gender blind), or, they exhibit an interest in the role of women in the global economy as workers and as citizens of developing countries. For example, Afshar and Barrientos (1999) suggest that,

> The impact of globalization on women has often been complex and contradictory, both in terms of their 'inclusion' and exclusion.' To be understood it needs to be analyzed not only at the global but also at the local and households levels. Feminists have been disaggregating the specificities of women's experiences in the context of the global process, but this work has yet to find its way into much of the core debate over globalization. (p. 6)

The limited attention to gender in mainstream perspectives on globalization is surprising, in the context of the contemporary understanding that gender intersects with class, ethnicity, race, nationality, and sexuality at virtually every level of social life. One would imagine that given the popularity and intensity of debates around globalization, the intersection of gender with these processes would have elicited greater attention, and that widely cited works on globalization would, by now, include gendered analyses. Even scholarship that specifically focuses on gender and globalization has a somewhat limited focus: analyses are either based on ethnographic accounts of local phenomena, or, more recently, have expanded to include provocative work by feminist economists on the role of economic restructuring and the subsequent effects on women in developing countries. However, we still lack insight into the impact of many globalizing processes on other aspects of women's experiences, including in the industrialized world. That said, the contribution of studies focusing on globalization and gender have generated new understandings about transformations in the social order in the global arena. For example, we now recognize that "cultural forms are imposed, invented, reworked, and transformed" on a transnational level with often far-reaching and unintended consequences (Gupta and Ferguson 1997, p. 5). This realization clearly points to the complexity and dynamism characteristic of globalization. Globalization is not just *one* process that can be succinctly captured and used to predict future phenomena. The processes of globalization are realized on the ground and in local contexts – but the actual progression itself is influenced, reworked and constrained through international, national, and local sites and actors (Freeman 2001). Ignoring gender in discourses on this phenomenon, leaves us with an incomplete understanding of some of the most dominant processes underlying globalization (Chow 2003).

Moving gender to the center of globalization analyses, allows us to develop new perspectives on the relationship between globalization and material, economic, political and social life. A gendered analysis provides insights into the association of processes, markets, nation-states and transnational entities with individuals. It highlights aspects of markets, transactions, and political movements, which are feminized or masculinized, and allows for speculation about the underlying causes for these processes. A gendered analysis exposes how social constructions of gender are manipulated, perpetuated, and negotiated and to what extent, within globalizing processes. Importantly for this discussion, a gendered analysis also exposes the implications of this phenomenon for the lived experiences of families, as well as their ideological representations. As Pyle (2005) states "A critical globalization study examining the relationship of globalization to women's lives must look at women's lives in the contexts of their families, communities, nations, regions, and internationally to fully understand the factors involved. Incorporating gender as a central category of analysis and utilizing such a multileveled analysis can lead to a more comprehensive understanding of globalization – both of its effects and the forces in motion – to reshape it. It can also shed light on the complex relationships among women from different countries and classes, revealing both the tensions and the similarities." (p. 250).

By including gender, we are able to gain insight into power differentials, and how unequal power relations are exacerbated or mediated through global processes. A focus on the relationship between gender and globalization allows us to understand that gender is a pivotal point for, and of, global restructuring (Nagar et al. 2002).

Gender legitimizes certain social institutions and processes that are associated with men and masculinity, in contrast to those that are concerned with women and femininity. Certain areas of production, for example, are increasingly dominated by female labor. Particularly in developing countries, such processes are legitimized, in part, by appealing to gendered discourses and evoking traditional gender images. For example, Talcott (2003) describes the highly gendered Colombian flower industry, where the invocation of women's "nimble fingers" are thought to be "better suited" to the "delicate work" of cutting flowers – a discourse that disguises the hazardous nature of the job. Wright (1997) also provides an instructive example by tracing how the success of *maquiladora* production in Mexico was achieved through a persuasive gendered discourse on "disposable women."[4] Women were depicted as working only on a temporary basis and earning wages for luxuries such as "lipsticks" instead of working to support their families. Since they were portrayed as temporary, they were not assumed to require any form of long-term investments and thus, no education or training was provided for them. Their low wages were publicly legitimized in the pursuit of capital accumulation by larger global entities.

Feminist economists are increasingly suggesting that a gendered analysis of globalization can uncover how "inequality is actively produced in the relations between global restructuring and culturally specific productions of gender difference" (Nagar et al. 2002, p. 261). Further, scholars such Nagar et al. (2002) and Wright (1997) illustrate that as neo-liberal states reduce the provision of social services, much of this work is taken over by women and moved to the "female" realm, usually conceptualized as the household, the family, and the community. In both industrialized and developing societies, a number of factors, including income insecurity have forced an increasingly higher number of women into the labor market. Particularly, low-wage women are often willing to take on precarious work without entitlements or additional benefits due to economic need. Governments characterized by a variety of economies have created conditions for employers that make it easier to let workers go, and to "downsize." This has facilitated reducing

---

[4]Maquiladora refers to a type of factory that imports materials and equipment on a duty-free and tariff-free basis for assembly and then re-exports the products, typically back to the country from where most of the products originated. The northern border of Mexico is a major maquiladora site for the production of U.S. goods. Typically, profits do not benefit the host country, in this case Mexico, but instead, flow back to the investor country.

benefits and rights for existing employees and resorting to a "cheaper" labor force to cover core work (Standing 1999). By increasingly emphasizing cost-cutting competitiveness, globalization has allowed companies to find new means to lower labor costs. This has also resulted in the move by companies to different types of subcontracting work, such as outsourcing and home-based work. This "informal" sector of work, those jobs without regular wages or benefits, has grown in proportion to the "formal" sector and has increasingly become associated with female workers. The economic restructuring of business and industry and its implications for workers and their families will be examined in greater detail in the chapter on work-family linkages.

The changing nature of women and men's ties to the market and to production may create, reconstitute, and deepen inequalities between groups and particularly, the sexes. For instance, at times various groups are in relations of conflict, as can happen in the context of employer-domestic worker scenarios, where large groups of women are employed by small groups of men. However, these transformations can also result in other outcomes. At times, undesirable conditions may encourage individuals to come together in forms of solidarity to resist and to take action (Talcott 2003). For example, some feminists point out that women are not just passive victims of global forces that sweep them into lives of oppression and exploitation, and instead women are active agents who resist and form new versions of womanhood and motherhood under changing conditions (Pyle 2005). However, while agency is often invoked in discourses on the relationship between actors and their social conditions, others, such as Talcott (2003) illustrate that agency, from a transnational perspective, is far more complex than the simple act of women asserting their will in certain situations. Not every woman or man, for that matter, can resist and choose among multiple options (Beneria 2003). Instead, individual's agency maybe constrained by cultural, social, and economic factors and contradictions that can undermine the potential for change (Gunewardena and Kingsolver 2007).

3.3 Masculine and Feminine Discourses

Mainstream approaches to globalization persist on emphasizing its "masculine" nature. The primary focus continues to be on the "public" and formal arenas of economics and politics, while ignoring the more "private" spheres of the household.[5] For example, Nagar et al. (2002) describe that,

> Research and discourses on globalization are peculiarly masculinist in that they serve to construct the spaces, scales and subjects of globalization in particular ways. Specifically, discourses of global capitalism continue to position women, minorities, the poor, and southern places in ways that constitute globalization as dominant. Images of passive women and places (frequently southern but also de-industrialized places in the north) are

---

[5] A large feminist literature has now disproven the public–private dichotomy by illustrating that it is impossible to dichotomize the concepts. Public and private spheres are closely tied to one another.

constructed and simultaneously serve to construct discourses of globalization as capitalist, as Western-centric, and as the only possible future for the "global economy." The result is "capitalist myopia" by which researchers assume that global capitalism is all encompassing and they cannot see, or consider salient, other noncapitalist, nonpublic spheres and actors. (p. 262–263)

In those occasions when gender is acknowledged in mainstream approaches, it is incorporated in a simplistic manner that allows class, regional and generational differences to be obfuscated. For example, globalization may be deemed as "oppressive" for women across temporal and geographical lines (Kelly 2001). Compounding this problem is the fact that development organizations may appropriate these interpretations and transform them into well-intentioned but, at times, culturally inappropriate and disastrous programs for women (Kelly 2001). Moreover, Marchand and Runyan (2000) point out, "Even as the private sector is valorized over the public sector more generally, the private realm is hyperfeminized in relation to not only the state and the market, but also civil society in which it is rendered either invisible or highly subordinated. Ironically, however, the private realm has become highly politicized as a site of and for restructuring processes" (p. 15).

As an example, Marchand and Runyan (2003) cite the contemporary case of middle class American women who are caught between mainstream gender discourses that cast them, simultaneously, as autonomous, self-empowered working women, thereby devaluing their contributions to their families, and popular rhetoric that emphasizes family values and intensive mothering.[6] These dichotomous representations have brought about a crisis for many American women wherein they are caught in the practical realities of their lives, which require them to work for economic and ideational reasons, and discourses that admonish them for not investing enough time into their families. This discourse has also lead to multiple conjectures about the dichotomization of the private sphere of home and the public sphere of work. While such a theoretical separation has lost credence in academic circles, positing the private against the public still remains popular in mainstream perspectives. However, as debates on gender representations illustrate, in today's world, the private is public and that which we have deemed as public has become private. It has become virtually impossible to speak of gender and gender roles as only pertaining to one or the other sphere. These contradictions are also found in the developing world, where conflicting gender representations characterize the social landscape as well.

Gendered analyses of globalization in the developing world have highlighted how women's triple roles in production, reproduction and community management have intensified and been expanded through global indebtedness, structural adjustment policies, and the popularity of neo-liberal development strategies (Marchand and Runyan 2000; Nagar et al. 2002). They have also brought to the forefront the fact that women's work for pay has not necessarily resulted in a rearrangement of domestic roles, but for many women just in an increase in their responsibilities.

---

[6] See Bianchi et al. (2000) for an interesting exposition of how the intensive mothering model has been growing since the 1960s.

Recent accounts point out that some of these analyses are also flawed as hegemonic "traditional" depictions of men, and women's roles do not take into account scenarios where men are unable to find work and women take on multiple tasks for family survival (Nagar et al. 2002).

Other gender-specific phenomena are also emblematic of the current situation. For example, as in certain parts of the world women have increasingly become poorer (the feminization of poverty), they have come together at times to share care work and other basic provision for their families. Importantly, in certain instances, this has led to collectivized political action and resistance movements by women against the globalizing forces that they perceive as destructive to their lives and their families' well-being. These types of movements indicate that new constructive phenomena can emerge out of potentially devastating situations.

Despite the obvious gendered overtones of globalization, mainstream analysis of the relationship between globalizing processes and gender discourses remains inadequate and relegated to "feminist scholars." Feminist scholars, themselves, have questioned if this marginalization is not part of a wider hegemony of globalization discourses where mainstream (male) discourses are privileged over their (female) contributions. Freeman (2001) suggests that

> What is called for as well, then, is a feminist re-conceptualization of globalization, whereby local forms of globalization are understood not merely as effects but also as constitutive ingredients in the changing shape of these movements. A feminist re-conceptualization of this sort requires a stance toward globalization in which the arrows of change are imagined in more than one direction, and where gender is interrogated not only in the practices of men and women in local sites but also in the ways in which both abstract as well as tangible global movements and processes are ascribed masculine or feminine values. (p. 1013)

Furthermore, while scholars point out that some aspects of globalization and gender are acknowledged and investigated, such as networks and trade flows, or investment, and migration, other areas, such as the effects of ideational movements and the emergence of transnational social networks of women have been virtually ignored. In today's advanced technological environment, knowledge on "women's issues" can spread through immediately through international conferences, a web presence, or media coverage. New conceptualizations of "appropriate" gender roles can instantaneously travel the globe. We know little about how these types of messages are received, interpreted and acted upon in local, national and transnational contexts. Without analysis of how women and men actually perceive and interact with globalizing forces in their families and communities, fundamental aspects of globalization remain hidden from view, and leave us with only a partial picture. Again, this raises questions and concerns around the hegemonic privileging of certain activities over others. A feminist perspective on globalization seeks to identify, deconstruct and obliterate the hierarchical dualism of masculinity and femininity, the public and the private, the culturally valued and the culturally de-valued. A gendered analysis is, thus, a key determinant for understanding the interaction of globalization with family matters.

3.4 How Did We Get Here? Contributions of Family Studies and Gender Theorists

Feminist analyses of global markets have focused specifically on the gendered division of labor where men's work is accorded more status than women's work with respect to pay and status. Of primary interest is the actual work that men and women perform, and how that is perceived and rewarded both from an ideological perspective as well as in more practical, financial terms. In the global context, gender representations, linkages to hierarchies of power, and constantly shifting types of work and work contexts, require dynamic forms of analyses.

The starting point for fluid conceptualizations of gender, stem from the "doing gender" perspective that was first introduced in the late 1980s. The importance of this concept lies in its emphasis on the active construction of gender in daily interactions. In a pivotal article West and Zimmerman (1987) explained,

> We contend that the 'doing' of gender is undertaken by women and men whose competence as members of society is hostage to its production. Doing gender involves a complex of socially guided perceptual, interactional, and micropolitical activities that cast particular pursuits as expressions of masculine and feminine 'natures.' When we view gender as an accomplishment, an achieved property of situated conduct, our attention shifts from matters internal to the individual and focuses on interactional and, ultimately, institutional arenas.....Rather than as a property of individuals, we conceive of gender as an emergent feature of social situations: both as an outcome of and a rationale for various social arrangements and as a means of legitimating one of the most fundamental divisions of society. (p. 126)

This approach to understanding gender continues to remain relevant, and becomes even more apparent when viewed through a historical and cross-cultural lens. The "doing gender" perspective emphasizes processes of "situated behavior." Gender becomes a moving target that is continually constructed and used in interactions – it is not a fixed entity. The "accomplishment" of gender relies on individuals behaving is such a manner that fits with normative expectations of appropriate gender behaviors. In other words, men and women are expected to exhibit certain characteristics and styles of behavior that distinguish them from one another. From a "doing gender" perspective, these characteristics and behaviors may be defined quite differently, depending on time and place. Normative guidelines rely on socio-historical context, and they guide and regulate appropriate gender behaviors.

Sullivan (2006) points out that while a large feminist literature has now incorporated the "doing gender" approach into analyses of family and household relationships, the main thrust of these works focuses on "how contextual behaviors lead to the reproduction of existing structures of gender inequality, rather than on their possible contribution to processes of differentiation and change in those structures (p.11). In other words, most analyses concentrate on understanding how existing gender constructions are replicated in families rather than how to bring about change with respect to gender roles. In order to understand some of the current processes, it is instructive to look briefly toward history and the material conditions that have led to the contemporary interest in gender roles, specifically on the household level.

The short synopsis that follows focuses on the United States due to the influence of American feminist scholars on the initial discussions about gender ideologies.

Much of what is believed in the West about the "appropriate" roles of men and women can be traced back to the era of industrialization. The fundamentals of the argument, which is primarily feminist in nature but has spread to more mainstream perspectives, can be summarized briefly as the following: In the Western world, the movement toward industrialization was accompanied by a growing distinction between paid and unpaid work, a distinction that became increasingly associated with men's (paid) work and women's (unpaid) work. As Western societies moved from primarily depending on an agricultural foundation toward a strong industrial base, the very nature of work changed. Where in agrarian times, women and men worked together to maintain the farm and the household, industrialization moved work out of the home. This form of work became increasingly valued and as society moved predominantly toward a market economy, money became the primary currency (Hattery 2001). As the need for factory labor grew, men's work became more valuable and led to a societal discourse around naturalized roles for men and women. Moreover, a pervasive discourse around a "natural" division of labor became legitimized by highlighting biological differences between the sexes. Women's biological ability to bear children increasingly became consistently equated with an equivalent ability to rear children. In the public perception, this was thought to make women infinitely more suited to attend to the "private" sphere of the household and family.[7] Men, on the other hand, were believed to be biologically better disposed to working in the harsh environments of factories and, in general, in the "public" arenas of work and finance. This brought about a context where the contributions of men came to be perceived as more valuable for families and society due to the primacy given to the importance of earning money (Hattery 2001; Moen and Sweet 2003). Women's most important input became their domestic one. However, by working for "free," their labor became undervalued creating inequality in families. These 18th and 19th century developments gave birth to an ideology about gender roles and the division of labor in families that continues to persist in U.S. culture.

Feminist scholarship on families has focused extensively on exposing this inequality between the sexes, and on understanding the perpetuation of traditional normative models of gender. Feminist scholars have also pointed out that despite popular conceptualizations that evoke a mythical relatively recent past characterized by clearly defined gender roles and breadwinner-homemaker families, historically, most American families were not able to adhere to this dominant model. Minorities and low-income families, while aware of these hegemonic representations, were unable to participate in these clearly defined domestic behaviors. Instead, in order to survive, low-income and minority men and women had to create other types of family constellations that included women working outside of the home and men sharing in domestic household activities (Coontz 1992).

---

[7]In colonial America, it was thought that men were more suited toward childrearing, especially teaching children values and morals.

Significant social changes in industrialized and developing societies, compounded by the spread of feminist ideologies, have led to the notion of appropriate gender roles in families becoming a hotbed of argumentation. A limited perspective has continued to adhere to biological arguments about the "natural" division of labor, while other standpoints have suggested that the dominance of traditional gender roles can be traced to their functionality (Parsons and Bales 1955 in Hattery 2001). Critical of these biological and/or functional approaches, feminists have identified the ideological construction of the "breadwinner-homemaker family" with its accompanying gender role constructs as particularly oppressive to women (Erickson 2005; Hochschild 1989; Thompson and Walker 1989). This view has been exported by feminists to other parts of the world where social unrest, the incorporation of large numbers of women into the workforce, and the revival of fundamentalist movements have re-focused attention on the role of women in families, communities, and societies.

However, this mass-scale exportation of specifically American perspectives on "appropriate" and "inappropriate" gender ideologies accompanied with the identification of family as the site of women's domination, have evoked a counter response, specifically from feminists working in developing and non-Western parts of the world. These feminists argue that while national ideologies may perpetuate models of traditional gender constructs and families, women and men are not passive actors. Instead, they are actively engaged in constructing new models of gender and families for themselves (Pyle 2005). Globalization has led to multiple ideological and economic constructs and models becoming available to individuals. We cannot speak of a universal condition nor can we blame the institution of the family for women's and men's situations. Instead, contextual approaches reveal that a complex interplay of values, resources, and individual responses shapes gender constructions and practices.

3.5   Patriarchy on the Decline?

From an economic and social perspective, a truly significant effect of globalization is the incorporation of growing numbers of women into the paid labor force, both in the Western and non-Western world. This change is undermining the very foundation that has sustained gender ideologies in so many places. We are beginning to witness patriarchal ideologies being questioned, and very slowly disintegrating due to economic arrangements that do not accord the breadwinner in the household, historically the male, the right to dominance anymore. While this process is uneven and realized differentially, empirical and circumstantial evidence point toward a gradual realignment of gendered relations. Women's entry into the formal labor force, in such high numbers the world over, is destroying the illusion that men have a unique role as breadwinner and provider for the family.

However, most discussions on patriarchy fail to capture the ambivalent nature of these changes. Despite contemporary circumstances that facilitate societal transformations in gender constructions and gender roles, unequal relationships in families and their ensuing conflicts and negotiations still continue to dominate as a central part of gender relationships in households and society at large. Beneria (2003), for example, observes that contemporary gender negotiations are framed by a less strictly formulated patriarchal framework primarily for women in the Western world. In the past, Western men derived support for their authoritative position in the household from dominant ideology, religion, media and other such forms of discourse dissemination. Today, increasingly in the West, these discourses are not as stringent or as dominant anymore. However, they have not disappeared and, at times, regain vigor through nationalist and fundamentalist movements such as the "family values" faction in the United States.

Evidence from of other areas in the world such as the Dominican Republic (Safa 2002), and certain areas of the Middle East (Moghadam 2003) point to the use of gender ideologies as a form of rallying cry. On the familial level, gender praxis is changing due to practical considerations merging with new gender representations, promulgated through the women's movement and contemporary media. However, simultaneously, nation-states have been reviving patriarchal ideologies in an attempt to rally their populations. Safa (2002) for example, describes that process with respect to a new movement by the Dominican state that encourages men to be placed in leadership positions in organizational settings and discourages labor unions from supporting female candidates for those same jobs.

> What we are witnessing here is a reassertion of patriarchy and more specifically the male breadwinner model at the public institutional level such as employers, labor unions, and political parties.....It is also be seen in employers' preference for men in supervisory positions and in the reluctance of labor unions to support women's leadership....low-income women such as free trade zone workers may suffer from greater subordination at the public level than middle-class women because they are subject to class (and possibly race) as well as gender subordination" (Safa 2002, p. 25)

The Dominican example illustrates that it is simplistic to assume that the large number of women working has now universally equalized relationships for women and men the world over. The dynamics of unequal gender relations are closely linked to institutional and structural factors that affect the intra-household distribution of resources and the social construction of gender (Beneria 2003). Multiple studies illustrate that the mere fact that women may have access to resources, does not guarantee that they will have control over these resources. Traditions, norms and gender constructions interact with access to resources and power relations. These processes, in turn, shape gender ideologies and behaviors. For example, in a study of lower-class women in West Bengal, India, Ganguly-Scrase (2003) illustrates that women do not necessarily seek to be autonomous beings, independent of their families. They view their financial contributions as important to the collective, which they, in turn, perceive as the support system that aids them in accomplishing their desires for greater opportunities.

It is striking to note, that while there is much public and scholarly interest in the movement of women into the formal and informal labor force, and the implications of this phenomenon on a familial and social level, there is not an equivalent intense discussion on the effects of changes in women's roles on men. In much of the discourse on the transformative aspects of globalization and gender, the relational aspect of gender is being ignored. In fact, Connell (2005) explains,

> In both national and international policy documents concerned with gender equality, women are the subjects of the policy discourse…..In every statement about women's disadvantages, there is an implied comparison with men as the advantaged group. When men are present only as a background category in a policy discourse about women, it is difficult to raise issues about men's and boys' interests, problems, or differences. This could be done only by falling into a backlash posture and affirming 'men's rights' or by moving outside a gender framework altogether. (pp. 1805–1800)

Connell raises the often overlooked point that as we see women's roles change, ever so incrementally, *globally*, we need to also account for what is happening with men. Moreover, since both women and men are positioned very differently with respect to access to resources, and systems of prestige and power, responses with respect to role change and ideologies will depend on a multitude of factors and cannot be simplistically assumed to be uniform across the sexes. As he continues to state,

> Class, race, national, regional, and generational differences cross-cut the category 'men,' spreading the gains and costs of gender relations very unevenly among men. There are many situations where groups of men may see their interest as more closely aligned with the women in their communities than with other men. It is not surprising that men respond very diversely to gender-equality politics (Connell 2005, p. 1809)

Blanket assumptions about the experiences of one group, be they men or women, do not capture the inequalities that both women and men may face on a consistent basis. Still, cross-cultural evidence indicates that fundamental changes in gender roles are underway in many parts of the world. These transformations, have significant implications for families, and specifically the "nuclear" family that has been the subject of so much debate, research, and controversy.

3.6   What is Happening to the "Nuclear" Family

A subject of much debate is the contemporary state of the "nuclear" family. Castells (1997), for example, argues that the nuclear family is in crisis. The nuclear family he refers to, is specifically, the patriarchal nuclear family that in the United States has been upheld as the ideal, since the post World War II years, and similar forms of which are found in many other parts of the world. In his analysis, he cites multiple factors as coming together to slowly but fundamentally transform social life between men and women.

> The patriarchal family, the cornerstone of patriarchalism, is being challenged in this end of the millennium by the inseparably related processes of the transformation of women's work and the transformation of women's consciousness. Driving forces behind these processes are the rise of an informational, global economy, technological changes in the reproduction of the human species, and the powerful surge of women's struggles, and of a multifaceted feminist movement, three strands that have developed since the late 1960s (Castells 1997, p. 135)

He continues his argument by stating,

> By the crisis of the patriarchal family I refer to the weakening of a model of family based on the stable exercise of authority/domination over the whole family by the adult male head of the family. It is possible, in the 1990s, to find indicators of such a crisis in most societies, particularly in the most developed countries (p. 138)

As evidence, Castells points to an increasing acceptance of divorce, to growing numbers of diverse family forms, to the dominance of single-parent households and to the increasing number of children born out of wedlock. These are trends that are primarily found in the West, but some are also very slowly permeating other regions of the world. In particular, divorce and single-parent households are becoming, albeit slowly, somewhat more pervasive in certain other areas. Castells also notes that the decline of patriarchy has changed the manner in which individuals identify themselves and even affects their relationship with others. For example, men are increasingly expected to participate more fully in the lives of their wives, as well as their children. This phenomenon is not just reflective of changes in the United States and Europe, but is increasingly taking on significance in non-Western countries, many of which have until recently been characterized by dominant patriarchal ideologies. Castells suggests that family connections are being replaced by personal networks "in which individuals and their children follow a pattern of sequential family, and non-family, personal arrangements throughout their lives" (1997, p. 348). This suggests a model of family that is fluid and dynamic, where men are not "in charge" anymore, so to speak. It also denaturalizes family roles and, instead, highlights the performative, intentional and achieved nature of relationships. Building on Castells' argument, these trends point to the emergence of a new normative family model, which instead of being defined by exclusion and boundaries, is, instead, an inclusive model characterized primarily by choice.

It is important to note that while speculation and discussions, such as Castells' widely cited work on the erosion of patriarchy, are significant we should not forget that in many places, there still exists a significant gap between hegemonic ideals of patriarchy, and the lived experiences of women in their families, communities and societies. As men begin to lose their authoritative position in the household, they are also increasingly nervous about the growing economic and social independence of women (Chant 2000). A significant rearrangement of what are perceived as "natural" or even "religiously" ordained roles, can lead to resistance movements that seek to strengthen patriarchal relations. Globalization has contributed to this conflict by providing greater access to low-paying jobs for women, and weakening men's place in the labor market.

Globalization has also contributed to other social changes on the familial level. Through greater attainment of economic resources, women are able to postpone marriage or re-marriage, and become more capable functioning as the female heads of households. Opportunities for labor migration can also allow poor families to adapt to changing economic conditions by utilizing the labor of an increasing number of members of a household. A contemporary extended family may contribute to household unity and survival through the contributions of its various members from areas all around the world. Remittances may come in not just from men, as in previous periods in history, but from a variety of family members working both locally and transnationally. The pooling of these resources, at times can even lead to the advancement of some segments of certain populations that may never have had access to economic opportunities before. This is not meant to imply that globalization leads most poor individuals out of poverty (*see* Chap. 9 for this discussion), but instead I just wish to point out that both constraints and opportunities accompany globalization. An examination of globalizing effects reveals that it is critical to examine household strategies in a contextualized, nuanced manner, and not to assume that globalization affects only certain groups or levels of society.

3.7   The Divisive Issue of Female Labor and Family Equality

Feminists emphasize gender equality as a key to empowerment and success for women across the globe. This ideology stresses that women need to have access to paid employment in the same manner as men. Moreover, this belief is based on the understanding that both sexes have equivalent capabilities and need to be provided with the same opportunities. However, there is another strand of feminist thought, which highlights the differences between men and women, and how these differences influence the relationship of the sexes vis a vis each other (Gilligan 1982). This has led to a fundamental dilemma for feminists with respect to either highlighting differences, which can potentially lead to the perpetuation of gender inequalities, or to diminishing differences and, thus, losing some of the traits that have historically contributed to the well-being of individuals and families (Beneria 2003).

Disagreements on these issues are expressed foremost in perspectives on female labor and its effects on the household. Some activists and scholars assume that a potential outcome of large numbers of women working outside of the home, is a higher level of female-headed households. According to this line of reasoning, when women are working on a massive scale, men do not find stable employment and, consequently, leave their families, forcing women to take on the provider role. However, another view posits that wage labor empowers women and increases their options within the family, the community, and the larger society. Fernández-Kelly (1997) illustrates that neither perspective can be supported by empirical evidence universally. As proof, she cites the findings of studies of households who were part of the *maquiladora* program in Northern Mexico. These studies revealed that most of these households were characterized by a surprisingly high degree of adaptation and diversity, and did not move in a linear progression toward disintegration. She also points out that perspectives, which posit that women are universally empowered in their families through labor market participation and monetary earnings, do not necessarily hold true either. While ideologies about the sexual division of labor are changing, for many women in the developing world in particular, certain aspects of their lives remain fixed and inflexible. In many places, it is now accepted for women to work outside of the home. However, men have not necessarily embraced an ideology of increasing their domestic involvement. Women, thus, turn to other mechanisms to make their families function. For example, Chant (1991) describes that Mexican working class families often add young, single girls to the household who provide child care and take care of household chores for working mothers in exchange for room, board, and some form of education.

Despite gendered critiques of family life, ethnographic work reveals that in all of its various configurations, the family remains a strategic arrangement that meets certain social and economic needs for its members. Moreover, especially among the poor, and for many individuals in non-Western societies, working outside of the home is best understood as a strategy for collective survival rather than as a path for individual advancement (Kelly 1997). When economic times worsen, it is imperative that as many members of the household work as is possible. This can result in greater family cohesion than fragmentation – at least from a structural perspective. Individuals depend on one another in order to survive. For women, this trend tends to have mixed results. Young working-class women who live at home, may have the added advantage of deriving a certain self-worth from participating in the labor force. Yet, this very action often also prevents them from furthering their education. Older women, become burdened by a double shift of work while working-class men may also be affected. They lose some of their traditional power due to decreasing opportunities and are forced to take on domestic roles for which they have no ideological supports in their society. In all of these scenarios, however, the importance of bonded relationships becomes primary. Moreover, the negotiation and dynamism exhibited by changing families illustrates that gender roles are neither fixed nor uniform, but are refashioned depending on local conditions.

3.8 Vulnerable Women and Children

A critical and often ignored aspect of globalization is the reality that economic deprivation and widening income disparities can have particularly disastrous implications for women and children. The growth of an international entertainment and tourism industry has magnified demand for the trafficking of women, girls, and at times boys, for sexual purposes (Pearson 2000). The increasing numbers of individuals drafted, either voluntarily or involuntarily into the sex industry, has been likened by some to a contemporary form of slavery (Watts and Zimmerman 2002). While reliable data is difficult to come by, it is estimated that between 600,000 and 800,000 people, of whom about 70–80% are female, are trafficked from one country to another every year. Many more are trafficked within their own societies (Cree 2008). The conditions that promote sexual trafficking include poverty, sexual and familial violence, and gender-based discrimination, making women and children, particularly vulnerable. Traffickers primarily seek out the most vulnerable members of society such as orphans, women with disabilities, and children in order to make it easier to transport and exploit their victims once they have take them to their destinations

(Hodge 2008). The primary contemporary "sending" areas from which sex workers are recruited or coerced include Eastern Europe, the former countries of the Soviet Union, Asia, Africa, and some Latin American societies. The main recipients of sex workers are the United States, Europe, Japan and Thailand.

This issue has spurred complex debates about the extent to which sex workers choose this form of work, their roles as victims, and the thorny issue of human rights. Lim (1998) has suggested that policymakers almost exclusively focus on the prostitutes (the females), while ignoring the clients (the men) and the poverty that exacerbates the situation. Much of the problem can be attributed to the invisibility of trafficking and the sex industry in general. Traffickers work in shadowy venues and victims are often too frightened to contact the appropriate authorities. Some contemporary analysts have suggested that one solution to this problem would be to import the Swedish model of prostitution. In Sweden, prostitution is considered a type of male violence against women and children, and thus, is considered a criminal offense. The institutionalization of this law has led to a stabilization, and even somewhat of a decline in prostitution, when compared to neighboring Scandinavian countries that have legalized prostitution as a separate solution (Hodge 2008). The issue of sexual trafficking and the conditions that lead to this form of exploitation raises questions about linkages between women and children, their vulnerability under certain conditions, the context in which choices are made, and the distribution of resources and power in families.

For millions of women, particularly in the developing world, gender issues such as the division of labor in families, patriarchy, or the struggle for self-realization and autonomy are not the primary focus, nor are these issues that they can relegate time to. For these women, basic survival for themselves, their children, and other members of their families is of overriding importance instead. The economic circumstances of their families force them to seek any form of paid labor, and at times due to the lack of opportunities in their home areas, to go abroad.[8] This creates a situation where women must leave behind their children and other loved ones in order to preserve the well-being of their families. For these women, the ideal of the "nurturing wife and mother" is unattainable in the manner in which it is construed in so many places. Moreover, in the areas to which they migrate, nation-states set up formidable controls to ensure that these women are there only for the explicit purpose of providing certain types of labor. Policy is designed to specifically prevent these women from bringing their children or other family members to the labor-receiving state. Thus, the familial contribution of women who are employed abroad, to their families, is primarily an economic one; one that is not legitimized by dominant models of gender either at home or in their host societies. At times, they even become construed as "bad mothers" or "uncaring mothers."

The academic literature, for example, is replete with examples of why migration "harms" women or "benefits" them (Ehrenreich and Hochschild 2003), but again, one cannot universalize from specific examples. Later in this book, I examine some

---

[8]Opportunities is used loosely in this context as it may refer, as we have seen, to a wide range of low-paying jobs or even sex work.

of these representations with a closer focus on the relationship between work and family issues. For the purposes of this discussion, it is sufficient to point out that this situation provides an example where dominant ideologies of gender conflict powerfully with economic realities. Women, and women's "roles" are eulogized and idealized, and in so many places, used as a symbol, to measure the health of families, communities or even societies. As was noted previously, in the West this is the outgrowth of a specific 19th century model that has most often been attributed to industrialization. Industrialization led to the concept of separate spheres for men and women, and a hegemonic gender discourse, which legitimized the separation of work and family. Adhering to representations of traditional gender roles, of "nurturing wives and mothers" and "breadwinner-provider husbands and fathers" allows those individuals who do not fit this model, to be relegated to a lower less prestigious realm of society. In these representations, how individuals construct and "practice" family and gender roles, become pivotal forms of evaluation. Significantly, what is missing in virtually all of these gendered analyses, however, is a perspective on the role of children in families, and the viewpoints of the children themselves.

3.9 Globalization, Gender, and Inequalities

The processes of globalization can distort existing social constructions of gender, strengthen them, or can assimilate traditional and newer concepts into new amalgamations (Pyle and Ward 2003). The gendered nature of globalization is not just an intrinsic aspect of ideology or culture, but is also deeply embedded in social institutions (Chow 2003). However, Bhagwati (2004) suggests that globalization and its impacts, cannot and should not be discussed simply from the position of women's welfare. Instead, in pursuing the gendered nature of social change, societies need to consider the ways "in which women in that society and economy may be more vulnerable to the consequences of policy changes such as trade liberalization, projects such as the building of roads and railways or the provision of irrigation or drinking water, and indeed the myriad ways in which change comes. Rather than setting up roadblocks on every policy change, big and small, and demanding that each policy change be made conditional on an examination of its impact on women....it is more useful to think of policies that alleviate the totality of distress to women from the multitude of policy changes" (Bhagwati 2004, p. 87).

Globalization processes can affect men just as critically as they do women. Especially with respect to job security and entitlement benefits, men are increasingly at a growing disadvantage. The kind of work and labor force involvement that has until recently been primarily associated with women (low paid and "flexible") is spreading to work that in the past was associated with men (steady and unionized). In fact, some argue that we are seeing a convergence in the labor market experiences of men and women (Standing 1999).

But the story is not that simple. A growing body of evidence links globalization with increasing inequalities not just between individuals within societies, but also between societies (Freeman 1996). As we have seen, numerous female scholars have highlighted the inherent vulnerability of so many women, particularly poor, low-income and minority women, in both industrialized and developing countries. It is this group that is particularly susceptible to globalizing processes such as market fluctuations, labor force demands and other social factors, which are out of their control. Rodrik (1997), however, puts forward the standpoint that societies that emphasize strong social safety nets, such as the Scandinavian countries, are in a better position to deal with the potentially deleterious impacts of globalization. Since societies, communities, and families become increasingly destabilized in environments characterized by unemployment and underemployment, there is a growing need for the institutionalization of social policies and safety nets that most places are not interested in nor are in the position to provide. Incorporating gendered analyses into globalization debates begins to move the focus to social issues and the *human* condition. It raises moral questions about the basic rights for women, men and children to a certain standard of living (Beneria 2003). Gendering globalization studies and policies introduces a social justice perspective that questions if we should ignore the reality that an increasing number of women, men and children are living without steady streams of income, and without adequate means to provide shelter, sustenance, and medical assistance for their families. Incorporating social analyses into the globalization framework also highlights the impacts of globalizing processes as inequalities between groups continue to grow instead of to lessen.

In order to begin to solve some of these issues, we may want to rethink how globalization is approached, analyzed, and responded to. A gendered approach allows for the incorporation of new perspectives that include a multitude of representative voices. Pyle (2005), for example, recommends implementing a wide ranging social justice agenda, and, thereby, increasing certain forms of gender equality. Her suggestions include raising awareness and empowering more individuals to address the gendered issues of globalization, recognizing work such as caring labor; creating new heuristic measures and procedures that account for gender (such as government policies), and assessing risks that women may face and ascertaining their rights.

We also need to be sensitive to the lived experiences of *individuals* in order to formulate solutions. Connell (2005) points out that while it is common to blame "men" for the ills of the world, the men who historically have benefited from their position in society, need to be distinguished from the men who provide much of the low-paid workforce in industrialized and developing societies. Men and women may have gendered experiences, but those experiences are mitigated by a wide ranging degree of factors. As Beneria (2003) succinctly suggests, this perspective implies placing inequality, moral issues, preservation of the environment, individual and collective well-being, and social change and justice in families and societies at the center of scholarship, as well as in the public agenda.

Part II
Examining Linkages between Globalization and Families

Chapter 4
Global Migration and the Formation of Transnational Families

A critical feature of globalization is the movement of individuals, both within countries and across borders. As the process of global integration accelerates, we are witnessing a growing number of people on the move. While migration is not a new phenomenon, it has grown in volume and impact since 1945, and especially since the 1980s (Castles and Miller 2003). Due to growing inequalities within and between societies, large numbers of people are moving from rural to urban areas, and from developing to industrialized countries in search of opportunities and resources. Refugee flows, the growth of global organizations, and the creation of new free trade areas are also contributing to significant international migration. While actual migration numbers are low in proportion to the global population, the impacts of migration are significant. Most individuals migrate as families or in groups, and their leaving and resettlement has crucial social, political, and economic implications for their home and receiving societies. International migration provides the basis for the creation of new forms of transnational families and the movement of information and capital.

Migration is recognized as an economically, politically, and socially complex phenomenon. International migration produces large flows of monetary remittances from the industrialized world, and allows workers from all walks of life to find new opportunities that are usually not available in their home societies. Globalization has facilitated this process, in part, through the opening up of free trade zones, and the ease of transportation and communication technologies. The large flows of individuals between societies has, however, led to increased hostilities between native-born citizens and migrants in many places, creating political tensions and restrictive policy responses. Globalization has also transformed the relationship of migrants and those they leave behind. Historically, migration was associated with the severing of familial, community and societal ties. However, in the contemporary environment, migrants have many more options for maintaining relationships to their home societies, in contrast to even just several years ago. Ease of travel, combined with media such as the Internet, and video conferencing, allow individuals who leave their homes to stay in touch with loved ones in previously unimagined ways.

Recent extensive international migration has had predictable and, at times, unintended consequences for both sending and receiving societies, and is associated with restructuring societies, politics, and economics (Castles and Miller 2003). While receiving societies benefit from the availability of cheaper labor and high skilled workers, immigration has also been perceived as highly disruptive to the social fabric. In recent years, we have witnessed a serious global backlash against migration as the perception of many, that migration favors immigrants over the native citizenry, has deepened. However, low birth rates in industrialized countries coupled with the aging of their populations, enormous pay differentials between various parts of the world, and increasing ethnic strife guarantee that individuals from the developing world will continue to want to migrate to the industrialized world, and that this phenomenon will grow.[1]

The significant impacts of migration have not gone unnoticed by scholars of globalization. While migration and its concomitant effects have long been a focus for anthropologists interested in identity studies, and for demographers concerned with the flow of individuals across borders, economists and political scientists have, more recently, also addressed the impetus and consequences of international migration in particular. Specifically, the role of remittances in global economic flows has elicited attention among migration scholars. For example, Pessar (1982, 1999) has suggested that while sending remittances home is not a new phenomenon, the more intense and frequent interactions that result from these contacts make contemporary migration quite different from migration in the nineteenth century. Feminists have also highlighted the gendered nature of the recent migrations. An increasing number of women are leaving their families and home societies behind, in order to find financial and employment opportunities abroad.

4.1 The Demographics of Migration

According to United Nations estimates, approximately 191 million individuals, or 3.0% of the world population were living outside of their native countries as of 2005 (United Nations 2008). http://esa.un.org/migration.index.asp?panel=1 Of those, approximately two-thirds were living in industrialized countries in contrast to the developing world, where about 1.5% of the population are not native born. From a global perspective, the U.S. currently has the highest actual number of immigrants. This phenomenon can be attributed to changes in the U.S. Migration Act of 1965 that ended migration quotas based on national origin. Besides the U.S., Canada, Australia, New Zealand, Argentina, and Israel are also considered major migration societies (Castles and Miller 2003).[2]

---

[1] Migration may also increase due to climate changes that could make certain regions uninhabitable.

[2] There is some terminological confusion between migrants and immigrants. Migrant is often used to describe an individual who leaves a place and goes to another without reference to direction, purpose, or duration. Immigrant most commonly refers to an individual who leaves one society behind to live and/or work in another.

A recent report by the U.S. Census Bureau indicates that there are approximately 38 million foreign born individuals in the U.S., constituting about 13% of the population (2008). This is a significant increase, given that in 1970 approximately 4.7% of the population was foreign born. Comparatively, Australia's population is composed of approximately 23% immigrants, and in Canada the percentage of immigrants is close to 18%. All of these countries are characterized by a *proportionally* higher immigrant population than the U.S. In some countries, such as England, urban areas specifically attract immigrants. For example, in London, 28% of the inhabitants were born somewhere outside the United Kingdom. In terms of actual number of immigrants, the U.S. is closely positioned with Russia, whose high migration rates, at 16.8%, are primarily attributed to the fall of the Soviet Union; change that transformed internal migration into international migration (United Nations 2008). The U.S. and Russia are followed by Germany, which has 7.3 million migrants. Other countries, including Saudi Arabia, France, Canada, Australia, India, and Pakistan are also major receivers of migrants ranging from 4 to 7 million individuals each.

Certain areas of the world are particularly affected by labor-related and/or refuge migration. For example, when compared to their native born populations, Middle Eastern countries have the highest proportion of foreign born. In the United Arab Emirates, approximately 68% of individuals are foreign workers (Freeman 2006). While several countries such as Turkey, Egypt, and Jordon are sources of migrant labor, the Gulf Oil states are the receivers of this labor. Political instability in Afghanistan has also resulted in this region becoming the globe's main source of individuals who flee, seeking refugee status (Castles and Miller 2003). Africa, Asia, and Latin America are also characterized by complex internal migration patterns that affect both the local region as well as the broader global landscape.

Many countries, including the U.S., also have large illegal immigrant populations (Castles and Miller 2003). Undocumented workers migrate from poorer countries in order to find jobs in agriculture and mining. Estimates hover around the 11 million mark for the U.S., but credible statistics are missing for both the U.S. and other countries. Of the approximately 11 million undocumented immigrants in the U.S., about 6.2 million are thought to be Mexican (United Nations 2008).

The demographics and skills of contemporary migrants vary widely. Currently, most global migrants come from China (35 million), India (20 million) and the Philippines (7 million), which are considered developing economies (International Organization for Migration 2005). There is also much variation with respect to educational attainment and professional skills. For example, 60% of immigrants to the U.K. are professionals, while Freeman (2006) has estimated that as of 2000, 45% of the U.S.-based Ph.D. economists and 55% of U.S.-based Ph.D. natural scientists who were younger than 45, were born in other countries. This is, at times, referred to as the "brain drain" – the migration of highly skilled workers from the developing world to industrialized countries. Some estimates claim that nearly one in ten adults from developing countries with professional degrees in medicine, or who hold PhDs, now live in Europe, Australia, or the U.S. (Lowell et al. 2004). In contrast, many of the immigrants from Mexico to the U.S. had not attained the equivalent of a high school diploma.

4.2   What is "Different" About Contemporary Migration Patterns?

Today's migration differs significantly from the major waves of migration that characterized the late nineteenth and early twentieth century. One major area of difference pertains to the proportion of migration in relation to the global population. The total of individuals immigrating today, while formidable in actual numbers, is actually proportionally much less than those who immigrated at the turn of the century. For example, from 1901 to 1910, 8.8 million individuals came to the U.S., in comparison to 9.1 million in the period from 1991 to 2000 (Freeman 2006). However, in 1900, the U.S. population numbered approximately 76 million people, while the world population is estimated to have been about 1.6 billion. By 2000, the Census indicates the U.S. population was close to 282 million, while UN figures indicate that the world population had reached 6 billion individuals. In terms of scale, today's migration numbers are relatively insignificant in comparison to migration patterns of just 100 years ago.

Today's migration is characterized by several other fundamental changes as well. Historically, immigrants tended to be primarily men in search of wage labor. However, today's immigrants are just as often women, and in the industrialized world, female immigrants now outnumber males.[3] In the U.S., migration is still centered around family reunification. Between 1990 and 2002, 65% of legal immigrants entered the U.S. under the category of "family preference." In contrast, in Canada during the same period, the equivalent proportion is estimated at about 34% (United Nations 2008). In European countries and Japan, migration revolves around temporary work or, as it is sometimes termed, "guest labor."

Perhaps, the most profound difference in today's migration patterns pertains to the flow of immigrants. Throughout the nineteenth century, most immigrants were primarily poor Europeans. In contrast, today's immigrants stem almost exclusively from developing countries who move to wealthier societies in search of work, or who flee their home countries, seeking refugee status abroad due to war and ethnic conflict.[4] Contemporary immigrants include highly educated, highly skilled workers and temporary or guest workers, who are primarily represented in the agricultural sectors as domestic servants, and in mining work. While these immigrants perform much-needed labor for their host countries, their status has become highly contentious resulting in heated debates about the need for regulation (Ruhs and Chang 2004). In addition, to these various categories of legal and illegal immigrants and guest workers, there are approximately 2 million international students who study at universities outside of their home countries. Approximately, one quarter of those students come to the U.S., primarily from China and India (United Nations 2008).

---

[3] The United Nations (2008) estimates that exactly 50% of all global immigrants today are female.

[4] According to United Nations (2008) estimates, global refugees number around 11.4 million people.

Tourism is another arena with major international flows of people: According to the World Tourism Organization, in 2004 some 760 million individuals traveled to international tourist destinations (Freeman 2006).

4.3   The Effects of Migration

High rates of migration have very specific effects on the host or receiving societies. As Castles and Miller (2003) point out, people move primarily in families or small groups, not just on their own. Thus, their migration can have profound social and economic effects on the sending and receiving societies. In receiving countries, migration is almost always tied to economic opportunities. This leads most immigrants to settle in urban and industrial areas, creating enclaves of individuals from the same country, region, or even village. In terms of demographic effects, since most immigrants are of working age, immigrants serve to lower the age of the population. Freeman (2006) points out that low birth rates coupled with the aging of their populations is going to lead to serious labor issues in the industrialized world, despite high migration rates. As these populations age (with Sweden and Japan at the forefront), migration rates at the current level will not be sufficient to make up the necessary labor and financial contributions (United Nations 2008).

New immigrants usually bring needed labor and skills to their host societies. For example, sectors of the economy in need of low-wage workers, benefit from the use of immigrants. We will examine the complicated debates around this issue later on. Until then it will be sufficient to say that migration can also add to the technological edge of the receiving society. As immigrants with skills move to receiving societies, creativity and knowledge are enhanced. For example, almost 60% of the growth in American Ph.D. scientists and engineers over the last 10 years has come through international migration (Freeman 2006).

Migration has other serious economic and social implications. While there is dispute if migration raises the socioeconomic development of receiving societies, the importance of remittances and the new ideas that often accompany them, is significant (Hadi 1999). The World Bank (2008) estimates that approximately $283 billion officially recorded remittances flowed to developing countries in 2008. The top three recipients of remittances were India, China, and Mexico, followed by a long list of countries in the developing world, including the Philippines, Poland, Nigeria, Egypt, and Pakistan. Some scholars note that remittances are as important to nation-states as exports, which in the past, were the most significant contributors to the gross national product (Orozco 2002). While a slowdown in remittance flows would be expected to reflect global economic conditions, remittance flows have proven to remain relatively resilient in comparison to government aid and private capital (World Bank 2008).

Remittances have local consequences: they allow families in sending societies to survive, and at times prosper, they may lead to changes in roles within families, and they can allow household members to engage in new productive activities. Immigrants also send back to their home countries, a host of new ideas about issues such as gender relations, the role of the individual in civil society, and the value of education and developing certain skills. It is important to note that a wide range of variables are tied to the positive and negative effects of migration, including education, occupation, land ownership, religion, and sociohistorical moment.

Mass migration from the developing to the industrialized world has stoked debates on ethnicity, race, and the role of multiculturalism and diversity in most societies around the globe. Immigrants are often culturally distinct from the populations of their receiving societies. They may be agrarian, speak other languages, practice different religions, have varying cultural traditions, and be distinct from the host population due to their physical appearance.[5] Their status (and depending on the host country, even that of their children even if they are born in the new country) is that of "noncitizen" or immigrant, and they may suffer from discriminatory practices.[6] Moreover, in response to the negative sentiments of many of their citizenry, a growing number of governments in receiving countries have been tightening the laws around migration and refugee status. A common public perception in the U.S., Canada, Australia, and Europe is that especially low-skilled immigrants will burden the social services sectors of society while taking away jobs from natives. In the U.S., this debate has been recently further obscured by a mainstream tendency to speak of legal and illegal immigrants as one group.[7] Media portrayals of "immigrants" jumping over fences and "strong" mayors and police who "crack down" on these individuals have fueled the public sentiment that migration should be curtailed. Most of these portrayals, sadly, do not clarify the important role that low-skilled immigrants play in the economy.[8]

How immigrants are perceived, legally and culturally in their host countries, depends a great deal on the ideology of that society. In the classic migration countries like the U.S., Australia, and, Canada, immigrants have been traditionally seen as permanent residents who are to be assimilated into society (Castles and Miller 2003). In other places, such as Europe and the Middle East, immigrants are thought of as temporary or guest labor and, as such, are not accorded the right to remain permanently in those areas. Laws are geared against family reunification and permanent residence, with countries in those areas asserting that they are not open to migration. A multitude of complex factors has contributed to an increasingly complicated sociopolitical environment, as guest workers attempt to remain in those countries.[9]

---

[5] For example, in France the issue of the head scarf that many Muslim women choose to wear is a highly controversial issue because it is perceived as making a religious statement in a secular society.

[6] All children born in the United States automatically receive American citizenship.

[7] This is a highly complicated discussion due to a long history in the U.S. of ambivalence with respect to assimilating immigrants into the mainstream of society and the rising rate of, particularly, Hispanics. See, Freeman (2006) for some interesting statistics.

[8] Most of these portrayals have very strong racial overtones with an emphasis on the "otherness" of immigrants and their non-European roots.

[9] For a comprehensive discussion about these issues, see Castles and Miller 2003. For example, many European countries are currently struggling with guest workers and refugee populations that refuse to return to their native countries despite financial incentives.

International migration is also tied to a pervasive discourse around the rights, legality, contributions, and cultural values of immigrants, with dominant images of the poor immigrant who "steals" the rightful job of the native born becoming ever more prominent in both migration and nonmigration societies. Immigrants are often blamed for all the various ills of society, including crime, drugs, and decaying social values. In societies that are not constructed around an immigrant ethic, issues of national identity have been severely tested as populations become increasingly multicultural. And around the globe, this phenomenon has spurred the rise of nationalistic and fundamentalist movements seeking an "authentic" identity based on "traditional" representations and beliefs.

4.4 The Gendered Nature of Migration

While decisions about who, when, and where to migrate are complex, and depend on a wide variety of factors, such as individual choice, family membership, economics, and even coercion, we are increasingly witnessing an unprecedented massive movement of women from developing to industrialized parts of the world. Recent research has begun to focus on the motives behind this phenomenon. Specifically, there is interest in how the changing economic and political conditions in sending and receiving societies impinge in varying ways on men and women, and disproportionally influence their reasons for immigrating. For example, some scholars have highlighted the fact that export-led production in developing countries has differential gender impacts. In particular, off-shore production increases international migration by "creating goods that compete with local commodities, by feminizing the workforce without providing equivalent factory-based employment for the large stock of under- and unemployed males, and by socializing women for industrial work and modern consumption without providing needed job stability over the course of the women's working lives" (Pessar 1999, p. 580). Scholars such as Mahler and Pessar (2006) and Hondagneu-Sotelo (2000) suggest that the decentralization and deregulation of manufacturing production coupled with the growth of "global cities" (Sassen 1994, 2002) and a demand for professional services, which require low-wage service labor, have contributed to the consistently increasing migration of women from the developing world. Many of the low-paying, unstable jobs that are now available in the industrialized world to immigrant women, are jobs that in the past were considered as the natural duties of middle-class housewives.

Since large numbers of females in the Western industrialized world have entered the paid labor force, but have remained primarily responsible for the care work and domestic labor in their families, their solution has been to "outsource" this work to immigrant women. The phenomenon of large numbers of women working outside of the home has occurred without a concomitant change in policies or professional outlook and expectations on the part of governments or workplaces (Lutz 2002). As a coping response, much of the labor that was once performed by middle-class women in the home is now relegated to the market place, where it is bought directly as goods and services or as hired labor.[10] Sassen (2003, 2006) even suggests that we are seeing the return of a significant so-called serving class in the global cities of the world. This demand for workers has resulted in women immigrating from developing nations to the industrialized world in search of employment in either the service sectors or in manufacturing (Parrenas 2003). Moreover, globalization and concomitant transnational migration have also fueled a booming sexual services industry. This often ignored aspect of migration is associated at times with voluntary migration, but is most often characterized by coercion, exploitation and even violence, as girls and women are duped into participating in the international sex industry.[11]

In the last several years, the U.S. has proportionally received more immigrant female workers than other host countries. Espiritu (1997) attributes this movement to economic restructuring and the expansion of industries that rely principally on women, such as health care, service, microelectronics, and apparel. She argues that immigrant women are preferred over males due to ingrained preconceptions and stereotypes that women from developing countries are willing to work for lower wages, are not looking for job advancement, and are better suited in terms of their psychological makeup for certain types of detail-oriented jobs. In a frequently cited quote she relays the views of a White male production manager in an assembly shop in California:

> Just three things I look for in hiring [entry-level, high-tech manufacturing operatives]: small, foreign and female. You find those three things and you're pretty much automatically guaranteed the right kind of workforce. These little foreign gals are grateful to be hired – very, very grateful – no matter what. (Hossfeld 1994, p. 65 as cited in Espiritu 1997)

Racist and gendered notions seem also to be at work at higher levels of the occupational ladder. For example, Waldinger and Gilbertson (1994) found that female immigrants from countries such as India and Japan were not able to translate their education into higher occupational success in the same manner as their male counterparts. Men continue to dominate as managers and professionals while women with equivalent or, at times, greater qualifications rarely make it into those ranks. Pessar (1999) concludes from these findings that "succeeding" in America is still primarily a male story.

Sassen (2006) points out that immigrant women, especially in the large global cities where they tend to locate, are invisible, isolated, and disempowered. In the

---

[10] It is important to point out that upper class women throughout the world have always employed others to perform domestic labor and that poor women have traditionally been burdened by a double shift in the home, including in the U.S.. What is different about the current situation is the breadth of need, especially for child and elder care among the middle-classes.

[11] Globalizing forces have also contributed to a spike in sex tourism and the trade in women for sexual services. There is much academic dispute on whether girls and women make this choice consciously or are coerced into this type of labor. It is sufficient to say here that it seems that both phenomena are coexisting.

past, many of these same women would have entered a local labor market, earned wages, and been able to use these earnings to renegotiate traditional roles in the family. Instead, she suggests, today's immigrant women are partaking in *survival circuits* that integrate the economic survival of families, communities, and even governments dependent on remittances sent home from these women. On the other hand, Sassen (2006) also points to the access of these women to wages and salaries, and the feminization of labor and business, as potential opportunities for the restructuring of gender hierarchies. In fact, research has shown that women are much more likely than men, to assume active roles with respect to organizing and activism in their communities, once they resettle (Hondagneu-Sotelo 2000). This foreshadows a greater role for immigrant women in the political and economic arenas of their host societies in the future.

4.5 The Role of Families in Migration

Migration results in the emergence of what are today referred to as "transnational families." Families may be dispersed geographically, but are able to reconstitute and redefine themselves at certain points, depending on material and emotional necessity, as well as practicality. Most commonly, family members live apart from one another, but hold together through a shared feeling of collective welfare and unity. Theirs is a strategic response to globalizing conditions that are affecting every aspect of social, economic, and political life (Bryceson and Vuorela 2002). Differences between generations and genders may be magnified or diminished, and individual family members employ varying strategies to consciously maintain, extend, or limit relationships. This points to the critical role of agency "whereby individual immigrants, their families and communities chart their way through new transnational spaces" (Bryceson and Vuorela 2002, p. 24). Nonetheless, it is important to remember that individual's agency is constrained by access to resources and power hierarchies. Both, the immigrants and those who stay behind, are caught in a constantly shifting set of relationships. Their sense of unity and identity is continually being negotiated and reformulated through their dispersal. Bryceson and Vuorela (2002) argue that various members of the same family may imagine their family differently, depending on their particular interpretation of "family stories and sense of belonging" (p. 15). This fluidity leads to a constant negotiation of roles and relationships throughout a family member's life cycle. It is important to point out that while migration may be a constantly shifting process, for many individuals, migration also involves loss: loss of place, loss of relationships, and loss of a sense of belonging that may never be claimed in the same manner, even upon return.

Strikingly, scholars from different disciplines view the migration decision and its relationship to household affairs, often from narrow perspectives. For example, Pessar (1999) points out that the economists' limited focus on the immigrant household's cost-benefit analyses fails to recognize that these decisions are not made just on the basis of the market economy. Instead, the decision to immigrate is also the result of a family's household economy. When a family decides if a family member should immigrate, it will weigh social concerns (such as a daughter's reputation) with economic benefits. This process is occurring even in parts of the world where families traditionally would never have let their children go abroad to work on their own. A recent article in the New York Times (December 22, 2008) documented the growing number of young and single Middle Eastern women who flock from poorer home countries to the United Arab Emirates to work as flight attendants. In a previous, more traditional Middle Eastern cultural context, it would have been almost unfathomable for a family to allow their unmarried daughter to live in another country and work on her own, but these sorts of decisions are becoming more common. Families are recognizing that it may be of benefit to the group to pursue new forms of migration, even though they deviate from standard cultural practices.

While families are a crucial location for understanding migration decisions, it is deceptive to assume the unitary nature of family decisions. A strong feminist scholarship on family relationships (see Chap. 2) has revealed that from an external perspective, family decisions may seem consensual, beneficial, and reciprocal. However, many families are organized along hierarchical power lines, separated by gender and generations, resulting in migration decisions that are distinctly gendered and generationally based. For example, Hondagneu-Sotelo (2000) has highlighted the fact that the mechanisms and strategies with which individuals and families respond to migration opportunities and challenges, are highly dependent on familial and community circumstances, and that these are always gendered phenomena. The decision about who should migrate depends on a multiplicity of factors. Under certain circumstances, it may be considered advantageous for the men to immigrate due to their access to social networks and the power that is accorded to them in their families. At other times, depending on opportunity structures, it may be the older (or younger) women in a family that take on the migration journey. There is growing recognition that men and women, even in the same family, may have completely distinct social networks, and that it is their network that can assist them with migration decisions, logistics, resettlement, and future success (Hondagneu-Sotelo 2003).

It is noteworthy, however, that contemporary migration is characterized by a growing movement away from traditional patriarchal norms that encouraged the father or the men in the family to immigrate. For example, in 1992, Pierrette Hondagneu-Sotelo writing about migration and gender explained:

> In family stage migration, patriarchal gender relations are embedded in normative practices and expectations that allow men and deny women the authority and the resources necessary to migrate independently. Men are expected to serve as good financial providers for their families, which they attempt to do through labor migration; patriarchal authority allows them to act autonomously in planning and carrying out migration. Married women must accept their husbands' migration decisions, remain chaste, and stay behind to care for the children and the daily operation of the domestic sphere. These normative patterns of behavior, however, are renegotiated when the departure of one family member, the husband, prompts rearrangements in conjugal social power and the gender division of labor in the household. (p. 394)

Less than 20 years later, while many of her observations still hold true, it is increasingly women who undertake labor migration. This phenomenon, which is on the rise, promises to initiate changes in family roles, unimagined previously. It is important to note that migration can have very disparate effects depending on if (1) the man/father in the household immigrates; (2) the woman/mother in the household immigrates; (3) the young adults in the household immigrate; or (4) if the couple or the family immigrates together.[12] Migration is also affected by age and the life course.[13] Except for feminist research, these distinctions are often not made in the migration literature. Moreover, the length and distance of the migration matter. For example, migration from Egypt to the United Emirates to fulfill a 2-year labor contract is quite a different phenomenon from migration from the Philippines to the U.S. for permanent resettlement.

It is important to note that most countries still base migration laws around the notion of the male-dominated family, with women and children deemed as "dependents." Thus, in many areas of the world immigrating women do not have the legal right to bring in their husbands, since the "natural" home residence of a woman is with her spouse. Other gendered notions are often at work in migration laws as well. For example, in the late 1970s, Britain enacted a law where all women arriving from the South Asian continent had to undergo a mandatory virginity test at Heathrow airport. This law, which remained in place for three years, was thought to stem the tide of "illegal" immigrants and refugees (Castles and Miller 2003). While the law was ultimately repealed, it does illustrate how gendered and racist notions can conjoin to create particularly unpleasant conditions for immigrants.

When couples or families immigrate, the migration may affect familial relationships in unexpected ways. For example, traditionally based marriage patterns may be disrupted through spousal separation, disputes over roles and new domestic arrangements. In particular, couples that move from the developing world to the U.S. or Europe often find themselves, as Hondagneu-Sotelo in the quote above suggests, in situations that require a rearrangement of gender roles. These couples may attain much greater gender equality than is the norm in their home society. While this does not happen uniformly and can be associated with a great deal of marital discord, the pattern is clear. Moving to the West introduces new ideas about the role of women in the family and community to immigrants who stem from societies where that may not be the norm. Further, economic circumstances often necessitate

---

[12] A virtually unexplored phenomenon is children immigrating without their parents. For example, some well-to-do Asian parents send their children to the United States to attend school in order to give them a better chance at entering the U.S. universities. They are at times referred to as "parachute" children. See, Orellana et al. (2001) for a discussion.

[13] Elder (1999) points out that "the life course of individuals is embedded in and shaped by the historical times and places they experience over their lifetime" (p. 3). In addition, the developmental effects of transitions differentiate according to when events occur in an individual's life (Elder 1999). Variables such as migration history, timing, generational status, and geographic location of settlement must be considered when interpreting the experiences of immigrant individuals and families.

that these women work outside of the home, leading to a rearrangement of roles in the domestic sphere (Kibria 1993).[14]

Women's access to wages can lead to control over household decisions with respect to budgets and the division of labor. However, in situations where women have a job, and their husband's do not, or when women earn more than their husbands, men will often exacerbate inequalities in the domestic realm. Feminists have explained this phenomenon as resulting from men feeling displaced from their traditional role as providers (Kelly 1991). At times, in those cases when international migration leads to the improvement of women's status, it has the converse effect on men. Men commonly lose some of their power and privileges both within the household and the community (Fouron and Glick Schiller 2001).

It is a fallacy, however, to assume that women's migration to the industrialized world is uniformly accompanied by improvements in women's status. Migration can lead to shifts toward greater gender equality, but that outcome is dependent on context: economics, the couple's relationship, and a multitude of other factors. It is often not recognized that when lower-class and immigrant women work outside of the home, their employment is not usually associated with self-empowerment, but is primarily the consequence of economic need and an expression of their vulnerability (Pessar 1999). In certain professions immigrant women are the preferred form of labor due to their lower market value – they are often found in the lowest and most insecure sectors of the economy. Feminist interpretations that question these women's desire to maintain gender norms and traditional families instead of working toward gender equality, also often do not acknowledge that the struggles of these women represent acts of resistance to more powerful dominant forces that threaten the very existence of their families.

While migration may not always have instantaneous benefits for family members, it can over time lead to increased opportunities (Bacallao and Smokowski 2007). For example, in certain cases, immigrant women are increasingly partaking on a more intense level in community and social action activities. Hondagneu-Sotelo (1994) has suggested that as immigrant couples move away from traditional gender roles, women become more involved in community and civic affairs. This social participation leads to an improved status for the whole family as women tend to be particularly skilled at finding and employing financial services and social supports. Women are the ones who integrate their families into the new society by building relationships with other women around social issues. As women strengthen their social networking skills, their own status continues to grow in their families and ethnic communities. Immigrant women often do not access formal institutions of power such as political parties in the same manner as men. Instead, they come together around social concerns (Dion and Dion 2001). Given the growing accessibility of women to networking through communication technologies and their involvement in community affairs, it is very likely that immigrant women in certain

---

[14] It is interesting to note that when immigrants from Northern Europe or middle- and upper-middle class Chinese move to the U.S., they are surprised by the "traditional" gender ideology that so many Americans embrace.

places will become an increasingly stronger voice for themselves, the men in their lives and their children.

4.6 Children and Migration

A completely understudied aspect of globalization and migration is the effect of these processes on children (Fass 2005). While there is a great deal of interest in the West on the development of immigrant children (i.e., the children who are born to immigrant parents, or immigrate with their parents to receiving societies), we know very little about the children who are "left behind" in today's migrations.[15] An examination of the history of migration reveals that family migration has never been a process in which the whole group necessarily moves together to a new place. On the contrary, history indicates that much of this process was traditionally concerned with the reassembling of families over time, and with maintaining connections with those family members remaining in the home community, even when this separation was associated with great distances. In particular, concern about reuniting with children has led to various forms of chain migration.

With today's instant communication capabilities, the loss associated with migration over great distances has been somewhat alleviated by allowing family members to stay in close touch. The staggeringly high migration statistics indicate that new labor opportunities resulting from globalizing forces allow and encourage both men and women these days to leave their families behind in order to earn wages that can then be sent back home. For example, over the last several years, large numbers of women have left their children and families in the Philippines to travel to all corners of the world, often times for many years at a time (Ehrenreich and Hochschild 2003). These women immigrate in order seek economic and career opportunities that will allow them to provide a better life for their children and loved ones. However, if this transient migration is beneficial or detrimental to the development of their children has become a controversial issue.[16]

4.6.1 The Issue of Transnational Mothering

As the movement of women from Latin America, the Philippines, India, Scandinavia, and Ireland to provide childcare and work in domestic arenas in the U.S., Europe, and Saudi Arabia, grows, scholarly analysis and public policy has

---

[15] Children who immigrate at a young age with their families are most commonly referred to as the 1.5 generation (Rumbaut 2006).

[16] It is important to note that while men have historically been the "immigrants," we have not seen a concomitant interest in the effects of this migration on children's development.

begun to take limited interest in the effects of mothering on the children of migrating women (Mortgan and Zippel 2003). Ethnographic evidence indicates that the children of migrating women are generally left in the care of substitute mothers, their fathers and/or extended family. They are thought to benefit, at least materially, from the remittances of their mothers. Parrenas (2001) refers to this form of motherhood as "commodified motherhood": the relationship between the mother and her child or children is maintained through gifts, money, and paying for an education. However, it may be potentially fallacious to apply Western conceptualizations of "good mothering" to these situations. While Westerners emphasize physical closeness and direct involvement as crucial in the upbringing of a child, this is a model that cannot be maintained by migrating mothers since in most cases they are not allowed legally to take their children with them.

Instead of vilifying migrating women as "bad" or "uncaring" mothers, it may be more appropriate to gain a deeper understanding of how "good mothering" is defined by these women themselves. For affluent Westerners, it may be very difficult to understand the conflicts and dilemmas that poverty and the lack of opportunities create for adults and children. As increasing numbers of women migrate and leave their families behind, they are in the process of creating new versions of "good mothering." It is important to point out that a somewhat similar process is at work among low-income women in industrialized societies. Many of these women work long hours at shift jobs just to make ends meet. They are unable to live up to societal ideals that value the constant contact between women and their children.[17] They are also in the process of attempting to create other forms of "good mothering" that may appear somewhat different than what middle class researchers and policy makers understand as the norm.

In an overview of the historical patterns of migration and children in the U.S., Paula Fass (2005) makes an interesting correlation between contemporary ideals of family preservation and reunification, and public policy that encourages this pattern of behavior. She points out that the 1965 Hart-Cellar Act was based, in part, on the concept of bringing families together. Thus, in most American's minds, the concept of women, specifically mothers, leaving their children behind, is appalling. However, globalizing forces and social policies are not concerned with the intimacies and intricacies of family life. Families must adapt to situations and use the opportunities that present themselves to persevere. Historically, the migration of a family member to another part of the world, most often implied a permanent separation. Today, with the ease and choices of multiple modes of transportation and communication, children can be periodically reunited with their migrating parent.

Discussions of transnational mothering and "good" mothering, must be examined from new perspectives that place a mother's relationships with her children within a specific sociocultural context. Further, mothering cannot be analyzed in

---

[17] The intensive mothering model extends even to the political sphere in the United States. Several years ago, a close advisor to the then President, George Bush resigned citing "wanting to spend more time with her teenage son" as the reason. This decision was applauded in the media with only a few feminists questioning this premise.

isolation from other family and caring relationships. For example, recent research on Filipina women who work abroad in places such as Singapore, illustrates that these women feel very close to their families and to their children, even though they are geographically separated from them. Their physical separation is legitimized by their feeling that working in another country is ultimately going to lead to a better future for themselves, their children and their families (Asis et al. 2004). Significantly, many of these women also point to migration as a means of pursuing personal goals that would not have been achievable in their home societies. From this perspective, transnational migration can provide a multitude of opportunities as it allows individuals to intertwine personal and familial goals. In this particular example, women function as active agents that seek actively to improve their situations by combining personal fulfillment with economic opportunities. While this is obviously not always the case, it is still important to recognize that increasingly women are taking charge of their situation in life and enacting new behaviors, or at least behaviors that differ from the traditional norms of their societies, in order to alleviate their own and their families' circumstances.

Globalizing processes have also served to produce a new generation of multi-national children who are familiar with often quite differing cultures. We know little about their experiences and the benefits and challenges that may ensue from a more international upbringing.[18] The limited research on the effects of female migration indicates that children of immigrant mothers exhibit the best outcomes when they are aware of their mother's contributions and sacrifices, when they have a strong support system of caregivers, and when they share a healthy relationship with their mothers (Parrenas 2001).

The observations rendered on migrating working mothers are not meant to minimize the potential feelings of loss that many of their children must experience. However, given the growth of the phenomenon, it is suggested that there seem to be coping mechanisms at work that have not been explored in depth and we, thus, need to be careful about applying our own ethnocentric notions of mothering or parenting in other contexts.

4.6.2 The Success of Immigrant Children

While the lives and outcomes of children of migrating parents who leave them behind in their home society has not elicited much academic or mainstream interest, research in the West has focused sharply on the experiences of children growing up in immigrant families. This scholarly interest both in the U.S. and Europe can be attributed to larger policy concerns with assimilation and educational outcomes

---

[18] Obviously, this is a very different international upbringing than the family that moves its children to another country due to parental employment at a high occupational level. Still, it is interesting to pursue the question how children are influenced by the greater international exposure they receive through their parent's migration if they stay behind.

for this group. For example, numerous studies conducted in the U.S. indicate that immigrant children are at two ends of the spectrum: they either outperform the native population with respect to educational achievement and grades, or they are unable to stay in school and never receive a high school diploma (Forrestand Alexander 2004). Scholars such Ruben Rumbaut (1997, 2003) postulate that many immigrant children, cognizant of their parent's sacrifices in order to provide them with a better life, try to work hard and be successful. However, over time the combined effects of a lax work ethic among many American youths combined with deleterious influences such poverty, drugs, and alcohol, lead to a decline in achievement.

The statistics on immigrant children's achievements are somewhat deceptive. There are wide achievement gaps between various groups, leading some to postulate that it is not just the immigrant experience that influences children, but also the socioeconomic context in which they find themselves. For example, Forrest and Alexander (2004) point out that an estimated 27 million children in the U.S. live in low-income families. When issues of poverty are combined with migration, it becomes extremely difficult to sort out which variables have a more profound effect on the well-being of children. Similar concerns are part of the national and scholarly agenda in European countries. The perceived lack of assimilation into local societies is primarily associated with cultural issues: that immigrant groups from very "different" cultures do not assimilate well. However, recent work indicates that the underlying causes may be much more complex and can be attributed to issues of discrimination and prejudice (Bernhardt et al. 2007).

4.7   Issues of Cultural Identity

Cultural identity formation is another significant aspect of the migration experience. Identity formation is an important aspect of any discussion on globalization and family matters, because identity formation, at least in its initial stages has traditionally been linked to family relationships. According to Erik Erikson (1963), the single most important developmental task facing young people is creating a coherent sense of identity. In order to develop in the most positive manner, Erikson argued, there needs to be a fit between an individual's sense of self and the social environment in which he or she functions. This popular model, which provides the basis for much of developmental psychology, assumes that young people develop their identities in a culturally homogenous environment where they move between social spheres. However, today's heterogeneous, transnational world, throws into question the whole process of identity formation (Suarez-Orozco and Suarez-Orozco 2001). Globalizing processes and the rapidity of technological change raises questions about how and where identity is formed. This issue becomes particularly complex in the context of migration, where individuals are confronted with various choices in terms of identity. For example, immigrant children need to construct identities that will allow them to succeed in a multitude of settings such as homes, school, and work. However, there may be wide cultural gaps between these settings as different languages, ways of behaving and ideologies characterize each of these spheres – particularly for those from new societies (Dion and Dion 2001).[19]

Identity and its linkages to migration have long been of interest to both scholars and policymakers. In migration societies such as the U.S., a hegemonic ideology advocates assimilation into mainstream culture. This requires a shift whereby immigrants begin to see themselves as belonging, first and foremost, to their new host society. They are expected to learn the language and the culture in order to "blend in."

Ackroyd and Pilkington (1999) suggest that there are four important aspects to understanding identity formation in individuals: One, individuals do not have one fixed cultural identity, but instead a spectrum of shifting cultural identities; two, individuals are involved in a continual process of representation, which is foundational to their identity formation; three, that cultural identities and representations must be understood as being constructed in a globalizing context; and four, that every individual exercises agency (within certain social limits) to fashion a unique cultural identity. Crucial to this understanding is that individuals have a variety of identities to choose from; these can include gender, age, class, educational level, and other such markers.

Certain identities such as ethnicity may shift depending on context. For example, a child from a Dominican household may identify as being black under certain circumstances, or, as Hispanic under another. An Asian child may identify with one cultural tradition in one setting, while emphasizing another practice when with others from his or her country of origin. As individuals move between settings, they are often aware of their shifting identities and through that process produce new hybrid identities.

Ackroyd and Pilkington (1999) point out that this process also validates the social construction of identities. Globalization has greatly facilitated this process. Concepts of imagined communities gain legitimacy through contemporary processes that link individuals over wide territorial and interest-related spaces. As technology and communication capabilities accelerate at an ever-increasing speed, so does the ability of people to create, recreate, and ascertain their identities. There are ever more choices to be drawn upon and negotiated. For example, Rosenau (2003) points out that "As distant developments become ever more proximate, the emergent epoch enables people to develop new, more flexible constructions of themselves. Their orientations, practices, and lives are still shaped by macro structures, but the latter are now more numerous and flexible than in the past, freeing (even forcing) people to shoulder greater autonomy and to evolve new identities and shifting allegiances. The decline of tradition and fixed systems of roles and norms of behavior has led to the imposition of an inescapable and unrelenting

---

[19] It has been pointed out that moving from one socio-economic class to another can also have profound effects on identity formation. See Rayna Rapp for a clear exposition on class in America.

autonomy on many people, just as the Internet and other technologies have enabled individuals to greatly expand the range of their interpersonal relationships beyond face-to-face contacts and thus to participate in the formation and enlargement of groups, in an ever more networked world." (p. 24)

As has been discussed, today's migration experience differs substantively from the same phenomenon even just 50 years ago. Many of today's migrants are transnational; they are able to stay in constant touch with their homes through regular visitations and ever more available and cheaper communication technologies, such as the Internet. They are involved in a constant process of relaying ideas, money, and new concepts about individuality, families, work, and the like. Simultaneously, they are linking up with others like themselves, sometimes due to geographic proximity, but increasingly over ever expanding distances. Through these multiple connections and influences, they are able to pick and choose among new hybrid identities. As we move forward, these choices only promise to grow. Our somewhat static conceptualizations about identity formation are quickly becoming outdated, particularly with respect to immigrant children.[20]

Many contemporary European nations are also struggling with the issue of identity formation and its consequences on children. These societies are confronted with the problem of "temporary" immigrants (their guest worker and refugee populations) whose children were born and have been raised in Europe. In migration countries such as the U.S., children born to immigrants receive citizenship upon their birth. Thus, from a legal and ideological perspective, these children are now part of the citizenry. They are raised, at least from an ideological stance, to believe that they have equal rights and opportunities as the native born population.[21] However, in the European situation, many immigrant children are confronted with a complex paradox. These children, for the most part, do not have citizenship, and even in those cases where they do, are usually still perceived as "foreigners." However, the children of immigrants *are* for all practical purposes part of the European societies in which they have been raised. They attend school there, play with "native" children, are exposed to European ideals with respect to gender equality and family relationships, and, in general, have no wish to return to the home societies of their parents.[22] On the other hand, these children are also exposed to the values of their parent's home cultures.

Gender can also be a significant issue for immigrant children. For example, in the case of girls in particular, they may wear the headscarf or value traditional roles in the home, depending on the culture of their parents. Young men may want to

---

[20] Current statistics indicate that 48% of children under the age of 5 in the U.S. are either immigrant children or nonwhite. This highlights the need to better understand identity formation in individuals from nonmainstream backgrounds.

[21] There are obviously many complicating factors such as race, ethnicity, national origin, etc. that come into play. And yet, I would argue that this is still the hegemonic discourse – all are equal and all have opportunities. This is obviously not the case, as for example the work of Suarez-Orozco, C. and Suarez-Orozco, M. (2002). *Children of migration,* Harvard illustrates.

[22] There is a large body of work on the immigrant children and their relationships with their parents. See for example, A. Booth et al. (1997)) *Immigration and the family.*

participate in the social life (e.g., dating and premarital sex) of their host societies but want to marry "traditional" brides.[23] Multiple complications arise from this situation. The children are an amalgamation, a hybrid of identities. Nonetheless, Suarez-Orozco and Suarez-Orozco (2001) postulate that immigrant children may be at an advantage in today's globalizing world with respect to identity formation processes. They point out that earlier assimilationist models that assumed unilinear development have lost their utility. Instead, all individuals need to operate within multiple cultural contexts these days. Immigrant children are advantaged, from this perspective, as they acquire competencies that allow them to move and be at ease in multiple cultural contexts.

However, the situation of immigrant children globally, remains complex. On the one hand, they fit in, and on the other, they are outsiders in the very societies in which they are growing up. This situation is coupled with rising sentiments among the various citizenries about the need for "national purity," assimilation, cultural understanding and the like. Obviously, sociohistorical moment, education, culture and country of origin, religion, and a myriad of other factors also complicate interpretations of who the immigrants and their children are, and their respective role in society.

What is rarely highlighted in these disputes surrounding immigrant children is that children and their identities can, at times, become the arena where cultural battles are negotiated and fought. On the one hand, they are seen as an important element in the transmission and retention of elements of their families or communities culture. Children are, at times, taught forbidden or ancient languages, brought up with certain rituals and beliefs, and are the focus of attempts to retain local traditions. This often occurs in binary opposition to the formal education that is taught in schools. Children – both their minds and their bodies – become used in debates about fundamental cultural values, ethnic purity, minority self-expression, and other such issues (Stephens 1995).

4.8   Family Change and Migration

Contemporary migration resulting from a complex interplay of globalizing forces has refashioned today's migration for both sending and receiving nations. In particular, the gendered nature of today's migration stands out as having significant implications for associated ideologies pertaining to families, gender roles, and even parenting. Historically, men migrated abroad and sent remittances back to their families. Today, it is quite common for women from developing countries to move, either temporarily or permanently, to places where they feel they can make enough money to send back home. Women work as childcare workers, with the aged, as nurses and teachers, and even in the sex industry. These women work in other places in order to raise their families' chances for success and prosperity. They

---

[23] See for example, Bernhardt, Goldscheider, Goldscheider and Bjeren, *Migration, gender, and family transitions to adulthood in Sweden*, 2007.

mostly work in countries where strong norms favor a conjugal unit centered around the raising of children, and where dominant sentiments reject the idea of a lack of physical involvement of parents, especially mothers, with their children.

While immigrant women are not able to fulfill Western middle-class ideals of motherhood, they support their families in ways that are often invisible to outside observers. In order to accomplish this mission, women rely, in part, on hiring other poorer women or on intergenerational ties to assist with the care of their children. This model of an extended dependent family differs radically from the influential 1950s model posited by Talcott Parsons (Parsons and Bales 1955). At that time, he suggested that it was only the small nuclear family that would be agile enough to navigate through the modern social world. In contrast, in certain areas and cultures, the large extended family has continued to play a determining role for the lives of its members, especially the children.

For poor women especially, contemporary migration has brought about dichotomous changes. On the one hand, women are empowered to leave bad and/or poor situations, and they gain in power through their movements. On the other hand, women are the ones having to leave behind their children, families, communities, and cultures to take on jobs that often place them at the bottom or certainly near the bottom of their host societies. Research indicates, however, that even with all the known disadvantages, female migrants feel that they are doing the best possible for themselves and their families.

Strikingly, we know little these days about the experiences of men – both the ones who migrate and the ones who stay behind. There is a scarcity of scholarship about how shifting markets and changes in gender roles for women have concomitant effects on men. Economic and political discourse on migration remains gender-neutral, treating the migration experience as located purely on a theoretical level. Feminist research on this very topic, while highlighting these limitations, remains marginalized and underutilized, even in the creation of social policies that could alleviate conditions for all involved. Simultaneously, as has been explored in this chapter, migration is effecting enormous changes on the microcosm of the family *and* gender ideologies. Even markets have been influenced by these shifts in perception. While only 5 or 10 years ago, the ideal factory worker was male and foreign, for many involved in industry today, the ideal factory worker is female and foreign. This is not to imply, that this is necessarily a beneficial phenomenon. Instead, it should just be noted that these trends are precipitating changes in social relationships and ideologies at an ever accelerating pace.

Loss and dislocation remain an integral part of the migration experience. However, migration also means the forging of new ties, the creation of new identities and the pursuit of economic, and, at times, social opportunities. Ethnographic studies indicate that by studying transnational families we can learn more about how individuals construct notions of families to begin with. For example, Filipino domestic workers who go abroad often refashion their notions of family by forming ties with other Filipino domestic workers in their region (Asis et al. 2004). Kinship ties, however, tenuous, become an important part of their day-to-day conceptualization of families. What we learn from these experiences is that globalizing processes are helping reshape how migrants view themselves, their families and their communities. As receiving societies increasingly tighten controls around the rights and incorporation of immigrants, immigrants react to their marginal status by creating new transnational spaces and identities for themselves.

The growing international feminization of migration opens up new areas to be explored. Currently, much of the literature on migration focuses on the family members who migrate and neglects those relations who are left behind. For example, we know little about the men, children, and extended family members of those women who choose to migrate in search of economic opportunities. We would gain greater insight into gender and family dynamics if we knew more about how men of different social classes construct and adjust new masculinities in the light of changed circumstances. We also need insight into the networks that women form, both in their home countries and once they settle in their host societies. The Internet, in particular, is facilitating new forms of social organizing whose impact for migrants has not been explored. Pessar and Mahler (2003) point out that we also need research that explores how immigrant women deal with the relationship between legal vulnerability and the concerns of their families and communities. Many immigrant women, all over the world, have little access to formal power structures. As migration, and especially female migration grows, family and household relationships that have long been engrained as "natural constructions" in so many areas of the developing world, are and will be changing. It is difficult to predict how rapidly these transformations are taking place, and with what end results with respect to families.

Chapter 5
Work–Family Intersections in a Globalizing Context

The last several years have witnessed a burgeoning global interest in the relationship between the work and family spheres. This focus has been fueled by fundamental changes in the nature and structure of work, as well as sweeping transformations in gender and family roles. The worldwide influx of women into the formal and informal labor force, accompanied by significant adjustments in family arrangements have debunked more traditional approaches that work and family need to be conceptualized as separate spheres. Instead, more recent perspectives illustrate that work and family are closely interconnected, and that they are an integral aspect of globalization (Parasuraman and Greenhaus 2002). The relationship between work and family domains has extended beyond scholarly works to businesses and their employees. As organizations have increasingly gone global, work and its relationship to family life has come under scrutiny both in the West and in non-Western parts of the world, albeit for different reasons.

In the West, the work–family focus is dominated by the theme of dual-earner couples, work spillover issues, work–family stress, and the relationship between work outside of the home and the division of labor in the home (i.e., gender roles). Moreover, organizations have come under increasing pressure to be more "family friendly" as workers struggle with child and elder care issues (Perry-Jenkins and Turner 2004) and other logistical problems faced by single parents and dual-earner couples. In the United States, much public attention has centered on middle-class Americans and their desire for flexibility in work schedules, affordable high quality day care, maternity and family leave, and same-sex benefits. Many of these issues have also become a central focus in other industrialized countries, with many European countries developing policies that specifically encourage women to combine paid labor with family life.

In developing countries, the focus has been slightly different. As economies have opened up and multi-national corporations increasingly move their operations to these places, governments have relaxed rules and laws with respect to employment practices. Globalization is closely related to these changes. By increasingly emphasizing cost-cutting competitiveness, globalization has encouraged companies to discover new means of lowering labor costs, which includes finding the cheapest possible labor and, at times, those areas of the world that have the laxest environmental

B.S. Trask, *Globalization and Families: Accelerated Systemic Social Change,*
DOI 10.1007/978-0-387-88285-7_5, © Springer Science+Business Media, LLC 2010

standards with respect to production conditions. Moreover, the emphasis on cost-cutting and profitability has resulted in the move by companies to different types of subcontracting work such as outsourcing and home-based work. This "informal" sector of work, those jobs without regular wages or benefits, has grown in proportion to the "formal" sector and has increasingly become associated with female workers. Thus, the economic restructuring of business and industry as a result of globalizing forces has significant implications for workers and their families, both in the industrialized and developing worlds.

Specifically, the global phenomenon of the influx of women into the formal and informal labor force has become a contested and contentious issue in most parts of the world. Both in industrialized and developing countries, fundamental questions are being asked about the role of paid work in relation to domestic work. Essentially, this is a debate about how societies should best be organized at the intimate household level, as well as from more macro perspectives. Particularly controversial in almost every country, and at virtually every level of society, is the division of labor within the domestic realm.[1] Much energy, discussion, and controversy, revolves around issues of reproductive labor and gender roles.[2] This topic is dominated by a focus on housework, care work and issues of equity within families. It is, however, important to note that what constitutes domestic or housework is somewhat variable. Thus, what the American middle-class housewife deems as domestic work looks quite different when viewed from the perspective of a poor South Asian woman or a female agricultural worker in China. This fundamental difference makes it extremely difficult to compare certain aspects of the female experience in different parts of the world, and brings into question older feminist perspectives that assume women are similarly oppressed due to the prevalence of patriarchal systems. However, issues of care work – who will perform the labor required by children, the disabled, and/or the feeble elderly, are growing in importance in both the industrialized and the developing world, as women (who traditionally performed this labor) increasingly balance home life with participation in the paid work force.[3]

It should be noted that even within the same society, women and men located at different parts of the socioeconomic scale will experience the balance of work and family in a very different manner. This holds true for discussions of family and work in other areas of the world as well. For example, professional women in the developing world, who are able to hire domestic workers to assist with their reproductive labor, are in quite a different position from the low-income or poor women

---

[1] Among the wealthy, in most societies, domestic work is traditionally serviced out. This is also the arena where patriarchal ideologies are most engrained, in terms of preserving very traditional gender roles. However, as women's educational level rises, so do questions about the role of careers and employment even in these families.

[2] Reproductive labor refers to the labor that households need to care and maintain themselves and future generations of the labor force. It refers primarily to childbearing, the raising of children, and daily tasks that are needed to sustain household members.

[3] Issues around the care of the disabled are virtually ignored as the disabled are "hidden" from public view in so many countries.

in their societies. This difference is often lost in Western discussions about the developing world, which tends to be conceptualized as a homogenous unit. What we find is a fundamental assumption that women and men, in developing countries, experience their society based on cultural ideals instead of differences of social class, socio-historical moment, ethnicity and other variables. This is a surprising development given the intensity of the debates, specifically in the United States, about the importance of incorporating a matrix of factors into understandings of the social positioning and experiences of different groups.

5.1 What is Work?

A fundamental aspect of family life is work both within the family or household and outside of the family. Despite a great deal of controversy surrounding definitions of "work," a commonly accepted characterization states that work is an "instrumental activity intended to provide goods and services to support life" (Piotrkowski et al. 1987). This definition usually entails participation in a market or a business organization. As was noted previously, definitions of "family" have also come under dispute. While family was previously conceptualized as a united group working in cooperation for the good of the collective, more recent scholarship has identified families as "a location where people with different activities and interests in these processes often come into conflict with one another" (Hartmann 1981, p. 368). Hartmann has highlighted the concept that family members are also members of gender categories. From this perspective the distribution of work in families is unequal as women tend to take on a greater degree of house work under the of guise of a shared division of labor (Hartmann 1981). Feminists have been quick to adopt Hartmann's views of the family and subsequently label the familial division of labor as oppressive and reflective of an engrained patriarchal system that advantages men.[4] This patriarchal system has allowed men to acquire greater social power including power in the intimate sphere of the family. The fundamental basis of this argument suggests that by not acknowledging women's work in the family, women's contributions are undervalued. Simultaneously, men's financial contributions are linked with greater power around decision-making.

Complicating the discussions on work–family linkages is the issue of unpaid work, which feminists in particular, have described as being primarily performed by women, thus creating different interpretations of work–family linkages than those laid out in older more traditional approaches to roles in families. The issue of unpaid labor and care becomes particularly critical in understanding the situation of poor and low-income women and children, especially those from the developing world. As Beneria (2003) points out, unpaid work is produced for use and not for exchange; it is, thus, often not acknowledged nor incorporated into work analyses.

---

[4] Hartmann was working from a strong Marxist-feminist perspective.

Women who are engaging in both market and unpaid labor are, thus, working double and triple shifts, often just to subsist.

5.2   The Changing Nature of Family Life and Family Roles

The last several decades have spawned an interest in the relationship between work–family linkages and gender. Interestingly, this focus was initiated by Gary Becker (1976, 1985), an economist, who drew scholarly attention to the societal aspects that encouraged women to enter the paid labor force. His analyses illustrated that the traditional division of labor in households was fundamentally unequal, that child care needed to be reconceptualized as "work," and that parenthood, especially motherhood, was accompanied by financial consequences (Drago and Golden 2005).[5]

In the West, the move to industrialization in the eighteenth and nineteenth centuries resulted in work patterns for men and women that have remained relatively consistent. These work patterns have been closely related to an ideology of domesticity for women, and of work outside of the home for men (Ferree 1991). Embedded in this construct is a structure where market work is organized around the ideal of an employee who works full time without substantial family responsibilities and who has a partner who takes care of dependent family members. This ideology is rooted in a belief about the inherent qualities of men and women: (1) that men are more competitive and aggressive, thus better suited to take on work in the paid labor force and (2) that women are more nurturing and caring and, thus, better suited for unpaid work in the home (McGraw and Walker 2004). While much has changed in industrialized societies, market and family work are still structured around these concepts, particularly for women with children. In the 1950s, only 16% of children had mothers who worked outside of the home full time. However, times have changed. Today, 59% of children have mothers in the paid labor force (McGraw and Walker 2002). Statistics for racial-ethnic women in the U.S. are even more staggering: African American women (78.35) are more likely than white women (76.65), Asian/Pacific Islander women (71.4%) and Hispanic women (65.85) to be part of the paid labor force (White and Rogers 2000). This phenomenal increase in the rate of women's labor participation, especially married women with children, can be attributed to a variety of factors in the U.S. and Europe. Initially, women entered the workforce due to changes in affirmative action laws and the feminist movement of the late 1960s and 1970s. However, the growth in women's employment has been sustained through increased opportunities for education for women, economic need, high divorce rates and a quest for self-fulfillment and personal happiness (Parasuraman and Greenhaus 2002).

---

[5] His work has come under extensive criticism from feminist economists due to his argument that the efficiency of a breadwinner/homemaker model of family was superior to that of a dual-earner family. However, I would still argue that his work is valuable because it initiated discussion on this topic in various fields.

The change in labor force participation has been accompanied by significant changes in family composition and family structure. As divorce has become more socially accepted, we have seen a rise in single-headed households, cohabiting couples, families that are taking care of a frail elderly and dual-earner couples. Thus, the model on which much workplace culture and policy has been predicated, the traditional single-earner breadwinner with a stay-at-home wife and children has become a minority with estimates ranging between 3 and 7% (McGraw and Walker 2002).

In the United States, while women are increasingly working outside of the home, they are also decreasing their involvement in the household with respect to domestic tasks and childbearing. Contemporary studies indicate that women's time spent on domestic activities such as cooking and cleaning has declined substantially between 1965 and 2000. Women are either lowering their standards for acceptable housework (Hochschild 1997) or they are purchasing the labor of other women to cook, clean and take care of their children (Ehrenreich and Hochschild 2003). Remarkably, women, including women in the paid labor force, are spending the same amount of time or even more time with their children as they did 40 years ago. Bianchi et al. (2007) found by studying time diaries, that working mothers prioritize their relationship to their children over other activities such as housework and time for themselves. In order to privilege the relationship with their children, women juggle multiple tasks simultaneously, and spend less time with their spouses.

Most contemporary women and men continue to struggle to balance both work and family life. While the bulk of research has concentrated on women, it is becoming more obvious that men are also increasingly taking on family-work responsibilities (Coltrane 2000). Men, at least in the American middle and upper middle class, are increasingly embracing an egalitarian ideal that, in theory, encourages men and women to participate equally in the paid labor force and in housework and childcare. This is, at times, referred to as "gender role convergence" (Moen 1989). Men are also under more pressure to adopt a new model of fatherhood. Until recently, a man's status and self-worth was primarily determined through his role as a breadwinner-provider. In an ethnographic study of middle-class men, Townsend (2002) argues that this definition of a good husband and father perseveres. However, today's new ethos, in the U.S. in particular, encourages men to also participate in all aspects of childcare that until recently were under the complete purview of women. In the contemporary American context, many men, as women, are also juggling dual roles and responsibilities. Interestingly, recent research indicates that when men and women's family work hours and paid work hours in dual-earner families are combined, they actually work approximately the same amount of hours (Bianchi et al. 2007). However, men tend to place their energy into paid work, while women are more likely to emphasize family work (Crittenden 2001).[6]

These types of findings have drawn public attention to disparities in gender roles and have raised questions about analyses based solely on statistical computations

---

[6] This brief review focuses primarily on the United States. However, particularly in Europe, this topic has elicited much attention by national research institutes and policy makers.

of the number of hours worked in and outside of the home. This newest research has also directed focus to the fact that until recently family work has been unrecognized and undervalued (Perry-Jenkins and Folk 1994; Crittenden 2001). The devaluation of family work raises concerns about social conditions that diminish parental contributions, and public policies that allow this situation to persist. In particular, the lack of affordable quality childcare is linked to an ideology that still encourages the breadwinner-homemaker model, and that penalizes working parents. Increasingly, the issue of elder care is also linked to similar factors. As our society ages and becomes increasingly diverse, more and more families are in the position of having to care for aging relatives. Current social policies in the United States do not allow for parents to easily assume these responsibilities. While these policies are somewhat more generous, in other Western countries such as Canada, Germany, France, and the Scandinavian countries, economic concerns are overshadowing any attempts at their expansion.[7]

Contemporary work–family analyses are dominated by two other themes: a family/developmental psychology emphasis on the effects of parental employment on family life, and an organizational focus on the role of the worker (Bowes 2004). More recently, the strategies that workers/family members use to balance work-life issues have also generated some interest. In part, these foci can be attributed to a concern on the part of both researchers and businesses in the actual mechanisms that increase productivity and allow workers to attend to their familial obligations while also maintaining a satisfactory quality of life. For example, a growing body of work documents that flex-time or part-time work is becoming more popular, especially with women (Pocock 2003; Barnett and Garesi 2002). Sometimes also referred to as the "mommy track," women are reducing the hours spent at work in order to spend more time with their children.[8] Other individuals are starting home businesses or combining multiple streams of income, in order to finance their lifestyles. Other less popular strategies include job sharing, and taking advantage of leave entitlements. However, some research also suggests that workers are nervous about taking advantage of formal work–family provisions due to the feared perception by colleagues and superiors that they are not adequately committed to their jobs (Hochschild 1997; Pocock 2003).

A very limited body of work highlights the effects of women's work on community participation. As women devote an increasing amount of time to the workplace and their families, they are less and less engaged in community affairs (Hochschild 1997). This has contributed to an increasing fragmentation of communities in Western societies. Friendships and networks are now forged in the workplace, instead of through volunteer activities. Pocock (2003) has documented the same phenomenon in Australia. As middle- and upper-class families lose those

---

[7] See Crompton et al. (2007) for a discussion of these issues in the European sphere.

[8] This phenomenon has led to new discussions about those individuals who choose to parent vs. those who remain childfree. In fact, there are some who argue that it is not gender anymore that matters in terms of career advancement but the choice to have or not have a child.

connections in the West, they become increasingly dependent on buying services from others. We shall examine that phenomenon more closely further on.

5.3 The Changing Nature of the World of Work

The changes in family composition and roles have been occurring, accompanied by simultaneous shifts in the world of work. Competitive pressures due to incorporation into global markets have forced businesses to reduce their workforce, find cheaper labor, and become more competitive. This, in turn, has put pressure onto workers who must work harder in order to increase their productivity and retain their jobs. In addition, the advancement of new communication technologies, while facilitating certain types of work, have also served to break down the work–family boundary. Work can be conducted from home, and employees have become more accessible to their employers. These changes have put pressure on both sides. Employees are under greater stress to retain and excel at their jobs, while businesses are under pressure to improve their productivity and raise their profit margins. These changes are closely tied, in various ways, to globalizing processes. In search of cheaper labor, organizations have moved work to new parts of the world and have started to rely on outsourcing as well as the subcontracting of work. This process has re-focused interest in work–family issues for those both in the industrialized as well as developing worlds.

Scholarship reveals that contrary to popular notions, all of these economic changes are not chipping away at the importance and value of families cross-culturally. In fact, Creed (2000) illustrates that in many places, the institution of family seems to be of growing economic significance. In part, due to globalizing processes, paid labor is in the process of shifting from the factory to the home in a variety of settings. For example, in the West telecommuting is a growing popular phenomenon, while in other regions of the world, multinational corporations and local businesses, for better or for worse, are encouraging the move of production into home-based settings. In part, this phenomenon is the result of ever-increasing demands for cheaper production costs and the need for a lower-wage work force. The consequences for workers are mixed. Depending on their economic and regional situation, workers now need to combine wage labor with subsistence production and other economic activities. What we find then, is that in our globalized context, work has become more flexible, but that very same flexibility can have unintended consequences. As capitalist economic forces reach all corners of the globe, the generation of new income makes some workers more desirable than others, and can make it necessary for low paid workers to supplement various work arrangements with multiple sources of income to act as a safeguard against uncertain times. Due to these intimate linkages between survival and economics, families may be even more essential these days than in the late 20th century. People need multiple streams of income from varying sources to make ends meets, and families provide the nucleus for these activities.

5.4   The Feminization of the Labor Force

Feminist scholars have highlighted the fact that the majority of the workforce in new sectors in emerging economies that are generated by the expansion of global trade and production, are women. In fact, a variety of studies have documented a preference for female laborers. Women continue to be heavily represented in low-wage production for export sector jobs, and in informal employment in low-wage, labor-intensive manufacturing jobs. These include lower-tier subcontracting chains, micro-enterprises, and self-employment. Specifically, women work in clothing and tourism industries, electronics components, data entry, financial services call centers and flower farms and fruit orchards (United Nations 1999). Large numbers of women are also increasingly found in the service sector. These jobs include services tied to global markets such as data entry and data processing in mail order businesses, airlines and rail systems, tourism, credit card providers, and other financial services such as banking. In some areas, such as the Caribbean, the service sector is completely represented by women (United Nations 1999).

Systems of flexible production rely primarily on women's labor through the use of temporary contracts, part-time work, and unstable working conditions. Sassen (2006) refers to this phenomenon as the *informalization* of work in the global economy. In this scenario, employers downgrade work by removing it from factories and moving it into worker's homes. Women and immigrant workers are the primary individuals affected by this move because they are usually more willing to take this type of work on, and because they are often more vulnerable. Paid work is moved from public to more private settings, where labor costs are cheaper and work conditions more difficult to monitor. While heavily criticized, this type of work contributes to low-cost production for global markets and is "tied to the volatility of global capital's mobility in search of the lowest cost location" (Beneria 2003, p. 78). Most of the individuals who particularly work in the informal sector, have little security or bargaining power in relation to income, working conditions, and benefits (Pearson 2000). The contemporary interrelationship of this type of work to the global economy also means that these new employment opportunities make workers more vulnerable to economic declines. If one sector of the economy collapses, among the first to be affected are its most vulnerable members, including those employed in low-wage and informal sectors.

Initially, scholarly approaches emphasized the exploitation of women by multinational industries by taking advantage of female stereotypes associated with female laborers and through their incorporation into low-wage and informal work. As discussed in Chap. 3, however, this "women as victims" approach has been recognized as too simplistic, and has been replaced with a new understanding that women are not just passive victims of exploitative situations (Ong 1987). More recent emphasis has been laid on the opportunities and challenges that women's employment in the paid labor force can generate, including women's increased independence and bargaining power within the family unit. Some studies have even revealed that some women's increasing economic power has allowed them to resist political forces and to stand up for their families in larger community settings (Kabeer 2000).

Beneria (2003) suggests that the links between the rapid formation of a female labor force across the globe should not be seen as purely a response to structural and economic factors. Instead, the multitude of women entering the work force is also a response to new gender constructions that emphasize the need for women to be financially independent and attain greater bargaining power over their own lives. Nevertheless, of concern to many feminist scholars and activists is the fact that despite a large numerical presence, women remain confined to low-wage employment. As was mentioned previously, an important aspect of globalizing processes is the trend toward more flexible labor, including part-time and home-based work. According to United Nations statistics, women are over-represented in each of these sectors (United Nations 1999). Further, in many developing and rural areas, a disproportionate number of women continue to perform a large portion of domestic work. Unpaid labor includes agricultural family labor, domestic work and volunteer work (Beneria 2003). Recently, the role of children in domestic labor has received increasing attention. Especially in the developing world, young children, and particularly girls, perform much of the domestic and carework, if their mothers are working outside of the home (Mensch et al. 2000). This phenomenon will be examined further on in this chapter.

The worldwide rapid feminization of the labor force is a phenomenon that is leading to a variety of culturally specific responses that have not been examined as a totality, nor with the intensity that is required to adequately understand them.[9] The feminization of the labor force is significant on multiple levels. Gender images are being negotiated, revised, and at times, reaffirmed according to local traditions and global trends. Thus, we find that the working of women outside of the home has evoked different responses, depending on regional as well as class location. Women in developed countries who belong to the middle or upper classes are enjoying a relatively advantageous position in the global economy. They are able to access educational training and higher levels of employment in unprecedented numbers. Meanwhile, women who are less educated both in developed and developing societies are taking on menial jobs that often exploit their labor for minimal financial returns. We, therefore, cannot generalize about the "condition of women" due to globalization.

Some studies illustrate that in certain areas where women are employed in lower level jobs, such as in Southeast Asia, the high rate of female participation in the labor force, viewed from a longer term perspective, has generated some improvements in women's wages and has led to a higher degree of female equality (Seguino 2000). In other areas, where female labor is plentiful, such as in Mexico, large scale manufacturers have taken advantage of the situation by offering low wages to women and by expanding informal sector work (Fussel 2000). As the public sector

---

[9] Much of the work on this topic is based on large national surveys that do not adequately capture the nuances of family life.

shrinks in poorer countries, women are usually expected to pick up the slack with respect to the provision of services and by finding alternate sources of income.

As one means of assisting low-income women in the developing world, microcredit programs have become increasingly popular over the last several years. Microcredit is extensively endorsed by transnational institutions as a means for alleviating the poverty conditions of rural families, and is perceived as an inexpensive way to incorporate women into the mainstream economy (Eisenstein 2005).[10] Supporters of microcredit suggest that women learn entrepreneurial skills and capacity building by participating in low-cost financial services. Microcredit traditionally involves the lending of small amounts of money to individuals, who are then grouped into small clusters, may borrow from the group fund, and are charged a minimal monthly interest rate.[11] While microcredit programs have become very popular, specifically in South Asia and more recently Africa, critics of the system suggest that the central tenet of this movement is the dismantling of public safety net programs. As responsibility for the alleviation of poverty moves to the private sector "the adoption of microcredit signals an acceptance of the permanency of the informal sector and the abandonment of any notion of genuine economic development" (Eisenstein 2005, p. 508). These same critics also highlight that microcredit has been viewed primarily from the standpoints of the lenders, and not from the perspectives of the borrowers. Ethnographic evidence indicates that many of the women who participate in microcredit programs often borrow money, which is then used by their husbands. Women take on the credit risk, and are simultaneously forced into the informal economy in order to pay off the debt. Due to the extreme poverty conditions in which so many of the borrowers find themselves, they are often not able to repay their financial obligation and, thus, enter into a cycle of repeated indebtness.

These conflicting perspectives on the relationship between work, the feminization of the labor force, and poverty, have led to a significant debate on the interrelationship between women's earning, their working conditions, export-oriented growth, and gender equality (Beneria 2003). There are those who optimistically suggest that globalization is reducing inequality between the sexes with respect to access to jobs, educational opportunities and wages (Dollar and Gatti 1999). Another point of view is represented by those who argue that economic growth is actually based on the persistence and support of gender inequalities, which include low wages and poor working conditions for women. There are several studies that illustrate that those Asian economies that have grown the fastest also have the widest earnings gaps (Seguino 2000). Complicating some of these discussions is the worldwide rise of female-headed households and their role in society and the marketplace.

---

[10] The origins of microcredit are primarily attributed to Mohammed Yunus, an economist who began this practice in the village of Grameen in Bangladesh in 1977. By 1999, his Bank (Grameen Bank) had 1,000 rural branches and extended to 45,000 villages lending more than one billion dollars to his two million members, of which 94% were female (Eisenstein 2005).

[11] Typically the group interest rate is between 12 and 24% a year based on the flat calculation method.

5.5   Female-Headed Households

Around the world, approximately one-fifth of all households are headed by women and one-half of all women between the ages of 15 and 65 are now working in the paid labor force (Ehrenreich and Hochschild 2003). While in areas like the Eastern Caribbean, there is a long history of female-headed households and constructions of masculinity and femininity already incorporate these ideas into local culture, in most parts of the world, female-headed households are viewed as an aberration and with suspicion.

As seen earlier, research in the 1970s and 1980s was characterized by a signifi-cant increase in dual-earner couples and rising rates of male unemployment. These two trends highlighted the importance of women's contributions to the family economy and led to optimistic predictions about the gains that women would make. Heidi Hartmann (1987), for example, celebrated the increase in female-headed households since she assumed that women *chose* to take care of their own families instead of relying on men. She along with other well-regarded feminists such as Karen Sacks presupposed that women's earning capabilities allowed them the choice to resist gender subordination in a family situation. However, what we have witnessed in recent years is that while female-headed households have become increasingly prevalent around the globe, they are almost always associated with high degrees of poverty (with the Scandinavian countries as the exception).

In order to augment the family economy, women are often forced to integrate increasingly complex combinations of financial sources. Despite the fact that they are primarily the consequence of economic strains, female-headed households are under continual scrutiny and are often blamed for all the ills of society.[12] And, yet, as Creed (2000) points out, most members of these households actually subscribe to the mainstream notions of domesticity that their societies value. He suggests that this phenomenon reflects a new "value of particular family arrangements in an economic context where multiple incomes are needed to support children and/or aging parents, and where the state is less willing to help" (p. 344). Nevertheless, female-headed households defy notions about the "appropriate" role of women and men in society.

The trends that accompany globalization have in large part altered the relation-ships of women to the market place. This has led to changes in gender roles and gender relationships and has transformed conceptions of gender both within fami-lies and across societies for women and men. But these changes have raised new questions about "how are women affected as the relative weight of their paid labor time increases and that of unpaid work diminishes?" (Beneria 2003, p. 83). Specifically, Beneria (2003) raises the question whether behaviors that have tradi-tionally been thought of as "feminine" such as cooperation, nurturance, and selfless-

---

[12] Nowhere is this more evident, than in the welfare to work discussions of the 1990s where "wel-fare mothers" represented through images of young Black women with babies, were highlighted as the primary recipients of welfare and social services.

ness will get transformed through women's greater incoporation into the marketplace. Feminists argue that these characteristics, far from immutable, are socially constructed and, subject to transformations. Therefore, we should begin to see the behaviors of men and women converging substantively in the labor force, and ultimately also in the domestic sphere.

A substantial work–family literature points to increasing trends toward equal end results for men and women who participate in the paid labor force. Working for pay now allows women to escape abusive marriages, marry later, and acquire power within relationships. But again, this situation holds true primarily for women with a certain degree of education and with relatively substantive jobs. In some areas of the world, such as many of the societies of the former Soviet Union, participation in the labor force has led to a revival, at least in the public discourse, of patriarchal attitudes and behaviors.

A somewhat different response is found in much of the Islamic world. There recent strides in opportunities for women have resulted in a great deal of interest in men's and women's "proper," "religiously" dictated positions in families and society. For example, among middle-class Egyptians, roles are changing due to the high influx of women into the paid labor force. As a result, on the intimate level of the household, men are beginning to take on duties that veer against the public dialogue on the appropriate nature and position of men and women. "Celebrity" sheiks blare messages across television screens focusing on the role of women as wives and mothers, and men as protectors and providers for their families. However, the economic situation is such that most middle-class households require women to work outside of the home.

In order to navigate through the contradictions of ideology (under the guise of religious discourse) and the financial realities of day-to-day life, many of these middle-class women have adopted the head veil when they move about in public. By wearing the veil, these women make a public statement that they are "conservative" women, who are "modern" enough to work outside of the home. These women have found a mechanism for, so to speak, moving between worlds. Their husbands also benefit from their wives' adaptation. They can point to their veiled wives as paradigms of virtue, instead of making excuses about why they are "allowing" their wives to move about freely in the outside world and to work outside of the home (Sherif 1996; Macleod 1993).[13]

The phenomenon of veiling among Egyptian middle-class women is an example that cautions us about making universal assumptions about the role of work and its relationship to family life. In different places and various sectors of societies, men and women negotiate the demands of the basic domestic tasks of family life with the need to earn enough money to survive and prosper. In the analyses of global phenomena, we always need to be mindful of social location and how that influences interpretations of the actions of others, particularly those in non-Western areas of

---

[13] You may also refer to my article in *Anthropology Today* (1999) on this topic. There is a large literature at this point on women's roles and their reasons for veiling throughout the Muslim world. See for example. Moghadam, V. (2003). *Modernizing women: Gender and social change in the Middle East*. Lynne Rienner Pub.

the world. As the Egyptian case illustrates, what may be perceived in the West as the "oppression" of some Muslim women due to their recent adoption of the headscarf, has very different connotations for the women themselves. What we are witnessing is a negotiation of gender roles, at both the ideological as well as praxis levels. Women are redefining contemporary circumstances by drawing, in certain cases, on traditional practices – but with reformulated meanings.

5.6 Where Does Girl's Labor Fall?

A complex and rarely discussed subject with respect to work and family is the specific issue of girl's work. Particularly in the developing world, young girls are often burdened with multiple domestic responsibilities that do not allow them to participate in the community or to attend school. This, in turn, restricts their future options and opportunities for self-empowerment. For example, ethnographic evidence from Ethiopia illustrates that even when girls are given the opportunity to attend school, they are often found to be absent due to pressures to cook, care for siblings, and engage in other household responsibilities. Often times, these girls need to take over the responsibilities of their mothers who are juggling responsibilities outside of the home due to their engagement in the market economy, or participation in community work (Woldehanna et al. 2008). Interestingly, this situation holds true even in cases where mothers are more highly educated. In the absence of affordable and accessible childcare, women rely on their daughters, in particular, to take over domestic responsibilities while they are engaged in paid activities outside of the family. These girls' activities do not show up in research studies and statistical documentation. Often times, girls are subsumed under the category of "children" and since they are participating in unpaid labor, their duties are not documented and, thus, ignored.

In areas devastated by HIV/AIDS, these issues become even more prevalent as growing numbers of AIDS orphans take on the responsibilities of caring for younger siblings. Due to the fact that there is a greater impact of poverty on female-headed households and there are more barriers to labor force participation, children in female-headed households are under greater pressure to combine household labor with schooling. In areas where boys are engaged in agricultural work, which is considered "men's work" and requires long hours with heavy physical activity, they may also be forced to forego educational opportunities. However, as a general trend, there are fewer demands on boy's labor than on girls and it is primarily girls who are denied opportunities to enhance their lives (Woldehanna et al. 2008).

Numerous examples illustrate that cultural norms shape parental views toward children's work. For example, for many parents in the developing world, children's involvement in the household or in the paid labor force is regarded as natural, unavoidable, and, often crucial, with respect to the family economy and skills acquisition. Children are made to work in order to support the family and they simultaneously acquire the skills to survive in the future. These attitudes are slow to change. However, new policy initiatives that specifically target girls' education are starting to bring about changes in this perception. There are multiple examples from around the world that affirm that investing in girls' education leads to lower fertility levels, delayed age of marriage, better health for the young women and their children, increased societal and political participation, and greater societal productivity (Bouis et al. 1998).

Many of the initiatives to empower girls and improve their lives, are based on relatively simple ideas. For example, some new programs in countries such as Ghana and Bangladesh include free after-school and weekend tutoring as well as an affirmative action program for girls that gives them preferred employment opportunities in local government offices, if they finish the eighth grade. These types of initiatives are changing the attitudes of parents toward their daughter's educational opportunities. Also, having schools in nearby proximity assists in encouraging parents to send their daughters to school (Glewwe 1999). If a school is located relatively near to the home, parents are much more likely to allow their children, and in particular, their daughters, to combine home and school responsibilities.

Another successful example comes from Burkina Faso, where a creative new program called The Milles Jeunes Filles (MJF) was introduced through a collaboration of the Ministry of Family and Social Welfare, the Ministry of Health, UNFPA, and the Population Council.[14] The goal of the program was to educate adolescent girls between the ages of 14–18 in order to create a stronger workforce. Initially, the program was conceptualized in a limited fashion that would allow the girls to acquire some working skills to be used on farms and in the family. However, the success of the program has led to a rapid expansion that now includes training in reproductive health, money management, literacy and environmental studies. Approximately 2,000 girls have attended the program and have spread the skills and knowledge that they have acquired to their families and communities. Parents have come to recognize the advantages that are to be garnered by sending their daughters through this training: the girls have better skills they can use at home and they are able to increase their earnings. This has changed fundamental assumptions about having daughters and their social worth. External evaluations of the program have highlighted the self-empowerment and networking that has resulted from girls' participation in the training. (Brady et al. 2007). The example of The Milles Jeunes Filles program illustrates how in a non-Western part of the world, work–family issues are intimately intertwined and can be supported through relatively simple initiatives.

A different approach can be found in the example of a pertinent case from the South Asian context where collective empowerment is understood as the key to challenging obstacles to female education and oppressive gendered work conditions (Gupta and Sharma 2006). Launched in 1988–1989, and now covering 9,000 villages and 60 districts in ten states, this government implemented a development initiative called *Mahila Samakhya*, a rural women's empowerment program. What

---

[14] Burkina Fasso is considered one of the poorest countries in the world.

makes this project unique is that it is not a service delivery program. Instead, this program seeks to increase the capacity of girls and women by raising their awareness and confidence, gives them information about their rights and entitlements, and trains them in the skills to access these. The underlying foundation is that incorporating the voices of girls and women into the actual development of the program, will aid them in bettering their status and lives. Participating women have ascribed the success of the program to the fact that it has let them "come out of their houses" (Gupta and Sharma 2006). Women have been able to develop new skills such as public speaking, leading training workshops, understanding bureaucracies, and interacting with all levels of governmental employees. These new roles have allowed girls and women to reconceptualize themselves as being productive on multiple levels than just as wives, mothers, and caretakers. Today, these women are able to mobilize women's collectives and they recognize, that through their involvement they may be able to thwart government corruption and assist in making other developmental programs work. They have also understood that it is through their work that other rural women will become aware of their rights to food supplements, housing subsidies, and employment opportunities.

These examples indicate that in different areas, local context and culture matters. Varying approaches are needed to assist girls and women develop new work roles *and* new conceptions of themselves, their talents, and their roles in a globalizing society. The examples from the Indian program also point to the challenges in attempts to draw parallels into the situations of women within and between societies. For example, even when comparing generations, the circumstances may be quite different. Moreover, while international development programs often target women in their initiatives, this approach ignores the internal dynamics of families. When women are drawn into the paid labor force, the domestic activities of the family remain to be resolved. Women either take them on as another burden [what Arlie Hochschild (1989) refers to as the "Second Shift" in the West], men become increasingly involved in domestic activities, children, specifically girls, take on new responsibilities, or family work itself is subcontracted to someone outside of the family.

5.7   Care Work and Women

Turning again to some of the contributions of feminist economists and their focus on the unequal intra-household distribution of resources due to power differentials, reminds us that the definition of "work" that is popular with family scholars and many economists, is often gender-blind, as it does not take into consideration domestic and care work (Woldehanna et al. 2008). Yet, as the number of women in the paid labor force continues to grow, the issue of care work has become increasingly visible and contentious. Particularly in the West, many feminists have had conflicts with policymakers regarding the appropriate role of women in families and the labor market, with respect to their relationship with their children, and particularly the lack of inadequate childcare. While care work for many families also includes the care of frail elderly, the disabled, and other sick family members, those topics have not led to quite the same heated and controversial arguments as the issue of childcare. Much of the work–family literature has focused on working parents, and specifically on the extent that women need to be present and involved in their children's lives.[15] In most Western societies, where families are often nuclear with little support from extended family or community members, the work of caring for children has fallen primarily on the parents, and specifically the mothers (Pocock 2003).

Working mothers in the industrialized world have devised multiple strategies for coping with the care work for which they are still traditionally responsible. Some women rely on female relatives like their mothers and sisters, as well as close friends, for assistance (Spain and Bianchi 1996). Other women, particularly middle-class and professional women are increasingly turning to low-wage workers to assist them with child care and housekeeping responsibilities. Scholars have characterized this continued gendering of care work primarily as relationships 'between women' (Rollins 1985 in Mattingly 2001). Care work provides insight into the differentiated roles within families and the role of the state and the market in influencing private situations and dilemmas. The growth of the occupation of care work "marks a commodification of a service once performed without wages by female family members, and a shift in the location of caring work from the family to the market. The need for private solutions to women's double day attests to the absence of state provision of caring labor for the families of working mothers" (Mattingly 2001, p. 373).

Increasingly, women who are financially able, are employing other women to assist them with their household, and specifically care work responsibilities. This need for labor has prompted an enormous migration of women from developing countries to developed countries in order to seek work as child care workers and domestics. As we have seen in a previous chapter, women from the Philippines, Sri Lanka, Mexico, Ecuador, Peru, and other Latin American countries are working in the United States, Europe, Canada, and the Middle East in order to improve their own and their families' lives by earning wages. It is important to note that there is a striking lack of concrete statistics given the informal nature of many of these arrangements. Nonetheless, the significance of this phenomenon is beyond doubt (Ehrenreich and Hochschild 2003). As part of this contemporary phenomenon, women from developing countries now often have a much easier time finding employment abroad than men do. This, however, necessitates these migrant women to leave behind their own families, with the raising of children being relegated to the extended families, or to the men in their lives. We, thus, have a situation where the care of children and the elderly has been removed from the core or nuclear family to either low income native or foreign workers in the case of middle- and upper-class women in the industrialized

---

[15] There is a growing fathering literature on the benefits of fathering for men [see, Palkovitz (2002) for example], but much of this literature has stayed within the confines of a 'fathering' dialogue and has not extended to broader discussions within family studies, economics, or anthropology.

world, and to extended family, "other mothers," men, and children in the case of women from the developing world.[16]

On the one hand, globalization has intensified the market for care work. For individuals in affluent areas, the availability of low-wage workers to take over care work has allowed, in particular, middle- and upper-class women to take on employment outside of the home. Simultaneously, women from poorer areas are now able to find jobs that, theoretically, could empower them due to their ability to earn wages. Zarembka (2003), however, points out that care workers are often in positions that do not allow them to protect themselves. Instead, they are vulnerable to exploitation and may have to work under conditions that they find intolerable. Nevertheless, paid domestic work is an important component of a new international network of caring labor (Mattingly 2001).

Individuals who migrate for this type of employment may find themselves in positions of powerlessness from which it is extremely difficult for them to extricate themselves. Instead of attaining economic independence and broadening their opportunities, they may find themselves in jobs with unregulated conditions, low wages, and at times sexual exploitation. Scholars such as Sassen (2006) and Chang (2006) further elaborate on the problem of care work by positing the critical view that by removing care work out of the family domain we are encouraging an even more highly differentiated and impersonal division of labor. From this perspective, the commodification of care threatens the fabric of basic social relationships (Zimmerman et al. 2006).

Bhagwati (2004) contradicts the assumption put forward by many of these feminist scholars that removing care work from families leads to a situation of exploitation. Instead, he points out that, often times, for women from very poor societies, the opportunities that are presented through working abroad outweigh the disadvantages. Women who go abroad earn more money for their labor, are exposed to new ways of thinking about issues such as traditional gender roles and patriarchal authority, and are able to enjoy a more "liberating environment." Bhagwati also points out that this perspective, popularized through Arlie Hochschild's "global care chains" (2001), implies that the nuclear family plays the same role in other societies as it does in the West. And yet, the social scientific literature explicitly describes many places where the extended family plays a crucial role in childrearing, and mothering is not just relegated to the biological mother. It is also important to note that the "intensive mothering" model that is currently so pervasive, especially in the United States, is a contemporary phenomenon. In a recent work, Bianchi et al. (2007) illustrate through the use of time diaries, that working mothers currently spend as much time with their young children as stay-at-home mothers did in the 1960s. This finding translates into a much more significant investment by mothers into their children in the U.S. today. Further, as was stated in the introduction to this chapter, in our current model, men are expected to be highly involved

---

[16] Heymann (2006) also documents that in certain cases, there is no one to take care of the children. They are just left to themselves.

in childcare alongside women. We should, thus, heed Bhagwati's argument, that particularly from a cross-cultural perspective, our hegemonic ideologies about family, gender and children's roles, cannot necessarily be uniformly applied to other parts of the world. Moreover, we should be extremely cautious about drawing conclusions about the lives of women, men, and children in other societies based on Western models.

5.8   Care Work and Children

In the U.S., the U.K., and Australia, scholars, policymakers, and social service professionals are taking increased notice of the extent and nature of children's unpaid, informal care-giving responsibilities in the family (Becker 2007). Specifically of interest is children's labor that goes beyond regular household duties. In part, growing attention to this phenomenon can be attributed to the mounting number of children who are forced to be engaged in care work, due to the crisis brought on by the epidemic of HIV/AIDS in sub-Saharan Africa. An increased scrutiny of children's care work responsibilities has, however, brought on varied policy responses to children in the West compared to in Africa.

Throughout the West, care that is provided within the family is rarely conceptualized as work. This is based on an understanding of the provision of care as an extension or provision of love and obligation – not as a formal arrangement requiring financial outlays (Becker and Silburn 1999). However, informal caring relationships *are* work and of concern to local, national, and international policymakers. According to a recent estimate, the replacement value of care provided by family carers for a year is approximately $306 billion in contrast to the cost of formal home care in the U.S., which is estimated at about $43 billion (Arno 2006). There are currently no statistics for either the West or other parts of the world that detail the economic and social contributions that children provide through their care. Care work by children is not labeled as work and, thus, goes unrecorded and unmeasured. One aspect of the problem is that there is no uniformly agreed upon definition of children's care work. In order to facilitate this discussion, we will therefore rely on the definition proposed by Becker:

> Young carers can be defined as children and young persons under 18 who provide or intend to provide care, assistance or support to another family member. They carry out, often on a regular basis, significant or substantial caring tasks and assume a level of responsibility that would usually be associated with an adult. The person receiving care is often a parent but can be a sibling, grandparent or other relative who is disabled, has some chronic illness, mental health problem or other condition connected with a need for care, support or supervision (Becker 2000, p. 378).

This definition has been applied to analysis of young caregivers both in the West and specifically, to understand the situation of families in various African societies (Becker 2007). This definition can also be usefully incorporated into understanding the care work of children in other parts of the world since it singles out those children who are engaged in a routine form of care as part of their daily lives, versus those who are in situations where they need to take on substantial amounts of care, often while still very young.

Due to global forces that highlight crises and topics of significance in other parts of the world, the relationship between children and care work is becoming an increasingly controversial topic. Malkki and Martin (2003), for example, point out that the privileging of the Rights of the Child by the Convention, lessens the value of the care that is provided by so many girls around the world to younger siblings and others.[17] The Convention also privileges the child-adult relationship and the education-to-work transition as the only appropriate path, despite a plethora of research illustrating that for many children, relations with adults are subject to negotiation depending on circumstances, and education and work transitions are frequently interrupted (Ruddick 2003).

Due to the "unseen" nature of children's care work in all societies, it is difficult to gather accurate statistics on this topic. In the West, census figures are often not representative because they rely on parents' self-reporting. In other countries, care is usually not recognized as a form of labor or work activity and, thus, not acknowledged. Estimates in the U.S. assume that approximately 3.2% of households with a child ranging from 8 to 18, or 1.3 million children, are engaged in informal care giving. The statistics for Australia and the U.K. are similarly striking, however, it is extremely difficult to compare data across nations due to different definitional and methodological issues. For example, surveys in Australia include young adults up to the age of 25 as "child carers."[18] We have no accurate figures for sub-Saharan Africa, but based on estimates of the HIV/AIDS pandemic, there is a great deal of speculation that an increasing proportion of the population will require care, especially when compared with Western countries, and that this will be provided primarily by children. UNICEF estimates that by 2010, more than 18 million children will have lost a parent to AIDS, and that less than 10% of children orphaned and put into risky positions due to AIDS will received some sort of local assistance (2006). Woldehanna et al. (2008) highlight these issues, and advocate that any social policies that seek to address development need to take into account the large proportion of carework that is being performed by women and children. Due to its unrecognized nature, women and children in caretaker positions are often not able to take advantage of economic and educational opportunities. This, in turn, has domestic consequences as their families continue to struggle in abject poverty, and at times, suffer even worse consequences. Most social policies in both the industrialized and developing world do not take care work into account, resulting in a major disconnect between the needs of families and programming when it comes to work–family issues.

---

[17] The Convention on the Rights of the Child will be detailed extensively in the next chapter.

[18] Becker (2007) presents an extensive discussion about the problems involved with using cross-national data and statistics.

5.9 Policies that Assist Families and Households

The relationship between work and families is determined by a complicated array of factors that include socio-cultural norms and values about the division of labor, the generational specificities of each household, and market place opportunities. However, ultimately the most crucial factor in determining who works and why is based on individual financial situations and perceived benefits, opportunities, and challenges. This makes the creation of work–family policies a highly challenging proposition in the global arena. For example, in some parts of the world, educating one's children may incur such a cost burden on a family, that schooling cannot even be considered as an option. Each member of the household is needed for his or her labor contributions. This is particularly true with respect to children being raised in rural areas of the developing world, and, often primarily girls. Social policies that attempt to provide educational and work opportunities, thus, need to be built on more nuanced understandings of the "generational ordering of social relations" (Alanen 2003). Moreover, what may benefit one member or one part of a household may, unintentionally, have negative consequences for another. For example, when work opportunities open up for women in certain sectors, it is the children, and in particular girls, who may become unduly burdened with domestic responsibilities.

Policies and programming must contextualize work and family responsibilities within cultural environments. Currently, exclusive American ideas about work are being exported to other areas, including Europe, Australia, Central and South America, Asia, and Africa. This exportation runs the risk of superimposing American values, which emphasize highly individualistic notions of family responsibility, onto places which value a much stronger collectivistic approach to families (Rapoport et al. 2005). As globalization spreads "paid" work to an increasing number of individuals in the developing world, other aspects of their contributions to their families become either devalued, or impossible to maintain. In particular, women are increasingly burdened with double and triple shifts that force them to work for pay outside of the home, while gender discourses legitimize the expectation that they are still to perform all of their domestic duties. As we have seen, in order to develop stronger work–family policies that support families as a totality, national agendas need to take into account paid employment, informal sector work, *and* care labor.

In the contemporary environment, the changing nature of labor force participation and the accompanying values of high productivity and job insecurity affect men in Western and non-Western contexts as well. In the United States, men are under increasing pressure to work long hours in order to retain their jobs, while losing their former security of earning a family wage. This stress is compounded by new ideals that value "involved" fathers and husbands. However, through an ethnographic investigation of middle-class American men, Townsend (2002) illustrates that despite the evocation of these new ideals, men are still primarily judged on their ability to be breadwinners and their primary valuation as fathers remains as providers. These trends make it difficult for many men to truly participate in a more equitable division of labor with respect to housework or to take advantage of policies such as paternity leave.

Among low-income families in the West and in the developing world, men have also seen an erosion of available employment for themselves. They are, thus, faced with the double bind of not being able to fulfill their traditional masculine role as breadwinners, and having to cope with new conceptualizations about their roles and those of women in families and society. Anecdotal evidence indicates that some men in those situations react negatively to a world in which they feel increasingly vulnerable and useless. However, in actuality we know little about the construction of new masculinities in the developing world, and the effects of globalization on male roles in different socio-economic and cultural contexts. We need research in this area in order to formulate policies that support all members of families. As the work world has been transformed, so has the domain of the family. And with changes in women's roles, the lives of the other individuals in their lives have also been altered. We need to deepen our understanding of these transformations and engage in a cross-cultural dialogue that utilizes the global platform in which so much of this change is taking place.

In concluding this chapter, I wish to point out a positive finding that is often not highlighted in work–family discussions: overall, parental employment has been shown to have positive outcomes in both Western and non-Western societies. For example, in the West, parenting has been identified as the key variable linking parental work and child outcomes (Bowes 2004). A small subset of studies have looked to the children themselves for their opinions on parental work, with generally positive assessments (Galinsky 1999). Parental work can introduce positive influences such as new ideas into the household and there is some research that indicates that individuals benefit from taking on multiple roles (Barnett and Hyde 2001). Thus, it behooves us not to view the work–family connection purely from a financial gain and social loss perspective. However, we need to engage in dialogue and action around supporting working individuals as they balance their work and family responsibilities.

These same findings with respect to parenting are also applicable in developing societies. For example, economic policies that create new income-producing opportunities for women under the correct conditions may improve the lives of children. There is increasing evidence that when women have more income, they invest it in their children's well-being. When mothers, however, are not supported through community or government structures, their investment in their own children can lessen with respect to nutrition, health and educational needs of their children. Also, as we have seen, children may be negatively impacted if their care-giving responsibilities in the household increase (Woldehanna et al. 2008). However, international examples indicate that social policies can go a long way to alleviate work–family stress. In developing countries, possible policy options include: cash transfers to encourage child schooling in higher grades instead of food-for-work programs; credit for labor, so that families can replace child labor with hired labor, and credit programs that directly target costs incurred through schooling. Given the widespread involvement of older children, especially girls, in childcare, implementing community childcare services would have a major impact in terms of freeing girls to pursue educational opportunities (Woldehanna et al. 2008).

In the West, and specifically in the United States, subsidized quality childcare would greatly improve working families' concerns about the well-being of their children while they work outside of the home, and simultaneously, remove an enormous financial burden from lower and middle-class families. Flexible work hours and more generous family leave would also help the many households that are involved in elder care or assisting a family member with a disability. People need to know that they can take time off from their jobs to perform their family duties without being penalized in the workplace. This requires a cultural re-conceptualization about the role of work in people's lives and how productivity is defined.

With respect to global companies, organizations need to consider how to increasingly work across transnational and cultural contexts. Globalization entails the potential for employees to be constantly on the move – in terms of business trips or actual relocations. Organizations need to find mechanisms to lessen the impact of these moves on individuals and their families. Moreover, improvements in telecommunications promise to transform the global workplace into a sphere that is increasingly less dependent on geographical location. A consideration of how budding forms of innovative technologies can be applied to improve individuals' and family lives needs to be part of the planning process. Further, an increasingly multicultural work force foreshadows that there will be new unforeseen issues to be dealt with. Varying ideologies about profit margins, productivity, authority, hierarchy, and even gender roles may come into conflict in increasingly heterogeneous environments.

Work–family issues need to be on everyone's radar – and not just with respect to productivity. Productivity is, in part, the outgrowth of just work conditions and a properly compensated workforce. Increasingly, around the world, the concept of life satisfaction is being coupled with the need for work. Global corporations can do much in terms of spreading wealth to underdeveloped and poor areas, while simultaneously assisting individuals find a more equitable work–family balance.

Chapter 6
Global Conceptualizations of Children and Childhood

Analyses of globalization, children, and childhood are currently only in the initial stages. From a superficial perspective, children belong in the "private" or domestic sphere. They are part of local environments and not directly influenced by globalization. In the eyes of many, globalization is part of the "public" sphere – it impacts macro processes and deals with shifting political economies, emerging markets, politics, and institutional arrangements. Upon closer examination, one finds that there is, actually, a multi-dimensional relationship between children, childhood, and globalization, and that it is analytically incorrect to dichotomize children and globalization into categories such as public vs. private, or domestic vs. international (Ruddick 2003). Also problematic is the current Western conceptualization of children as an age-specific group requiring the same resources, stimuli, and attention the world over. In the words of one prominent scholar on children and childhood, "In a period of scholarship emphasizing the historicization and de-naturalization of virtually every category of social identity (prominently including race, ethnicity, gender, class, and nationality) childhood has remained one of the most persistently biologized and universalized" (Stephens, 1998, p. 3).

Universalizing and biologizing approaches to children and childhood negates all we have learned about the importance of context, access to resources, and the variability of human nature. Globalization has produced a popular vision of what childhood is, and what children should do (Kuznesof 2005). From a Western perspective, children need to be "protected" from harsh environments and complicated issues, they need to "play," and they ought to go to school. However, this conceptualization of children and childhood does not mesh with the experiences of children in many parts of the world, raising complex questions about their lives and rights.

Conceptualizations of children and childhood are culturally determined, historicized, politicized, and transmitted between and within cultures. They differ over time and place, and are vigorously contested with respect to representation and reproduction (Malkki and Martin 2003). Yet, Western hegemonic representations of childhood, the nature of children, and the types of relationships they are capable of, are spreading. Governments around the world are increasingly examining, borrowing and adapting aspects of Western children's rights and child labor laws. Simultaneously, global markets are impacting children's lives across national

B.S. Trask, *Globalization and Families: Accelerated Systemic Social Change,*
DOI 10.1007/978-0-387-88285-7_6, © Springer Science+Business Media, LLC 2010

boundaries, regions, and social class. Cross-cultural contacts are affecting identity formation, and educational systems are being influenced by prevalent hegemonic depictions of "appropriate" or "successful" pedagogies for educating young people. By examining the close relationship between globalization, children, and childhood, we can learn not just about the influence of this process on the microcosm of the family, but also about the symbolic flow of information and values, and the potential for the manipulation of images and knowledge. We can also better our comprehension of linkages between local, national, and international forces, and, thus, may be able to better protect and enhance the lives of children worldwide.

6.1 The Spread of a Universal Concept of Childhood

Being a child is a universal developmental stage rooted in biology. However, childhood is a socio-cultural concept derived from specific values, beliefs, historical moment and geographical place. In order to reproduce itself and to survive, every society must produce children and raise them in some form of a safe manner. Yet, each society defines the period of childhood and its associated experiences differently. As a stage, childhood plays a strategic role – it is the basic foundation for socialization and the arena where groups, communities, and societies reproduce their identity (Fass 2003). The meanings of childhood are closely tied to local, as well as national and, at certain times, international beliefs and norms. Even within families, the whole concept of childhood can change with gender, family size, social class, education, and regionality. It matters if a child is born and raised in a city, a suburb or a rural area. In the case of individual children, kinship relations, religion, parental education, and family income are only a few of the factors that determine the experiences of childhood. Further, biology determines when a child is born – but it is culturally prescribed when childhood ends. Grew (2005) points out that childhood can also offer various protections, opportunities, and dangers depending on context. We can speak of a general group of children, but we cannot generalize to a shared experience of childhood even in the same society. Thus, there always exists a tension between the conceptualization of children as an abstract, idealized and universal group, and the lived experiences of children (Malkki and Martin 2003).

Philippe Aries is often cited as one of the first scholars to suggest that childhood has different meanings, depending on socio-historical time. He described our contemporary concepts of childhood as emerging as part of the early modern period of industrialization. In a much quoted phrase from his pivotal work on this subject, *Centuries of Childhood* (1962), he stated that "in medieval society the idea of childhood did not exist" (1962, p. 1). Using data from pre-industrial France and England, he argued that prior to industrialization, due to high child mortality rates, parents did not view their children through the same sentimental lens that we use today in the West, and instead children were regarded as miniature adults. While Aries' work has been heavily criticized since its publication, its value lies in alerting scholars to the critical nature of the social construction of childhood (Aitken 2001).

In our contemporary environment, however, the social construction of childhood is beginning to be lost. Due to global processes a worldwide, ahistorical concept of childhood, imported from the West, is spreading, which superimposes on children an image of a "universal category of biologically immature human beings" (Stephens 1994, p. 2). This conceptualization is exported to all corners of the globe along with assumptions about the appropriate socialization and education of children. Stephens (1995) suggests that these concepts are closely linked to other exported ideas about gender, individuality, and family relationships. Western constructions of childhood are intimately intertwined with debates about how to produce a future moral and cultured citizenry, and the role of individuals in production. However, how these concepts are interpreted on the local level varies widely.

In the West, childhood has become invested with heavy emotionality – children are revered, tenderly nurtured, and taken care of into adulthood. This image of the vulnerable precious child is sustained, encouraged, and fostered throughout the middle and upper classes.[1] An important feature of this representation has been the assumption of children as deserving to be treated as special, and as different from adults.[2] Children are to be segregated from adults and need to inhabit an innocent world of play and fantasy. They are to be kept out of the world of production and spared arduous tasks (Stephens, 1998). This hegemonic idealized depiction of children is spreading from the West to other areas of the world where, however, the resources to adequately replicate this form of childhood are lacking. And, even in many Western environments, resources that support an idealized form of child rearing have been declining (Ruddick 2003).[3]

6.2 The Pivotal Role of Child Development Pedagogies

Tied to the spread of concepts about children and childhood, is the move toward importing models of early childhood education, values, practices, and programming influenced by Western, primarily American, paradigms. For example, the World Bank, with the endorsement of 12 major international donor agencies, including UNESCO, USAID, and UNICEF, has published a "definitive" widely used handbook for early childhood programming (authored by Evans et al. 2000).

---

[1] Annette Lareau refers to this as concerted cultivation. She argues in her book *Unequal Childhoods* (2003) that middle- and upper-middle class families in the United States raise their children in a highly scheduled and regulated manner in order to provide them with the tools to be successful in life. She calls this concerted cultivation, while working class and poor families allow their children more freedom, termed by her as "natural growth." However, according to Lareau, "natural growth" results in working class and poor children not being able to function as well in society as children raised with "concerted cultivation" which impedes them from moving out of their social class.

[2] This representation becomes highly problematic in the U.S. legal arena, where there is constant dispute around the issue of trying children as adults, or as a unique category.

[3] In fact, there is some evidence that in certain very poor areas in the U.S. in particular, the lives of children are not that different from those of children from poor families in the developing world.

This handbook which draws on similar publications by UNICEF and other such organizations, concentrates on concepts and practices created for children in the U.S. Primarily, the handbook explores the concept of "developmentally appropriate practice," a phrase coined by the National Association for the Education of Young Children (NAEYC), which is the main umbrella organization for professionals working with children. Developmentally appropriate practice describes the ages and stages that children pass through, as well as the familial contexts in which they learn. Children's experiences are subdivided into several arenas including the physical, the intellectual, the emotional and the social spheres. Developmentally appropriate practice encourages certain types of actions on the part of adults in order to assist children to pass through these stages. A basic premise is that, universally, children pass through these stages and that culture only plays a minor role in their experiences. Thus, all children pass through similar phases despite living under very different conditions, such as in Los Angeles, California or in rural Mongolia. Research from neuroscience and developmental psychology provides justification for this interpretation of children's needs (Penn 2002).

The concept of developmentally appropriate practice now appears in books and training manuals for professionals who work with children the world over. On the basis of this perspective, the fundamental aspect of being a young child is brain capacity and its development. In fact, the World Bank handbook goes as far as to state that cultural variation needs to be acknowledged, but that breaches of developmentally appropriate practice need to be overridden by those who work with children (Evans et al. 2000). Penn (2002) points out that a careful examination of this handbook and others like it reveals that they are the product of what she describes as a "pick and mix" approach. "Pick and mix" refers to the practice of drawing on aspects of research studies, often in contradiction with one another, to provide justification for an argument. She describes one of the most widely cited studies on brain development by Chugani et al. (1987) which reported on the results of PET scans on 29 children with epilepsy compared to seven "normal" adults. Despite the fact that this study's research population represents a highly atypical sample, it provides the basis as "hard data" about the first 3 years of life, for a wide range of texts on developmentally appropriate practice, including the World Bank handbook.

This approach to early childhood has been quietly criticized by those who argue that crude extrapolations from limited studies do not provide the necessary justification for explaining behavior, since development varies, and is dependent on various factors, including context (Richards 1998). The concept of development is used as a general term for a complex phenomenon that results from the interaction of genetics, environment, and biology. Multiple influences interact at various levels and impact individual children differently. This makes it limiting, at best, to speak about developmentally appropriate practice as a universal concept. Developmentally appropriate practice is based on specific assumptions about society and childhood: it presupposes that individualism and selfhood are primary values, and that children are being raised in a nuclear family with a primary caretaker. It also presumes that children will be taught choice from a wide array of material resources (Penn 2002). Penn goes as far as to describe developmentally appropriate practice as "how to understand and bring up your child as an Anglo-American" (2002, p. 125). The problem, of course, is that by assuming that children everywhere can benefit from the same types of parenting and teacher interventions, we are ignoring the multitude of complex environments such as war, excruciating poverty, and HIV/AIDS in which children are being raised the world over.

Developmentally appropriate practice does not take into account problems such as extreme income disparities and horrendous social conditions such as the ravages brought on by pandemics and refugee status, but instead assumes that home visitation and parent education will assist poor families around the world in raising their children. As will be seen, however, there is little discourse, dispute, or even acknowledgement of the complexity of these issues. Instead, Western child rearing models, which emphasize developmentally appropriate practice, are spreading rapidly to the farthest corners of the globe.

6.3   Problematic Universal Concepts

The adaptation and implementation of Western child rearing techniques become even more complex when viewed through more localized lenses. For example, Wollons (2000) points out that child rearing ideals tend to be global these days in terms of their values, but local in their implementation. It would be simplistic to claim that Western ideals are becoming dominant around the world. Instead, there is a constant merging and reformulation of Western concepts with local practice. Moreover, locally relevant concepts and meanings are transformed in the process. Thus, discussions around teaching individualism and independence to children may be becoming more popular in non-Western societies – but they may be based on very different assumptions about what those ideologies and behaviors actually mean in the local context, than they do, for example, in the United States (Hoffman and Zhao 2007). What we find is that ideological hegemony becomes challenged at times on the local level, and gives space for local agency and voice.

The questions of hegemony and hybridity with respect to early childhood education also bring up the issue of universality. A popular point of view posits that when we are talking about the inherent nature of children, their development and their education, we know what is best for them not due to Westernization or the hegemony of American ideals. Instead, these ideas and ideals are based on a sound understanding derived from science. From this perspective, science now allows us to understand universal principles that pertain to all children throughout the world. This is one of the primary assumptions behind developmentally appropriate practice and education, and probably explains the increasing global popularity of this approach. Hoffman and Zhao (2007) astutely point out that the appeal of Western notions on child development and child rearing probably can also be attributed to a certain global competitiveness that associates these ideals and practices with more "developed" societies. Thus, the allure, at least for some, stems primarily from the origin of the idea rather than the idea itself.[4]

Hoffman and Zhao (2007) suggest as another possible rationale for the popularity of American-based early childhood models that there is a basic ethnocentric bias, which is inherent in the concept of universality values. Universal is equated with research that is developed primarily by Americans studying and working with American children. Thus, research is founded on the concept that *we* know what is best for children. However, such a perspective ignores the wide spectrum of culturally diverse lives, values, and conditions under which children live. This discussion is complicated by the fact that the flow of knowledge is not necessarily uni-directional, i.e., just from the United States to other parts of the world. For example, Hoffman and Zhao (2007) point to the case of Reggio Emilia as a program model that has become a worldwide phenomenon.[5] It is probably the case, however, that the United States and other Western nations play an enormous role in popularizing, legitimizing and spreading information in worldwide flows of childhood ideology and practice. It is not just the production of knowledge that is an issue, but also, and probably much more importantly, the control and dissemination of ideas and practices (Ambert 1994).

Discourses around early childhood development and care are also closely related to economic and political agendas of various societies. The issue of children's status, welfare, and requirements may, at times, be highlighted or subsumed under a more dominant economic agenda. It is often not clear if certain models of child development and care truly benefit children or, instead, further a social agenda that privileges global market economies.

To Western audiences in particular, ideals such as individualism, independence, and developmental appropriateness resonate and are appealing. However, some scholars argue that it is unclear to what extent these values may actually promote certain forms of Western market economies (Hoffman and Zhao 2007).[6] The concept of parenting itself relies on a specific socio-historical interpretation of what is appropriate in terms of behaviors and ideals. De Carvalho (2001) suggests that, worldwide, parenting has become a form of science, whereby parents "create" a product out of their children based on normalized, standardized, and expert-driven content. This "product" is tweaked and shaped in order to fill high status social positions.[7]

---

[4] This is particularly true in China where a whole literature on how to educate your children so that they will be able to study in the U.S. has become increasingly popular. In some of the most famous books, Chinese visitors to the U.S. have upon their return documented all of the "methods" that American parents use in order to prepare their children for higher education. Woronov (2007) reports that books such as *How Americans raise their daughters, How to raise your child to get into Yale,* or *Sports and art classes in American schools* draw enormous Chinese audiences.

[5] Regio Emilia is a child-focused approach to early childhood education that originated in Northern Italy.

[6] See Hoffman and Zhao (2007, p. 71) for an expanded discussion on this issue.

[7] The complexity of preparing children and adolescents in the U.S. to enter elite universities attests to this phenomenon. A whole industry has now built up around SAT preparation, college essay writing and preparing for college interviews. These services are only available to an elite group of children due to the high cost associated with them.

Contemporary U.S. child development ideology holds front and center, the values of being child-focused and teaching individualism. However, Hoffman and Zhao (2007, p. 71) argue that the underlying concepts of "social status, instrumentality, productivity, and institutional prerogative are implicit and generally, remain unchallenged." For example, while the values and practices that promote individualism are becoming increasingly popular around the world, the actual meaning of the term varies widely depending on context. This is illustrated by the example of a recent study of mainstream American parenting magazines that revealed a pre-occupation with raising "independent" children. These same advice magazines, however, portrayed adult-child relationships as power struggles that need to be "won" by the parents. The underlying assumption throughout these discussions is that a child's will needs to be negated, is a source of social deviance, and needs adult intervention to conform to more socially appropriate standards of behavior (Hoffman 2003). This interpretation of child-centeredness is diametrically opposed to a Chinese conceptualization of fostering independence in children. A cross-cultural, comparative study revealed that in Chinese interpretations children's will is thought to be strong and natural, and that this should serve as a guide to parents and caregivers. Adult control is interpreted as detrimental to developing independence (Lee 2001 in Hoffman and Zhao 2007).

A standardization of beliefs and practices around child development and parenting practices ignores the day-to-day realities of the lives of multitudes of children around the world. The "legitimacy" of the views of educators and other experts now increasingly dictate the relationship that parents, extended family, and other guardians and caretakers have toward children. Ironically, this move toward a homogenization of beliefs and practices ignores the very perspective it purportedly supports; those of the children themselves. This standpoint also does not incorporate and acknowledge the validity of local traditions, values, or circumstances. Maybe most importantly, what is missing from so much of the dialogue is a critical view toward what is considered "best practice" and its global exportation.

6.4 Changing Transitions to Adulthood

Some theorists such as Hengst (1987), Frones (1994), Cunningham (1995), and Aitken (2001) suggest that childhood as it was conceptualized in the nineteenth and early twentieth centuries in the West is again in the process of transformation. While during the last century, and the first part of the twentieth century, childhood came to be understood as a distinct phase of the life cycle, meriting special treatment and education, as well as a clear separation from the world of adults, especially the world of work, that separation is currently becoming more ambiguous.[8] In part, this transformation is potentially attributed to the lengthening of institutionalized educational

---

[8] In The U.S. Hall in 1929 was one of the first to identify adolescence as a specific phase in the life cycle requiring specialized attention.

control. Thus, the line between childhood and adulthood is not easily drawn anymore. Evidence for this notion can be drawn from historical aspects of the ideational expectations for middle-class American families. For example, before World War II, early marriages and boundaries around sexual relations created a clear passage way from childhood to adulthood: an individual was a child until he or she married, commenced sexual relations, and for men, entered the workplace. All of these events occurred within a relatively circumscribed amount of time (Frones 1994).

Increasingly in the West, the demarcation between when an individual passes from childhood to adulthood is unclear and depends on a multitude of interrelated factors, including financial dependence on parents, social class, religiosity, ethnicity, regionality, and educational level. As sexuality has become separated from marriage (normatively speaking) and financial dependence is lengthened due to educational needs, there is a great deal more variation as to when young people are now considered adults.[9] This issue is complicated by an increasing tendency to classify young people into multiple developmental groupings, including tweens, adolescents, and young adults, making it in some ways even more difficult to distinguish the line between childhood and adulthood in the West.

From a global perspective, the stage of life known as adolescence or youth is becoming a worldwide phenomenon. In terms of demographics, there are approximately 1 billion young people between the ages of 10–19, of whom 85% live in the developing part of the world (Bruce and Chong 2006). While in many regions, children until very recently moved immediately from childhood to adulthood, we are witnessing a form of global social revolution with children staying in school longer and carving out a new social space, not unlike what occurred in the West in the early twentieth century. In part, this phenomenon can be attributed as a global response to the Convention on the Rights of the Child, which states that childhood ends at the age of 18, as well as the Convention to End All Forms of Discrimination Against Women. Both documents emphasize the link between human development and human rights, and advocate for protecting the rights and capabilities of young people, and the right to gender equality. Specifically, the Convention on the Rights of the Child provides the basis for a cross-cultural focus on late childhood and the need to protect and nurture adolescents in order to allow them develop their abilities (Bruce and Chong 2006).

The foundation provided by the Convention on the Rights of the Child, and the Convention to End all Forms of Discrimination Against Women, were furthered by historic accords signed in Cairo in 1994 at the International Conference on Population and Development, and the Beijing International Conference on Women in 1995. What emerged through these Conventions and the documents that were signed at the international conferences, were formal recommendations to governments

---

[9] It is important to note that historically in the U.S., there was also a great deal of variation with respect to marriage and the like due to early death of parents, financial dependence of younger siblings, etc. In fact, scholars such as Hareven (2000) have argued that life course timing was much more erratic in the past than in our contemporary world. However, in the pre-World War II example, I am referring primarily to the mainstream, accepted norms of the society.

and monitoring committees that highlight the relationship between young people, development, health, and social issues. These Conventions are often believed to be an outcome of globalization, and among the most significant influences impacting the lives of children and youths around the world.

6.5   The Complex Issue of Children's Rights

The loss of a clear line between childhood and adulthood in the West is attributed by some to the increasing concern over children's legal rights (Okin 1989; Archard 1993; King 1999). For the first time in modern times, children are being treated from a scholarly and, at times legal, perspective as independent beings – not as appendices of their families, an institution, or the state (Reynolds et al. 2006). From a global perspective, children's rights have become a dominant feature in the international dialogue, particularly since the enactment of the Convention on the Rights of the Child in 1989, which was ratified by all members of the United Nations, except for the U.S. Specifically children's rights are equated with human rights, which has sparked an intense debate on the effectiveness of campaigns to reduce social inequality and change existing power structures. Both proponents and opponents tend to subscribe to simplistic notions of universal children's rights that do not account for local complexities, variations and commonalities. Rights are realized in specific contexts and socio-historical times in a multitude of ways. Moreover, often times, the results of applying children's rights in a particular manner does not necessarily coincide with the initial objectives of the Convention (Reynolds et al. 2006). The "child" that was the focus of the Convention is one whose childhood is depicted in Western terms, one who needs to be socialized for its adult roles, not one who is already a social actor, who constructs meaning out of its life, and is already fulfilling certain responsibilities (Ennew and Morrow 2002).

With an eye toward this issue, it is instructive to briefly examine what is meant by "rights."[10] The universalized concept of rights that is found in the UN Convention on the Rights of the Child is based on a "construct of selfhood which presumes that the child is an autonomous self with a direct, unmediated relationship with the state" (Joseph 2005, p. 122). This directive assumes that self-interest is paramount, and that rights can be constantly renegotiated. This assumption is accompanied by the notion that a child is separate from adults and an equal. This concept of citizenship, rights and responsibilities stems from a Western historical model that privileges the citizen. The citizen bases his or her choices on rational decision-making and in the process attempts to maximize rewards and minimize losses. Critiques from feminists and scholars of color have suggested that these concepts of self and citizenship

---

[10] I have purposefully added the discussion on linking children rights and women to this chapter due to the fact that these discourses are almost always separated. While this is understandable from a Western feminist view, I believe it leads to false conclusions when applied to other parts of the world.

derive from a specific Western democratic tradition and do not apply to most of the citizenry of the world (Joseph 2005). This same argument can be extended to the representation of women's rights. For many women around the world, self-empowerment and self-interest are not the foremost goal. For these women, representations of self are intertwined with group interests, usually those of their families. They are not looking for "equal rights" in the sense that is promulgated by the UN Convention or the various women's movements. Instead, they need material and educational assistance in order to ensure the survival of themselves, their children, and others in their families.

It is important to note that different social groups have varying interpretations and employ diverse strategies with respect to implementing an agenda of children's rights. International organizations, local governments, development agencies and grass root groups use the notion of children's rights to further their particular agendas. For example, in the debate on child labor, varying groups substantiate their competing claims with an emphasis on children's rights. The International Labor Organization (ILO) opposes child labor and bases its argument on children's rights, while organizations composed of working children straddle the opposite side of the fence, and argue for the right of children to work in dignity and take part in decision-making with respect to their employment. The same language is being used with very different meanings and interpretations.

The concern with children's rights has been synchronous with the intensification of global interconnectedness in the 1990s and the first decade of 2000. In particular, certain issues have gained international prominence: the use of children as workers in sweat shops, as prostitutes, and as soldiers. Western middle class concepts of the role of children in the family and society have clashed dramatically with images of children from places such as Nairobi, Kenya, Mumbai, India, and Mexico City, Mexico. These images have brought about complex questions about the productive and reproductive role of children in contemporary societies, and have highlighted the extreme economic variation that may separate children in the same society, and, between societies. Today, Westerners are outraged by the sight of children working at very young ages or fighting in wars, but as Paula Fass (2003) points out, Western sensibilities have been formed through a complex history of slavery, an increased sentimentalization of childhood, and a greater commitment to the wishes and self-empowerment of the individual. Much of this change can also be attributed to the rise and spread of market economies, and concomitant needs of dedicated workers. It is important to note that these sensibilities did not take root immediately in the United States and Europe, but developed over time and spread slowly from the upper classes to other parts of various respective societies. In the U.S. case, our current conceptualization of childhood has resulted through a shift from the early American Calvinist child, perceived as primitive and unredeemed, to the child as an innocent being, an expression of God's love. This image in conjunction with the loss of the market value of children has moved contemporary representations of children into the emotional realm, making representations that clash with these images unpalatable to many Westerners.

For many contemporary individuals in the West, a child does not provide labor or old age insurance. Instead, the value of a child lies in the emotional satisfaction it brings for its caregivers. Its emotional well-being and societal preparation confer pleasure and, even status for its guardians. The child is a source of happiness due to the intrinsic qualities that it brings to its family, and is seen as the guardian of the future (Fass 2003). This conceptualization of childhood is, thus, the outgrowth of a specific set of historical and economic circumstances and solicits the question of how children and childhood are and will be perceived in other parts of the world.

The demand for cheap labor, the persistent search for new labor markets, and the need for resources continue to be integral aspects of globalization. These forces are bringing more work to children, and from one perspective, assisting them in gaining financial resources. These same forces also allow Westerners a deeper glimpse into the lives of children in other places. From the Western perspective, children should be carefree, in school, and not working. They would like children to play and be educated, and are offended and horrified at the thought of their exploitation. Nonetheless, the actual effects of employment on children's lives, the potentially deleterious outcomes of taking children who need to work out of their jobs, and their own perspectives on their situation are rarely part of the analysis or discussions on children's well-being and childhood.

An innovative contribution of the UN Convention on the Rights for the Child is the recognition of children's rights to participate in social life by expressing their opinions (Ennew and Morrow 2002). Children are encouraged to participate in decisions made on their behalf, express their opinions, have freedom of thought and religion and, also, to form relationships with others. This interpretation has led to an understanding of the extension of children's participation not just in family and community life, but also as a voice in national and global processes. However, due to a Western conceptualization of children as "innocent" and "blank slates," children's voices are often obfuscated for adult agendas (Stephens 1992). Thus, adults may form a "Global March Against Child Labour" (1998–1999), in which child workers refused to participate because they felt that their interests were not being represented accurately. Despite rhetorical pronouncements, children are often not taken seriously and not incorporated into decision-making processes that pertain to their lives (Stephens 1992).

The contemporary nation-state plays an important role in the global political and economic arena. However, it is also a highly complex source of cultural identity for its citizens, including its children (Ennew and Morrow 2002). On a broad level, the state that signs on to the Convention on the Rights of the Child tacitly accepts a relatively uniform, and thus, globalized conceptualization of childhood. Basically, it subscribes to the idea that all children are the "same" and that human identity is shared. On a secondary level, the nation-state passes on the notion of a national identity. Interestingly, international human rights law uniformly advocates the right to nationality as a fundamental right. And on a tertiary level, children of native, minority or indigenous groups are allowed the right to a non-national subgroup identity within the nation-state (Ennew and Morrow 2002).

What is rarely explored in discussions on the Rights of the Child is that children and their identities can, at times, become the arena where cultural battles are negotiated and fought. On the one hand, they are seen as an important element in the transmission and retention of elements of local culture. Children are, at times, taught forbidden or ancient languages, brought up with certain rituals and beliefs, and are the focus of attempts to retain local traditions. This often occurs in binary opposition to the formal education that is taught in schools, which are increasingly importing values and pedagogical techniques from a great distance, both geographically and culturally. Children – both their minds and their bodies – are exploited in debates about fundamental cultural values, ethnic purity, minority self-expression, and other such issues (Stephens 1995).

6.6   Linking Children's Rights with Women's Rights

Often missing in perspectives on children's rights are their ties with women's rights. For example, Malkki and Martin (2003) highlight this issue by referring to the ideas introduced by Sharon Stephens, a cultural anthropologist who was highly committed to the welfare of children, and who brought to the forefront the overlooked relationship between women's and children's rights. Stephens emphasized that when comparing the UN Convention to End All Forms of Discrimination Against Women and the UN Convention on the Rights of the Child, the convention on women's rights draws attention to the potentially oppressive nature of the family for women and the value of freeing women from traditional social roles. These roles are perceived as the basis for all kinds of discrimination against women. Interestingly, the Convention on Children's Rights suggests the opposite perspective: the family is to be strengthened as it provides a protective sphere for children and represents cultural traditions that are the foundation for their identity and socialization. What we find is a situation where many feminists fear that attention to children's rights will subsequently disadvantage women by weakening their ability to resist culturally supported hegemonic discourses about their appropriate roles in the family and the society.

Potentially problematic is also the fact that the Convention on the Rights of the Child upholds the family as the "ideal protective frame for children's well-being" (Stephens 1995, p. 35). This type of universalizing discourse does not allow for a consideration of circumstances where family life is less than ideal or may even be harmful for children (even though the women's rights movement acknowledges that this may be the case for women). It also does not acknowledge situations where other forms of care, nurturance and responsibility are taken over by other arrangements, such as community networks that provide for children. For example, ethnographic research on low-income African American families in Chicago (Stack 1974) depicts specific provisions where non-kin protect and take care of children in a nurturing manner. Ethnographic examples provide contrasting representations of how family and gender representations can be constructed quite differently in the same society, and move us away from universalizing paradigms that assume that all children are faced with similar circumstances.

The debate between women's rights and children's rights underlines the complexity of defining rights in a universal framework. Children's rights are intertwined with adults' rights in intricate power relationships. Further, as Stephens argued, while the category of "women" has been denaturalized and politicized, the same has not happened with the concept of "children." By remaining silent, she argues, feminists contribute to the universalization and heterosexualization of children. It is important to note this point because it is striking how the feminist literature and the women's movement have made immense inroads in deconstructing and denaturalizing gender and families. However, for the most part, children have been relegated to the sidelines in these discussions. Moreover, debates on families are widely divergent, depending on whom one is focusing on: women, men or children.[11] This disconnect is leading discourse, analyses, and policies, in, at times, conflicting directions. On the one hand, there is a pull to "strengthen" families in order to ensure the safety and care for children, and on the other hand, families are to be deconstructed in order to empower women. Most probably neither of these paths are universally productive for women and children, and the families they are associated with. Instead, we need to acknowledge context, life course, and individual circumstances in order to create supports for vulnerable children *and* women and men.

6.7   The Role of Gender and Generation in Children's Lives

Universalizing discourses can be particularly problematic because they presume that young people across the globe are being influenced in a homogeneous manner by deceptively similar phenomena. There are enormous regional, class, ethnic, racial and social differences between individuals and their ability to attain resources, ideas, and goods. Gender, also, plays a critical role in the lives of young people: in many places, particularly in the developing world, boys are culturally valued over girls, translating into a differential access to opportunities, resources, and education. While boys may be encouraged to attain an education and be provided with the necessary resources and time to pursue their schooling, girls are often forced to take on extensive responsibilities in the household and, depending on cultural context, are married at a young age.

Adolescence, which is often defined as the time that begins with the onset of puberty, can be particularly detrimental to the opportunities of young girls. Under the umbrella of protection, families and communities restrict the movement of girls outside of the home, which may increasingly limit their opportunities. For

---

[11]It is important to note the ungendered nature of most work on children.

example, a survey of Egyptian girls between the ages of 16–19 revealed that 68% of young women were involved in domestic work, compared to 26% of boys (Mensch et al. 2000). Especially in rural and low-income areas, girls take on increasing family responsibilities and may be forced to drop out of school. In some places, girls are now persuaded or forced into marriage and early childbearing. Examples from South Asia indicate that while families may encourage and support the education of boys, for example, girls in rural areas are often burdened with excessive household chores. A gendered perspective on the lives of young adolescents highlights the vulnerability that girls can face even in a global context, which is encouraging a strong shift in gender ideologies and gender roles in families and society.

Within the same household, children may occupy different social positions that can serve to restrict their personal and social development, thus making it difficult to speak of a general "youth culture."

Nevertheless, current Western scholarship treats youth culture as a distinctive stage that is somewhat isolated from its surrounding environment and, yet, plays an instrumental, influential role. In contrast to earlier philosophical treatises on generations that equated youth with the spirit of a time or a philosophy (e.g. the American "flower children" of the 1960s), today's analyses focus on the global nature of young people who supposedly share similar passions for certain goods (such as in the technological realm) and who subscribe to shared values across countries rather than within the same society.

Much current thinking indicates that for young people the traditional values and choices of their parents are increasingly irrelevant due to the rapidly changing global context within which they now have to make decisions. Through increased contact across cultures and geographical space, youth are influenced by multiple forces leading them, in the words of one scholar, to develop a bicultural identity that incorporates elements of their local surroundings with exposure to a larger global culture (Arnett 2002). The notion that youth people are more likely to adopt new ideas, and are more able to infuse change into traditional ones is appealing because it links personal, biographical time with wider historical phenomena and provides one form of explanation for the process of social change (Elder 1999). And historically, there is some truth is in this conceptualization – massive social movements have often been characterized by being heavily dominated by young people, be it the collapse of the Iron Curtain or the Civil Rights movement in the United States.

At times, the spread of youth culture has led to an association with political positions that seem asynchronous with Western, and often specifically, mainstream American ideals. So, for example, to understand the rise of fundamentalism both in the United States and abroad, one has to comprehend that at times this is a response to identity threats among certain groups of young people (Smith and Johnston 2002). However, it is important to remember that for a nation, a society, or a community, young people represent the future. They are the link to human continuity from both a biological and socio-cultural perspective and this makes their well-being and socialization such a controversial and significant issue.

6.8   Influences of Globalization on Children and Youth

Children and youth are impacted through globalization in an increasingly distinct manner. For example, Frones (1994) argues that the growing democratization of households in the West, allows children now to have a "voice" in previously unimagined ways. It is becoming more common, for example, to ask children to give their opinion and express their desires in certain realms of their lives. This is sometimes also referred to as the growing democratization of children's lived experiences. In the West, children are encouraged, and at times, forced to participate in decisions that affect their lives (such as in divorce cases), they are allowed increasing freedom of thought and choice (such as with respect to religion), and they also may form relationships and friendships with others who may not necessarily be in their parent's social sphere (such as social networking through the Internet). This general trend is coupled with an ever-growing media presence that targets children as a subset or consumer group, changes in family structure and formation, and new assumptions about upbringing and education. In fact, Oldman (1994) warns that children are now perceived as a group to be exploited, and that they have become an integral, commodified aspect of capitalism (also in Aitken 2001).

Children and youth also have increasing power as consumers. This is particularly the case in the West. However, this phenomenon is becoming more relevant in other parts of the world as well, as more children are exposed not just to traditional media such as television and movies, but have Internet and text messaging abilities. By no means does this discussion mean to imply that children and youth, the world over, have uniform access to consumer goods and communication technologies. In fact, quite the opposite situation exists. We have a growing gap between those young people who do have access to communication technologies and consumer goods, and those who don't. However, in both, the West and the developing world, more children have increasing access to money and the commodities that they are able to attain with their allowances or earnings. With available cash (however little) and growing exposure to Western goods and habits, young people are able to acquire various of forms of music, clothing that is marketed to them over multiple media, and different forms of technology. From a market perspective, they are seen as a group to be catered to as they can have a significant impact on household consumption. Moreover, aggressive marketing of consumer goods such as toys no longer focuses just on holidays such as Christmas and birthdays as times for making major purchases. Instead, there is a consistent flow of new products aimed at children, and brought to their attention through cartoons and celebrity placement (Ruddick 2003). Both in the United States and the United Kingdom, market studies have identified children as significantly influencing the purchases that their parents make (Rust 1993). They play an important role in the purchasing behavior of households even for day-to-day items such as detergent and food.

Robson (2004) points out that in our current discourse, children are dichotomized as active consumers in the Northern nations and as exploited overworked innocent beings in the Southern nations.[12] This suggests a viewpoint that is based in current conceptualization of child development, modernization, advancement, and globalization. It enforces a notion of a more barbaric past in the West where children were not treated as well as they are today. This representation ignores the fact that so many children in the industrialized world are living under poor conditions with inadequate health care and poor prospects for their futures. For multitudes of children, both in the West and in the developing world, a carefree consumption-filled childhood does not relate to the day–to-day realities of their lives.

6.9   The Problem of Child Labor

A complex and little understood aspect of globalization is the role that child labor plays, specifically in the developing world. Broad indicators suggest that child labor is on the rise despite international concerns condemning this phenomenon. The International Labor Organization (ILO) (2002) includes in its estimates that approximately 352 million 5- to 17-year-olds around the globe participate in some type of productive activity. Out of this group, about two-thirds of young workers are defined as "child laborers." Most of these children work either on family farms, in their families' households, in small manufacturing companies, mining or plantation agriculture. Children are often involved with the manufacture of carpets, garments, furniture, textiles and shoes (French and Woktuch 2005). A smaller but highly visible group of children live on the street engaging in a wide range of legal or illegal activities or are involved in prostitution.

Many individuals in the West, in particular, argue that lax standards in the developing world encourage the use of child workers in order to further economic advantages in the production of goods. The image of young children engaged in menial work under harsh conditions has aroused a broad emotional reaction in many activists in the West. Even individuals, who would usually not be that interested in social justice issues, have spoken out publicly and led crusades banning "third world labor practices" and even boycotting certain brands or corporations that supposedly rely on this type of exploitive behavior. However, a closer examination of this phenomenon indicates that the debates and issues are much more complex than popular imagery belies. For example, a popular measure, the World Bank's *Developmental Indicators,* uses the participation rate of individuals that are between 10 and 14. However, Cigno et al. (2002) point out that there are many children around the world that are under the age of 10, who work either full time or part time. The issue of age is compounded by definitional issues surrounding the term child labor itself.

A significant problem is that there is little agreement in the current literature on what constitutes child labor. International organizations such as the International

---

[12] Northern and Southern are often used as synonyms for industrialized and developing nations. There are no agreements on terms in the social sciences and there is much ambiguity related to this terminology.

Labor Organization (ILO) and the International Program on the Elimination of Child Labor (IPEC) offer a description of the difference between child work and child labor:

"Economic activity" is a broad concept that encompasses most productive activities undertaken by children, whether for the market or not, paid or unpaid, for a few hours or full time, on a casual or regular basis, legal or illegal; it excludes chores undertaken in the child's own household and schooling. To be counted as economically active, a child must have worked for at least 1 h on any day during a seven-day reference period. "Economically active" children is a statistical, rather than a legal, definition. It is *not* the same as the "child labor" referred to with regard to its abolition (ILO 2002).

This definition stems from the writings of Fyfe (1993, p. 4) which provides the basis for many of the writings on this topic. From his perspective, child labor is work that is detrimental to the health and development of children, while child work is that which detracts from the activities of childhood such as play and learning. He suggests that both child work and child labor are unhealthy for children, and a reflection of the developmental status of a nation.

Unanswered in these definitional debates is what level of activity constitutes the role of children working within households. Ethnographic sources indicate that millions of children are widely engaged in domestic activities, and that it is often not true that young children are not working. However, it is also important to note that children's work is primarily being evaluated through a Western lens. For many households, children's work is their primary source of childcare, provision, and income. However, such a contextual approach tends not to be a major part of the analyses of this phenomenon. Instead, we have a situation where strong voices, particularly from the West are seeking to develop and implement international standards with respect to children's work or labor. Meanwhile, there is a strong opposition, primarily from non-Western sources that argue that we cannot impose universal standards. Instead, they point out that context matters, and that we need to be more sensitive as to what work is, and to the role that work plays in children's and families' lives. These arguments underline the complexity of arriving at universal definitions of the capabilities of children and point to the widely varying conceptualizations of childhood. They also highlight the multiplicity of complicated relationships that families and households have to labor markets and forms of production.

6.10 Responding to the Issue of Child Labor

Most critics of children's work attribute this phenomenon to the poor circumstances of their families, who take them out of school and use them in whatever manner is needed to help sustain the household. They condemn this type of treatment of children as an infringement on their rights and as a form of subversion of their potential for development. The argument can be summarized as the following: while it may be true that the family is impoverished, that does not mean that children should be "exploited" to save the parents and/or siblings and other relatives. Instead, all children deserve the right to a "real" childhood, consisting of play, leisure time, and schooling. Children need to be protected and nurtured by adults and all other definitions of childhood are deemed as unacceptable. This leads Western critics and non-Western reformers basically to argue that all forms of child labor are unacceptable and need to be abolished (French and Woktuch 2005). Many of these discussions use broad economic criteria as the basis for recommending changes in the lives of children.

In this vein, using Fyfe's work as a foundational platform, an IPEC (2004) report determined that eliminating child labor and replacing it with "universal education" would result in a 22.2% net benefit globally by 2020 (Aitken et al. 2006). This statistic was further broken down to a 54% net economic benefit for sub-Saharan Africa, and a 9% benefit for Latin America. The analysis concludes with the observation that the elimination of child labor by replacing it with education will result in impressive economic benefits to the countries located in the Southern hemisphere and be accompanied by other "social and intrinsic benefits" (IPEC 2004, p. 4).

A series of ethnographic and observational studies, however, suggest a different conclusion. Aitken et al. (2006) working in Mexico, Katz (2004) in Sudan, and Punch (2004) in Bolivia advise that child labor needs to be understood in a much more contextualized manner and is not easily replaced by "universal education." While movements and protests against child labor are laudable, Ruddick (2003) warns that there may be unintended consequences to children and their families, when policies such as a complete abolition of child labor are enacted, without regard to the complexities of local environments.

There are other voices such as Levison (2000) and Myers (2001), who are challenging the promotion of a universal childhood and universal prescriptions for understanding and dealing with children's work. They argue that our current Western view of human development may be flawed or incorrect, and suggest, provocatively, that potentially the whole human experience, from the youngest age, is meant to be productive. From this perspective, children should have the right to participate in meaningful activities at all ages, that they benefit from by gaining skills and responsibilities, and that a purely duty-free existence may not be the appropriate basis for child rearing.

Drawing on evidence from the various social sciences the advocates for children's work argue that children's employment can actually be beneficial to their long-term physical and psychological health. They also point out that there are many instances of children who work, who may do so not just due to their family's economic condition, but because they enjoy the independence that an income can bring. Critics of universal concepts about children also argue that the focus of the child labor debates and outcries need to shift from calculating hours of activity in the labor market to a recognition of the type of work activities that children are engaged in. A different approach to children's work, for example, ascertains if certain types of work pose a health risk or psychological harm, while other types of wage work could be recognized as acceptable and, potentially, even beneficial (French and Wokutch 2005).

This varied viewpoint needs, however, to be accompanied by the recognition that certain types of non-wage work, such as the heavy domestic responsibilities shouldered by some girls, is actually detrimental to them, both physically, as well as with respect to their long-term development (Nieuwenhuys 1994).

While debates on child labor and child work are a useful starting point for analytical distinctions, it is difficult to parse out differences in practice. There are certain types of work such as mining and industry that pose clear hazards for children (and, actually, depending on the working conditions, for adults as well) and there does exist, at this point, a general agreement on the "worst forms of child labor," which include prostitution and soldiering. The parties on all sides concur that these are such burdensome, and potentially harmful activities, that no child should be exposed to them (French and Woktuch 2005).

There are other types of labor activity, however, that are not as clearly deleterious to children. For example, almost any kind of work (farming, mechanics, etc.) can be potentially dangerous if certain basic conditions are not met.[13] But this also indicates, that under the appropriate conditions, children could participate in these activities without causing harm to themselves. This ambiguity makes it extremely difficult to engage in conversations about "types" of work, and what is acceptable or not-acceptable. White (1996) suggests a potential categorical approach to this issue. He recommends that work be grouped into various categories, depending on if a work activity, even though it is potentially currently harmful to children, can be reformed in such a manner so as to allow the children to continue working; that work could be neutral in its effects; and / or that a work activity could actually be beneficial to the children who are engaged in it.

It is possible as Aitken et al. (2006) point out that as Western and non-Western cultures interact, new kinds of childhood can, and may, emerge that defy Western conceptualizations. Children are active agents that interact with their environments. On the one hand, their lives are shaped by their local living and working conditions. However, children also affect their environments – their voices and their actions at times result in unexpected change. It is, thus, instructive, to continually examine their various roles and the transformations and negotiations, which result from their daily interactions.

6.11 The Vulnerability of Young People in a Globalizing Environment

The experiences of youth, have never been, and are certainly not uniform today. Globalization, however, impacts various aspects of youth in specific ways. While, as we have seen earlier, child labor may be a complex and controversial

---

[13] Our current 9 months school model is a remnant of predominantly agrarian times when children were expected to assist with the farming work and especially the harvest. Despite this knowledge, the school calendar in the U.S. has not adjusted to the contemporary reality of most parents working outside the home, year round.

issue, young people who are working for pay may suffer from a completely different aspect of globalization as well. From a worldwide perspective, globalization brings with it mixed economic blessings for young people. In India, China, and parts of Asia, the gross domestic product per capita has risen by impressive margins. However, in other parts of the world such as sub-Saharan Africa, parts of the former Soviet Union and Latin America, the economic situation has stagnated or worsened (Wade 2004). On the one hand, new opportunities through economic restructuring bring work to places that earlier may have been neglected, under-utilized, or too far from centers of power and production. But that same fluidity also makes work more precarious. When companies decide to move their operations to a more lucrative, (i.e., cheaper labor location), young people are among the first to be laid off and lose their chance at economic stability. Flows of capital can just as easily move into a region as they move out of an area, resulting in general instability in local economies (NRCIM 2005). However, even in areas that have been characterized by prosperity and growth, there are often vast differences between rural and urban sectors. Thus, there are many areas around the world where young people are living lives very similar to those of their ancestors. This is worrisome, since globalization is creating ever widening gaps between those individuals that are connected to the global economy and those that are not.

Young people who enter the labor market are unprotected by seniority and experience and are often marked as outsiders to workplaces. It is young people who are often awarded fixed-term contracts or part-time work and they tend to become the first to face unemployment during times of economic crisis or uncertainty. This situation is particularly relevant for those youth who are at the bottom of the economic ladder and thus are at greatest risk. This positioning has consequences for their future familial status: those who are in precarious economic positions are more likely to delay or forgo permanent partnerships and parenthood (Blossfeld and Hofmeister 2005). In Western societies, young people from the middle upper echelons of society are delaying marriage and parenthood due to the increasing need for higher levels of education and training to attain professional positions that will allow them to live independently. In other words, young people, the world over, still want to partner up and have children, but it is increasingly not economically viable to do so. Thus, what we find is that childhood and youth are experienced in very different ways depending on the interactions of a multitude of personal, environmental, and socio-historical factors.

6.12   Children and Public Space

Discussions of the appropriate role and the rights of children and youth are also intertwined with complex issues of space. For example, the usage of public space is an arena that has not received much attention in discussions on children and childhood. Instead, homes, schools, and several other youth-oriented spaces such as playgrounds, are deemed as the only acceptable public spaces for children to inhabit.

Fear of strangers, terrorism, and violence lead many Western parents to shun most other places that are not deemed as "safe enough." Increasingly, Western parents pay to have their children play in "public" spaces, such as Kindercare or the Discovery Zone, which are deemed as appropriate for children, out of harm's way, and "off" the street. Katz (1993) and Davis (1997) suggest that these types of activities are actually a commodification of children's lives, legitimitized by creating fear in parents. Meanwhile, poor and minority youth are either forced to spend their time on the street or, through increasing public curfews forbidden from congregating in public spaces.

In a concurrent phenomenon, street children in other parts of the world have received much attention and publicity from international aid organizations due to their high visibility (Burr 2002). They are disdained for exhibiting traits such as independence and savvy, which are perceived as "not childlike."[14] Instead, street children's voices are often not legitimized in the international debate on childhood and children's rights. Stephens (1995) points out that street children are viewed with suspicion by Westerners because they undermine the Western conception that children need to be taken care of by adults. She further suggests that some Westerners now see children themselves as a risk – a risk that needs to be controlled and reshaped in order to increase social control.

Ethnographic evidence indicates that despite the widespread international interest in the UN Convention on the Rights of the Child and its emphasis on "hearing children's voices," this does not happen in reality. Article 12 of the Convention states that children's views need to be acknowledged and weighed in accordance with their age and state of maturity. Instead, the global model of childhood, which is based on a contemporary Western understanding of children, has created an international agenda that deems it wrong for children to be highly independent, to work, or to enforce their views (Boyden 1990). Yet, realistically, in many parts of the developing world, children have no choice but to defend themselves and to work. Children often leave impoverished rural areas in the attempt to find work in urban areas. For example, a study of street children in Hanoi illustrated that by leaving their homes and working on the street, children were able to amass a small income that allowed them to further their education and to send remittances back home. In contrast to Western perceptions, by being part of a group of street children, they were also protected, formed friendships, and developed a certain level of stability in their lives (Burr 2002). Evidence from Latin America reveals similar phenomena. In studies of street children, when asked why they were living on the street, most responded that they are assisting their families (Kuznesof 2005).

While street children have been a consistent part of the social landscape in many parts of the world for quite some time, it is only recently that these children have become vilified and even feared. The "epidemic" of street children stems in great part from government failures to provide adequate housing, minimum wages, medical care, and education for their populations. Children either leave or are sent

---

[14] In fact, having "street smarts" often has a somewhat "lower class" connotation in English speaking societies.

out of the home in order to find resources. The real reason that children are on the street is due to inadequate resources at home or because they are victims of violence. When viewed from a more independent perspective, one sees that children draw on their creative capacities to generate their own understandings of the world in which they exist (Smith 2004). This view is particularly important when one looks at children who have been victimized, and sees how they are coping with their world. Their reactions and responses will differ depending on circumstances and their own experiences, as well as their different capacities to make sense of what is happening to them. In order to understand and resist, they may create their own worlds. Boyden (1997) persuasively argues that children can be quite capable of creating their own communities and economies, even in dangerous circumstances

> Street children generally organize into groups, often with clear internal hierarchies and strong attachments to a territory. Group solidarity extends to the sharing of food and other goods and provision of protection and support in crises' (Boyden 1997, p. 196).

Interventions from international agencies that are opposed to street children and children's work, have little effect and may actually cause harm by trying to impose agendas that do not fit the circumstances. Sending children back to their homes because this is the "best" place for them, does not bring about the desired results in areas that are greatly impoverished and where there is a complete lack of opportunities for children and their parents. In the words of Hecht:

> Efforts at preventing children from working in the street threaten the position of poor urban children within the home. The more difficult it is for children to bring in resources to households that not only desperately need the fruits of child labor but morally expect them, the more vulnerable the child's status becomes.... Declaring the street out of bounds will only make the home less viable (1998, p. 198).

Returning to the Vietnamese example, Burr (2002) describes a fascinating case of two Christian-based U.S. aid agencies that worked with street children and did not try to change the children's lifestyles. Instead, these agencies set up non-formal night schools that ignored the children's illegal status.[15] The children were able to further their education and to keep earning an income during the day. At the children's suggestion, other types of educational training programs in areas such as mechanics were also established. This provided the children with an opportunity to learn a skill and to earn a livelihood. Burr describes an incident where a visitor from UNICEF, upon visiting one of these training facilities, then accused the aid organization of "encouraging child labor" and violating the children's right to an education (Burr 2002, p. 59). However, the Convention on the Rights of the Child actually stipulates that vocational training should be made available when appropriate. At the end of her ethnographic anecdote, Burr describes that one of the street boys who she had used as an informant and who had participated in the training,

---

[15] In Vietnam, all children must be officially registered. For example, when a child is born in the countryside, it may only live in the local region and not move to any other city. See Burr (2002) for greater details.

ended up working in a garage, renting a room with a study, and in general, was living a better lifestyle than he had ever experienced before. Burr's examples illustrate that improving people's lives requires an understanding of the circumstances in which they live. A blanket approach that universalizes the needs, beliefs and rights of individuals can have unintended consequences. This is true not just for adults, but also for children.

The debate about who are children and what is childhood is increasingly fought in an ideological space that is dominated by Western concepts about an age-graded system in which the younger members of society need parental protection and nurturing in the physical space of the home and the school, versus a non-Western reality of impoverished familial and societal conditions, poor or non-existent schools, and cultural beliefs in the value of work for children. The value of children's economic contributions to a household may actually, in certain circumstances, outweigh the value of their going to school by allowing the family to stay together or by improving their economic circumstances. Depending on the type of activity, children may also learn skills through working that they would not attain by attending school. As French and Woktuch (2005) point out in an analysis of the Brazilian shoe industry, it is often in the children's best interest not to take them out of the labor market, but instead to reform the conditions under which they are working. Taking children out of the labor market can have a whole host of unintended consequences, including jeopardizing their future ability to finance an education, providing them with work experiences, and forcing them into even less desirable forms of employment as they seek to restore lost wages through informal sector work. Instead of blanket prescriptions that attempt to enforce a universal conception of a work-free childhood, in the long run, it may be more productive to attempt to institute policies aimed at eradicating child exploitation and reforming the conditions under which children work in certain places and industries.

6.13 Emphasizing the Varied Dimensions of Children and Childhood

While we are faced these days with an impressive body of scholarship on conceptualizations of childhood, the effects of childcare on children, socialization, parenting, and the effect of parental work on child rearing, there is very little research on how these messages and actions are received, internalized and used by children themselves. In the nineteenth century in the West, child rearing and nurturing were removed to the private sphere of the family. This domestic arena was the site of social reproduction, discipline, and nurturant socialization. An important part of the then prevailing ideology was on creating a new properly educated labor force that would be able to take over at the appropriate time. One significant aspect of globalization is that this is not necessarily, or at least not always an important societal goal anymore. No particular labor force needs to be reproduced (Aitken 2001). Instead, labor can be found in different parts of the world depending on demand and expense. This changes the value of children, their educational needs, and the very nature of childhood.

Perhaps, most strikingly, an enormous child development "machine" has been built up specifically in the United States. Books and programs with definitive descriptions and prescriptions about what is "best" and most "appropriate" for children are increasingly popular. These are also exported around the globe influencing pedagogy, child rearing, programming and social policies. What is lost in this endeavor is an understanding of the importance of context, and that the situation of children, even just in our own society, can be quite different and complex, from that which is promoted in our scholarship, media, and practice. Once we turn to other parts of the globe, we see that varying notions of children and childhood are, at times, completely at odds with what we think is the best way to raise and nurture children.

The "ungendered" child is another challenge that has not been dealt with adequately in either academic work or policies and programming. As has been pointed out previously, there are many areas in the world where girls are at particular risk due to the cultural valuing of boys. They may be forced to marry at a young age, denied educational opportunities, and assume disproportionate care responsibilities. In the United States, we actually have the converse problem. At this point, there is growing concern around the situation of young boys, especially with respect to schooling. A privileging and concern with the achievement of girls has, according to some, left boys behind. This is reflected in current college enrollments, where approximately 60% of college attendants are young women. In our discussions and analyses of childhood and how to generate universal improvements in the status of children, we need to factor in the complexities of local contexts. A greater cross-cultural dialogue and an openness to understanding how other circumstances, cultures, and traditions influence children, would go a long way to not just benefiting children in other places, but also children in our society.

As webs of connection grow, informal communication and the influence of formerly less dominant institutions are increasing. We, thus, are faced with a simultaneous process: on the one hand, dominant institutions and organizations are spreading knowledge and values, while informal methods are gaining in strength. Both impact children and their experiences. Engagement is not just confined to family and community life, but also to participation in larger democratic processes (Ennew and Morrow 2002). Stephens (1992), however, points out that often times children's opinions and voices are utilized for adult goals and that the children are aware of this issue. The symbol of the pure vulnerable child is easily manipulated and used to further political agendas (Kjorholt 2002). As we continue to export ideas about children and childhood from the industrialized world to the developing world, we need to be mindful of how easy it is to use representation of children to further adult agendas while not necessarily working in the best interest of the children themselves (Levison 2000). We also need to acknowledge the power relations and dynamics between adults and children, and the necessity for creating bargaining frameworks that incorporate their voices about their lives into decision-making processes.

Chapter 7
Critical Issues Around Global Aging

The aging of the global population is unprecedented in human history and promises to play a critical role in globalization dynamics. According to United Nations (UN) predictions, by 2050, the number of elderly around the world will exceed the number of children for the first time in history. In some countries in the industrialized world, this historic shift has already taken place (United Nations 2002). This proportional reversal of old and young has direct implications on intergenerational relationships and intergenerational equity. Compounding this issue is that not only are more people living longer, but over the last 50 years, global life expectancy has grown more than over the past 5,000 years (Peterson 1999). Up until the time of the Industrial Revolution, approximately 2–3% of populations lived until the age of 65. Today, in the industrialized world, the percentages range between 12 and 14% of the population.[1] Demographic predictions suggest that by 2030 some countries will see the population of their elderly soar to 25 or even 30%. And according to demographic predictions for the world population, the number of elderly is estimated to reach approximately 21% by 2050, up from 10% in 2000.

This growth in the global elderly population is accompanied by several other noteworthy trends. Elderly individuals are less likely to be part of the paid labor force than in the past. For example, in 1950, one out of every three people over the age of 65 was likely to be working. Today, that ratio is less than one out of every five. However, this trend does not reveal the gender differential: in 1950, both in the industrialized and developing world, approximately 26% of workers aged 65 and older were female. By 2000, those figures had changed dramatically. In the developing world, approximately 29% of women aged 65 and older were working, and in the industrialized world, approximately 41% were in the paid labor force (United Nations 2002). These statistics reflect global conditions that, at times, encourage older women to work. However, more frequently they point to the financial necessity of women working for pay outside the home. These statistics also do not reveal the fact that in the developing world, a larger percentage of men and women must work more years to survive due to the lack of government social supports for the elderly.

---

[1] Sweden leads the industrialized world with an elderly population of 18%.

B.S. Trask, *Globalization and Families: Accelerated Systemic Social Change*,
DOI 10.1007/978-0-387-88285-7_7, © Springer Science+Business Media, LLC 2010

Globalization has increasingly raised our awareness about the demographic shifts that are profoundly restructuring our world. But it has also brought attention to crosscultural differences pertaining to conceptualizations of aging, the elderly, and their role in society. Increasingly, age and aging are understood as socially constructed, and informed and transformed, through globalizing processes. Age and aging are experiences that are laden with cultural meanings and symbolism and subject to interpretation and change. However, in the popular imagination, as well as in the scholarly world, it is considered, in general, acceptable to view chronological age as reflecting natural physiological age. In fact, most research on aging is conducted with a basic assumption about what aging "is" and who the "elderly" are. Public policy and programming approach aging in a similar naturalized manner. The elderly are viewed as a homogenous group, who are challenged by related issues with just slight variations in experiences. But as has been noted, other aspects of the human experience, such as gender and childhood are not natural constructions. How individuals define themselves and their place in this world is the product of a complex array of factors. Therefore, in order to comprehend the relationship among globalization, aging, and family issues, it becomes crucial to also "denaturalize" aging.

Aging and aging related concerns develop not just as the result of physiological occurrences but are the product of a complex set of interrelationships among cultural, social, and environmental processes (see for example, Baars et al. 2006).[2] With respect to globalization, older people all over the world are, themselves, in a constant interactive process between global, national, regional, local, and familial forces which influence the perceptions and realities of their experience. This relatively new perspective on aging has been referred by some as a "destabilizing" force: "one that disturbs and reconfigures conventional narratives about the meaning of growing old" (Philipson 2006, p. 48).

Globalization is also tied to very specific aspects of aging, namely the tensions around nation–state based policies with respect to demographic changes, as well as those that are enacted by global actors and entities (Philipson 2006). While there is recognition that the growing number of elderly will *affect* changes in both the industrialized and developing world, globalizing processes that include economic and political information and communication technologies are influencing the lives and economies of the elderly. As societies around the globe become increasingly multicultural through mass migrations, these countries are also faced with a new complex phenomenon: multicultural aging. As will be seen later on in the U.S. case, the statistics with respect to the diversity of the elderly population are staggering, and lead to predictions that aging as it has been conceptualized in the past will be irrevocably changed in the near future. This significant transformation can also

---

[2] A small but new body of literature, for example, has examined menopause from a crosscultural perspective and found that this stage of life is experienced very differently by women in various cultures. While in the U.S., the tendency has been to "medicalize" women and, until recently, prescribe them hormonal therapies, in other places women may barely notice the symptoms of menopause.

be attributed to another aspect of the globalizing process, the "glocalization" of phenomena, images, and representations (Robertson 1995). As Western images and products flow freely around the world, they are absorbed and reinvented in local environments. Aging and its accompanying images, concerns, and practices are an integral aspect of this process.

7.1 Reconceptualizing Aging

The acceleration of globalizing processes has highlighted aging as a phenomenon that transcends national boundaries. For much of its history, the study of aging was concentrated in the industrialized world. In fact, in the spirit of the last vestiges of modernization theory, Western concepts of aging were thought to spread crossculturally and, ultimately, create a uniform experience of becoming old. However, information and communication technologies have brought the issue of global aging to the forefront and revealed that, exactly like other phenomena, aging is interpreted in local contexts. Thus, we find that globalization has highlighted the suffering of the elderly in certain areas of the world, such as regions plagued by extreme poverty sub-Saharan Africa or in war zones. But, globalization has also spread new ideas about that which is possible in old age with respect to activity and lifestyles. What we find is that conceptualizations of aging are contested, recreated, and reworked as a result of globalizing processes. For example, Philipson (2006) points to the growing recognition of aging not just as a national issue to be dealt with within state borders, but instead as a global phenomenon, with implications for the world order. The recognition of aging as a global concern has, for example, lead to mounting worries about deepening global ties that could lead to a "politicization" of aging. These concerns have been tied to neoliberalism and its stance that private provisions are more beneficial than policies that are ordained and legitimized through states (Dannefer 2000).

Globalization and aging have also become interrelated with new understandings of risk. In the West, in particular, as growing older has become associated with being well-off and leisure, so have worries materialized about how to achieve this form of security. Phillipson (2006) suggests that this fear of risk has now been transposed not just onto older people but also younger individuals as they plan for their futures. Risks that were once the purview of governments, places of work, and social institutions now fall in the domain of families and individuals. For example, most workplaces in the industrialized world have moved away from promising lifetime employment to their workers. Instead, citizens are expected to take care of "themselves" by investing in private pension plans. The line of reasoning can be described as the following: should there be a catastrophe, it should be up to the individual to have old age security measures in place, instead of relying on public institutions or assistance to help bail him or her out. This redefinition of aging as "risk" is increasingly influencing perceptions of the aging process itself. Individuals are preoccupied with staying as young and as healthy as possible, in order to ward off any sense of potential dependency or misfortune.

A primary emphasis of earlier sociological studies of aging focused on old age as a "natural" stage accompanied by specific physiological processes, or on individual failures to adjusting to a new stage of life. In the contemporary context, focus has shifted to the role of states, and economic forces, in influencing the perceptions and status of the elderly. For example, Townsend (2006) explains how the dependency of the elderly has come to be constructed through retirement, poverty, institutionalization, and the restrictions of social and community roles. He terms this as an "artificial" structuring of dependency based on a fixed age for receiving a pension, the low level of subsistence that is possible to be sustained on a minimal pension, and the social push to retirement facilities for the many individuals who do not need that type of care. While aging has been perceived as primarily a static entity, one that is connected to these images of dependency, Castells (2004) also suggests that until relatively recently welfare states were perceived as vital to both controlling and assisting the elderly. Welfare states had a role in formulating a type of identity for the elderly – on the one hand they served as a form of control over the elderly and, on the other, as a type of remuneration. A lifetime of hard work resulted in the reward of being taken care of in older age Philipson (2006).

Sen (1995) also highlights the fact that just as dependency has been a dominant aspect of the social construction of the elderly population in the West, so has the assumption that the aged do not have anything valuable to contribute to society. In a dominant capitalist model, where productivity is measured by market value, older people are perceived as unproductive and, thus, not valuable, further strengthening the dependency model.[3] She points to the arbitrary line of 60 or 65 as the supposed period when "old" age begins and suggests that it is time to reassess conceptions of dependency as contingent on physiological age. Stereotypes of aging as a time when all individuals begin to decline do not capture the complexity of the human experience. A number of scholars suggest that globalization is leading to more fluid notions of aging that are not necessarily sustained by welfare states. In fact, these days, there is a greater divide between those older people who are able to take care of themselves by moving to care communities and retirement homes and those elderly, such as women in poverty and minority elders, who have few if any resources and securities besides those provided by the state or their families.

7.2 Growing Concerns Around the Elderly

7.2.1 Significant Demographics

The next several decades are going to witness an unprecedented growth in the number of individuals over the age of 60 and, in the industrialized world, an unprecedented drop in the number of children born. In order to understand some of the complexities

---

[3] Sen (1995) compares the lack of value of the contribution by elderly individuals to the undervaluing of women's domestic contributions.

of global aging, it is instructive to begin with a look at some of the specific statistics pertaining to the United States, and then to place them in a global context. According to the U.S. Census Bureau (2005), as last reported in 2003, 35.9 million people in this country were aged 65 and older equaling about 12.8% of the total population. Among this older population, 18.3 million were aged between 65 and 74 years; 12.9 million were aged between 75 and 84 years; and 4.7 million were 85 and older. The numbers are striking, especially when one considers that the aging population of the U.S. is on the threshold of a major boom. Census Bureau projections indicate that a substantial increase in the number of older people can be expected in the next 20 years, which will coincide with the first Baby Boomers turning 65 in the year 2011. By the year 2030, the older population of the United States is projected to be twice as large as it was in 2000, growing from 35 million to 72 million people. Thus, in the next 20 years, nearly one out of every five individuals in the United States will be 65 years of age or older. Even more striking is the prediction that centenarians (those individuals aged 100 years and older) are the fastest growing age-segment of the population. According to the United States. Census Bureau (2005), the number of individuals in this group has increased in the past several years from 37,000 in 1990 to over 50,000 in 2000. In 2005, the number of centenarians rose dramatically to about 67,000; the projected number of centenarians in the year 2040 is an astounding 580,605 (United States Census Bureau 2008). The dramatic rate of increase among this age group in the United States alone is enough to warrant special attention from aging scholars and entities concerned with the status and care of the elderly.

A significant aspect of aging demographics in the United States is their gendered nature, as women tend to live longer than men. According to a report from the United States Census Bureau (2008), in the year 2000, among people aged 85 and older, there were only 50 men for every 100 women. Following this trend, it is understood that widowhood is more common among older women than men. In 2003, women aged 65 and older, were three times as likely as men of the same age to be widowed. This proportion is higher at older ages and remains higher for women than men. Older men were much more likely than older women to live with a spouse. Additionally, older women were more than twice as likely as older men to live alone. As the older population of this country grows larger, it will also grow more diverse. Such changes reflect general demographic changes in the U.S. population as a whole over the last several decades. The percentage of foreign-born members of the aging community has increased as well. The United States Census Bureau (2008) reports that in 2003, 11% of the older population were foreign born. Individuals originating from parts of Europe and Latin America stood at about 35% each, while individuals from Asia comprised approximately 23%. Moreover, in 2000, 13% of the older population spoke a language other than English at home; among this group, more than one-third spoke Spanish. Projections indicate that by the year 2030, the composition of the older population will become dramatically more diverse. According to the U.S. Census Bureau (2005), the older Hispanic population of this country will grow rapidly from just over two million in the year 2003 to nearly eight million by 2030. This projected increase will make the Hispanic aging population larger than the older African-American population. The Asian population of the United States is projected to rapidly increase as well from nearly one million people in 2003 to four million by 2030.

Reports from the United States Census Bureau (2008) indicate racial and ethnic disparities among the aging population in relation to socio-economic conditions and living arrangements. In 2003, older Americans of European descent (listed as non-Hispanic Whites by the Census) were less likely than older African Americans and older Hispanic Americans to be living in poverty at 8%, compared with 24% and 20%, respectively. These rates were higher for women of European and African descent than they were for their male counterparts. Moreover, African American, Asian American, and Hispanic American women were more likely than women of European descent to live with relatives. Older White women and African American women were more likely to live alone (at about 40% each) than were older women of Asian and Hispanic heritage (at about 20%). These statistics point to the growing disparity *within* a population, such as in the United States, a fact that is often overlooked in country-wide statistics on aging. As the population grows elderly, significant inequalities between ethnic and racial groups, as well as the growing poverty among older women, will challenge dominant images of the aged as a homogenous group requiring uniform policies and programs.

While there is much concern surrounding the shifting demographics with respect to aging in the U.S., Europe and Japan face even greater crises at this point in time. A larger percentage of their populations are aging even more rapidly, and their public pension funds are more generous than those in the United States. The growth of the elderly populations in these industrialized countries has generated a great deal of worry about the sustainability of government-sponsored programs for health care and pensions. For example, the largest increase in individuals over 85 years of age is predicted to occur in Japan, where as of 2030, they will compose 24% of the older population. However, what is usually not acknowledged in Western aging predictions is that the elderly population in developing countries is also growing at an accelerated rate. According to UN population estimates, by 2025, most elderly people will actually be living in the developing and not in the industrialized world (Polivka 2001).

Aging populations are experiencing not just a phenomenal growth in numbers as was stated in the beginning of this chapter, but individuals are also living longer raising concerns about their quality of life. For example, currently, China has 12 million people over the age of 80 and the United States has nine million.[4] By 2050, six countries are predicted to have more than ten million elderly over 80 years of age: China will have 99 million, India, 48 million, and the United States, 30 million (United Nations 2002). While most individuals over 80 currently live in the industrialized

---

[4] China is followed by India at six million, Japan at five million and Germany at three million.

world, by 2025, 57% will live in the developing world. And by 2050, this estimate is expected to rise to 70%. Further, the number of centenarians is expected to rise dramatically. For example, by 2050 about 1% of Japan's population is expected to reach the age of 100 or more.

With respect to global demographics, there are also significant gender differences. Women have longer life expectancies than men: by the year 2000, there were 81 males per 100 females over the age of 60.[5] However, UN predictions estimate that the life expectancy of men in the industrialized world will grow over the next 50 years to 85 men per 100 women over the age of 60 (2002). In less developed countries, variations in life expectancies between men and women are not as great as in the industrialized world. Right now, among individuals aged 60 and older, the sex ratio is estimated at about 88 men per 100 women, with large variations between countries depending on a range of factors such as the effects of wars, famines, and health related factors. Some of this variation is predicted to decline over the next half century (United Nations 2002). However gender differentials impact every aspect of life including health, family caregiving, living situations, economic status, and the labor force (Kinsella and Phillips 2005).

7.2.2   The Relationship Between Aging and Fertility Declines

The importance of demographics with respect to aging must be understood in the context of fertility declines, particularly in the industrialized world. Currently, fertility rates have continued to fall to 1.56 children, far below the population replacement level of 2.06 (Castles 2003).[6] The drop in fertility has been explained as a direct consequence of improved health care and reductions in disease, making it possible for women to bear fewer children since fewer will succumb to illness and death. However, the decline in fertility has serious implications for the future population levels of Western societies. For example, if fertility levels were to stabilize for the next 100 years at 1995 levels, Germany's population would be approximately 17% of what it was in 1995, while estimates of Italy predict a population of 14%, and Japan at 28% (Castles 2003). In order to cope with this crisis, countries will have to increase migration and labor force participation. However, this will only partially stem the economic consequences from these dramatic population reductions. Analysts point out that it would take an enormous number of migrating individuals entering the labor force to subsidize the social expenditure of the growing aging populations. Such a mass immigration, in turn, will create a whole host of new social problems, many of which are

---

[5]There seem to be both physiological as well as social reasons for women's increased longevity. See, for example, Hooyman and Kiyak (2006).

[6]Castel's data are based on his analysis of statistics from OECD countries. OECD countries refer to those countries that are members of the Organization for Economic Co-operation and Development.

already starting to be experienced in the European context. Further, the dramatic shrinking of populations will have implications for the status and economic importance of countries in the world order.

7.2.3   Dependency and Social Welfare

The statistics presented above need to be evaluated in the framework of government formulations of dependency, which are expressed quite differently in various parts of the world. Currently, only three in ten workers in the global labor force receive any form of a pension which translates into the reality that a large percentage of men and women need to work more years in order to survive (King and Calasanti 2006). For example in Nigeria, only 1% of the labor force receives social security while in the industrialized world approximately nine out of ten workers are covered (King and Calasanti 2006). Thus, the entitlement to a secure old age is mediated in the industrialized world, through the employer–employee relationship and supported by the state. The same is not necessarily the case in developing societies, nor in the case of many women in either part of the world. Since women, and other vulnerable populations, have not been part of the paid labor force in most places, or they have primarily had lower paying, less secure jobs, they also usually do not have access to the security that is offered as the reward for a certain period of labor. The relationship between inequality and differential life chances are examined in the following section.

7.3   Inequality and the Life Course

Much of the study of aging in the industrialized world has been structured around the assumption of individuals following a traditional life course. Different stages of life culminated with an "orderly" transition from family of origin, to school, marriage, childbearing, and work (for men specifically), and, finally, to retirement (Dannefer 2003). Philipson (2006), however, suggests that globalization has transformed this linear model of individuals' lives. He points to the increase in risk in individuals' lives created through the loss of lifetime job security resulting from the globalization of finance and the movement of capital. Combined with the major migrations of the last several decades, individuals' traditional life courses have morphed into new nonlinear versions of aging. "Normal" aging markers, such as retirement, now occur earlier or later in life. Further, as societies become increasingly diverse, through the influx of large groups of immigrants coupled with intensified global networks, new conceptualizations and values pervade the mainstream, including different perspectives on aging and the aged. Philipson (2006) predicts that "ideas about the meaning of old age, when old age begins, and normative behaviors for later life, will demonstrate greater variation within any one society than has historically been the case" (p. 51). Some of these same phenomena will hold true for the aging citizens of developing nations as well.

7.3.1 Gender Issues

Around the world, the poor and many older women are marked by extreme vulnerability in older age. This stems from the problem that social production of inequality manifests itself in old age. Dannefer (2003), for example, has highlighted how advantages and disadvantages become cumulative over an individual's life course, specifically through the influence of the state in regulating and reproducing different life chances for individuals. When combined with factors such as systemic discrimination and prejudice, gender, race and ethnicity, and the lack of educational opportunities, old age can be quite a wide-ranging experience for individuals. As citizens enter the later period of their lives, social inequality becomes expressed as a decisive difference. We see this particularly in the growing phenomenon of the feminization of poverty in old age.[7] In most societies, economic security in older age depends on the accumulation of savings from income earned during the individual's lifetime as well as control over financial assets (Sen 1995). As Baars (2006) explains, we cannot attribute this phenomenon to the lack of effort on the part of women but must instead view it from the prism of the effects of various forms of inequality including social exclusion, poverty, labor markets, and pension systems.

Narrow definitions of that which is considered work, and what is rewarded with pay, has contributed to the labor of many women not being valued in financial terms. Even in developing countries, where much of what women do is directly tied to the subsistence activities and survival of their families, their labor still goes unrecognized and uncompensated. In the West, the move of work from the manufacturing sector to the service realm has translated, particularly into the growth of part-time jobs, an arena of work that is primarily filled by women. And part-time work in the West, is usually unaccompanied by benefits such as pension plans and old age insurance, leaving women in this form of work at a growing disadvantage as they age. Except for an elite group of professional women, most women have difficulty contributing to retirement plans and do not have the ability to amass financial resources.[8] In the developing world, especially where much of women's labor is in under-recognized, poor and peasant women have the added cultural pressure to bear as many sons as possible, in order to elevate their status and to provide them and their husbands with a form of old age insurance. This pressure exists despite the reality that it is usually daughters that take care of the elderly in these

---

[7] See the work of Ingrid Connidis for some wonderful examples of this issue.

[8] Often ignored in these discussions is that even women who work in professional jobs, often take time off for child bearing which bears detrimentally on their future earning potential.

societies (Sen 1995). For many of these women, childbearing takes precedence as the one form of security that they may benefit from in old age. However, as we shall see, globalizing forces are even affecting this very fundamental relationship.

7.4 The Crisis in Care

Global demographics raise great concern about the future of the elderly in the industrialized as well as the developing world where the populations of aging individuals are growing, but there are fewer public resources to draw on. Polivka (2001) points out that resources in developing societies constitute less than 10% of current expenditures in industrialized countries, and even these resources have dropped from previous levels due to cuts in revenues and expenditures. All of these countries do not have programs such as Social Security and Medicare and the generous social programming found in European societies. Compounding this issue is the fact that the elderly in developing countries are not just more numerous but also poorer and less healthy than in the West. They suffer from the same chronic conditions as elderly individuals in the West: arthritis, high blood pressure, heart disease, stomach ulcers, and lung diseases. In fact, statistics indicate that the rates in some of the countries in the developing world are vastly higher than in the United States. For example, a crosscultural health study indicated that 60% of elderly in Thailand and 49% of elderly in Indonesia suffer from arthritis compared with approximately 40% in the United States. Compounding the problem is the fact that most countries located in the developing world are characterized by very limited resources for their citizens for healthcare and restricted accessibility to health services. In order to provide much needed services, they will require resources from the West or else healthcare will become even less available for hundreds of millions of aging individuals. Of further concern in these regions is that young people are moving to urban areas, leading to more elderly living alone in rural communities. This situation, unfortunately, points to a crisis of care that is just as profound, if not more so, than in the industrialized world.

The crisis in care is compounded by growing concern among some about the negative effects of neoliberal globalization policies on developing countries. In many cases, these countries are unable to respond to their most vulnerable populations as their fragile safety nets disappear. While the development world and international organizations focus on children and the falling wages of working populations, there has been little concern exhibited for the status of the elderly. Some of this lack of interest, or benign neglect, can be attributed to a lack of familiarity with the staggering statistics and with the role that aging and the aged play, in general, in many of these societies. The "invisibility" of the elderly and their ascription to the "family" realm has kept them out of the public arena with respect to policies, programming, and financial support. In much of the developing world, in particular, the elderly are thought to be taken care of by their immediate kin. However, as family relationships and structures change through migration, work, and the rearrangement of roles, many of these elderly have no one to take care of their needs, radically worsening this situation.

In the industrialized world, a somewhat different trajectory is taking place. As citizens are faced with growing inequalities within their societies and states are gradually decreasing social supports for their elderly populations, a growing discourse is necessitating the need for family and community assistance. This has led to widespread speculation that within a relatively short period of time, both industrialized and developing societies will be engaged in relatively similar dialogues about the role and status of the elderly in their societies (Kim et al. 2000). However, as has been pointed out, discrepancies in access to resources makes this proposition somewhat questionable. Further, it is important to remember that family care often equates to "female care." Given the family and gender role dynamics that have been highlighted in previous chapters, this begs the question of how elder care will be handled in a doable and equitable manner in the future.

7.5 The Case Study of China

China presents an interesting case study with respect to the issue of care. Despite significant social, economic, and political changes over the last 50 years, patterns of familial caregiving have remained relatively rooted in ancient traditions. In China, children, and in particular sons, were raised with the responsibility of passing on the family name and providing financial care for their parents, also referred to as "xiao" (Zhan and Montgomery 2003). As part of the patrilocal system, girls, once married, were expected to take care of their in-laws as they aged. Despite changes in family law, the family system, with respect to responsibilities for elder care has, until very recently, remained unchanged. However, new research indicates that, increasingly, daughters are caring for their parents, especially in urban areas, and those elderly parents are also relying on them for financial assistance (Zhan and Montgomery 2003). While this transformation can be attributed, in part, to the changing family structure brought on by the one-child policy that was enacted in the 1970s, it also seems to be the outgrowth of globalization. As China has moved from a socialist to a free-market economy, and as businesses have increasingly privatized, the country has witnessed a steep decrease in jobs. As a consequence, job security and accompanying health benefits have decreased. Women, specifically, have been affected by the transformation of the economy. While many Chinese women have been part of the paid workforce since the 1950s, they have often worked in part time jobs without benefits. Thus, the economic reforms of the 1980s have been particularly detrimental for women who have lost their employment and health care benefits. As these women have aged, their status has become more precarious due to the lack of a pension. They have also had to rely, to a greater extent, on their one child for physical and financial care. Furthermore, since it is also women who themselves tend to be underemployed or without a job altogether, they are the ones who usually become the designated caretaker of the family.

This points to a growing crisis for older women in a society without minimal safety net programs for the elderly, like Social Security and Medicaid, as well as for younger women in general. Zhan and Montgomery (2003) point out, that while some younger women may benefit from incorporation into the global economy, older and unemployed women, or women with extensive caretaking responsibilities, are left in an increasingly vulnerable position. Unlike in the West, women in China cannot make claims on their husband's pensions. As they age, and their children move away through globalizing processes that encourage greater mobility, these women may find themselves in a position where they have no one to turn to for assistance except, perhaps, some other women.[9] What we find in the Chinese case is an example of the enormous impact that the intersection of familial, economic, and gender structures can have on ideologies and traditions, that have been thought to be relatively fixed and not subject to global influences. While the cultural norm of filial responsibility has not lessened, especially with respect to elder care, economic and social pressures are forcing younger people to follow employment opportunities leaving their aging parents on their own. We also see that again, it is the poor and women (and these two tend to come together) who are the most vulnerable in today's circumstances. Maybe most worrisome, however, is that we are only on the brink of impending changes and that, especially when it comes to issues, such as family relationships, and gender and the elderly in the developing world, there is little dialogue and action on these issues.

7.6   The Stress of the Sandwich Generation

The issue of carework and its impact manifests itself in various forms. Demographic and social research in the U.S., for example, increasingly points to the "sandwich generation" as among the most stressed and overworked individuals.[10] As workers increasingly care for both children and their elderly relatives, their own health and well-being suffers. A study by the Families and Work Institute's National Study of the Changing Workforce revealed that the percentage of employees who reported taking care of elderly relatives jumped from 25% in 1997 to 35% in 2002 (Neal and Hammer 2007). As individuals increasingly delay childbirth, the population ages, and a growing number of women participate in the paid labor force, it becomes more common for women and men to find themselves taking care of both children and their elderly parents and relatives, simultaneously. Since care is predominantly a female phenomenon, the crisis of care affects women disproportionately.[11]

---

[9] The focus is on women because men still have the advantage of acquiring a pension under the current system. Also, given the current ideology and structure of Chinese society, men have an easier time finding full time employment.

[10] There is a serious dearth of studies on this issue in both other Western countries and the developing world.

[11] In this discussion, however, it is important to point out that care is quite often defined differently in various studies. So, for example, there is evidence that men also participate in elder care, albeit in different ways from women. They may provide instrumental care such as money or transportation while women tend to take on day to day tasks. See Hareven (2000) for example.

Taken together with these demographic and social factors, the global trends of aging, globalization, and gender migration highlight the growing demand for care labor in the U.S. and other industrialized countries. This has been termed by some as the "international transfer of caretaking" (Parreñas 2001). As families and, specifically, women are increasingly combining full time paid work with family responsibilities, family care is serviced out to paid employees. Strikingly, care work remains simultaneously critical to families and societies, and yet, also invisible and undervalued (Zimmerman et al. 2006). In order to cope with the increasing demands of caring for dependent family members, there is an increasing reliance in industrialized parts of the world on immigrant women. These women provide care for children as well as the growing frail elderly population (Browne and Braun 2008). However, as has been seen, women who work as domestic laborers by providing care are particularly vulnerable and easily oppressed. Much domestic service is paid under the table without regard for labor laws, and involves elements of exploitation. For the most part, the home governments of immigrant women do not become involved in their situations, due to their societies' dependence on remittances. Concurrently, host societies have tightened immigration and residency laws in order to prevent many of these women from remaining permanently in their countries. We, thus, have a situation where neither their home governments nor their host governments intervene in the condition of migrant women working abroad. Browne and Braun (2008) raise the troubling questions of "Who [then] is responsible for immigrant women's social and economic well-being? And at a more macro level [they] ask: Do developed nations owe a debt to those nations whose workers migrate after receiving health-related training?" (p.21). In part, Browne and Braun answer their own questions by, rightfully, pointing out that at the bare minimum, workers need to be sufficiently compensated and protected for the care they provide. They also highlight the fact that cultural issues will increasingly play a role in these relationships, as the workforce itself diversifies and the populations that are being cared for become increasingly multicultural.

In this discussion, it is critical, however, not to view migrating women who take on care work, as the passive victims of globalizing forces (as they are so often portrayed even in scholarship).[12] Instead, it is important to highlight the fact that poor and working class women have a history of refashioning and creating new lives for themselves both in the past in the U.S., and today in societies around the world. The dominant feminist view of women as pawns of global forces that give them little choice but to follow market forces eliminates any form of agency or choice on their parts. While it may be true, that scores of women are forced to migrate due to economic scarcities, this does not imply that they are bound only to live in impoverished or marginalized conditions. The same global forces that induce them to move also provide new spaces for them to refashion their identities, and roles within their families, their communities and their host societies.

---

[12] Discussions of carework in the U.S. are particularly troubling since they are often founded on the unspoken assumption that women "should" be assuming these responsibilities and that by hiring other women, in this case, immigrant women to perform this labor, they are somehow passing on, what they should rightfully be doing themselves.

7.7 How Globalization Could Contribute Positively to Aging Issues

Globalization promises to bring some necessary focus to the significant issues facing aging populations around the world. For example, the spread of concepts such as age discrimination is finally gaining a larger audience as workplaces and states increasingly come under the purview of international law. However, the aging of the population in industrialized countries has been accompanied by neoliberal state policies that are systematically increasing the role of the private sector. Further, fears about dependency in old age have been elevated by reducing pensions and increasing job insecurities. As global populations age, issues of care are also becoming increasingly critical. In industrialized countries, delegating elder care onto households has significant implications for both women and men who have to negotiate complex demands on their time, both at work and at home. Virulent debates about "who" should shoulder care work have not brought about many productive results. For example, public disapproval of middle class and professional women in the industrialized world who employ and "exploit" women from the developing world who "perform their care work for them," are, often, misguided as well. These kind of disagreements actually do not assist families with the serious care issues that they are facing, and in fact, at times, even serve to again "naturalize" women's roles in families as primary caregivers. In an environment where most often, both men and women are working outside of the home, even strong norms with respect to gender equality, will not solve the fundamental problem of who will take care of domestic responsibilities be they caring for children or for the elderly.[13] As we have seen, this is an issue of growing concern in developing countries as well, were the lack of safety nets and the slow erosion of familial care has been promoted by globalization and its concomitant effects. Families in these areas are faced with the same growing dilemma of how to care for their dependent members, but often with even fewer available resources.

7.7.1 Beneficial Social Policies

The unprecedented demographic shifts in the global aging of populations have aroused concern about the types of policies and social changes that would prove to be most beneficial. Again, it is important to stress that, as we have seen, the elderly do not constitute one body or group and that a great deal of variation exists between and within societies. Peterson (1999) suggests some fundamental macro-approaches to dealing with the economic, social, and political challenges facing aging societies in the industrialized world. He points out that lengthening the time period individuals spend in jobs, growing the labor force through immigration, promoting higher fertility

---

[13] Interestingly, many of these arguments are founded on the basic assumption that this is work that should be kept in the family – but distributed differently. We have little discourse around the need for states to step in and provide policies and services that will alleviate the caretaking burden of working families.

rates, investing in the training and education of future members of the labor force, supporting intergenerational relationships within families and increasing government services and benefits to the most vulnerable populations while promoting personal responsibility with respect to saving for the future, would be potential strategies to ward off the aging crisis, soon to be experienced by virtually every country around the world. However, Peterson (1999) also highlights the fact that many of these strategies violate unwritten social contracts between the citizenry and its leaders. They overturn basic expectations about the role of governments in providing for individuals or they reverse dominant ideologies. I would add that they also serve to ignore some of the most entrenched issues with respect to aging: that in so many places, as we have seen, women and low-skilled, low-paid workers, are disproportionately affected by the aging process. It is these same individuals who provide care in families for the elderly, and it is these same individuals who themselves tend not to have adequate resources such as pension plans and assets that allow them to enjoy a dignified and somewhat more relaxed older age.

Any national formulations and policies that address the susceptibility and security of the elderly need to include poor women and other vulnerable populations as a primary focus. Further, in order to begin to solve some of the complex issues of the developing world, with respect to aging, local and global inequalities need to be approached in a systematic manner. In particular, the life chances of those elderly who live in developing societies, as well as those populations who live in the poorer communities of the industrialized world need to be improved. Philipson (2006) points out that "bodies such as the UN and the World Health Organization (WHO) will need to confront the power of International Government Organizations (IGOs), such as the International Monetary Fund (IMF) and World Bank, to impose social policies that result in drastic cuts in expenditure on services for groups such as older people" (p. 54). I would also suggest that governments need to start acknowledging care work in their policies and prescriptions. As the familial context remains and/or becomes the primary domain for elder care, caretakers (be they women or men) need to receive monetary compensation for their efforts. This would minimize the burden on governments and support efforts between the private and public spheres.

As we witness the emergence of new cohorts of aging individuals, we are also likely to be confronted with new visions of aging, of attitudes and of political and economic action. Globalization brings with it the added potential for transnational movements and ideologies. But, it also highlights the varying concerns of different sectors of the elderly, including poor women, minorities, and people with disabilities. As the Baby Boomers in the U.S. age, we are witnessing a reformulation of old age and its possibilities. However, as the poor in our society and throughout much of the world also enter their final years, we should be increasingly concerned with their situation. We need to harness the power that comes through globalization, not just to raise awareness, but also to effect changes that guarantee the basic dignity and rights of every elderly individual. The potential to effect this mission is within our grasp. A lack of consensus and action around this issue bodes poorly not just for vulnerable groups but for us as well as we enter into a world that is increasingly going to be faced by issues for which there is no prior model in human history.

Part III
Future Challenges and Opportunities

Chapter 8
Nation-States, Transnational Spaces, and Family Linkages

The global transformations of the latter part of the twentieth and early twenty-first centuries have been accompanied by critical debates about the role of the nation-state and its relationship to its citizens. As globalization has given rise to new types of concerns and problems, the lines between formerly distinctive realms of decision-making have blurred. Many of today's issues require for states and governments, at various levels, to interact with other organizations and institutions that are public and private in order to achieve their goals (Castles and Miller 2003). Despite transformations in the very nature, mechanisms, and goals of nation-states, families remain intimately tied to their activities. In a globalizing world, family issues with respect to migration, the aging of populations, changes in men's, women's, and children's roles, and declines in fertility become hotly debated political focal points, and are intricately related to policy decisions. In contrast to the past, however, as nation-states respond to these social dynamics, they are also increasingly bound to powerful transnational forces that may sway them in new and, at times, unpopular directions.

Boundaries between states have opened up since more economies have embraced international trade and capital flows. These phenomena have led to speculation that we are on the verge of a new global order, characterized by forces that circumvent and lessen the sovereignty of the nation-state (Appadurai 1999). As ideas, goods, finances, strategies, images, and people circulate ever more freely, it is becoming increasingly difficult to differentiate between a local concern and a global matter. Information and communication technologies have allowed us insight into far away places and have placed struggles and conditions of far away people into the purview of individuals, who, in the past, may never have left their home community. The connections of the global community are increasingly understood by everyone, and are incorporated into people's consciousness in previously unimagined ways. However, this phenomenon also has specific implications for conceptualizations of nation-states. Increasingly, the role of the state needs to be understood within a transnational framework, one that disentangles it from its territoriality (Gupta and Sharma

B.S. Trask, *Globalization and Families*: *Accelerated Systemic Social Change*,
DOI 10.1007/978-0-387-88285-7_8, © Springer Science+Business Media, LLC 2010

2006). As borders become more permeable, states have had to adopt new concepts of sovereignty.[1]

It may be useful here to refer back to Giddens (1990) who described two opposing perspectives on globalization. From one point of view, globalization is just the continuation of historical processes that have intensified over time. But from another perspective, globalization is real, different, and is realized on cultural, political, economic, and social levels.[2] From this vantage point, globalization is a complex set of processes that are characterized by contradictory forces. On the one hand, they pull power and influence away from the local and nation-state level, but, on the other, they simultaneously create new spaces for local autonomy and cultural identity. This analysis leaves room for an understanding that the nation-state is not necessarily disappearing or devolving, as has been suggested by some, but is instead in the process of transformation, specifically because of the processes and effects of globalization. Globalization is not just an external force. It is realized between and *within* nation-states with implications for individuals, families, and communities.

Most recently, globalization has been accompanied by the growing power of international regulatory organizations such as the International Monetary Fund (IMF) and the World Trade Organization (WTO). These transnational entities are often singled out as examples of presenting unique challenges to nation-states. Their purported function is to regulate, oversee, and even at times, control the actions of states, most specifically with respect to finances and markets. However, a growing number of these transnational entities are also concerned with a spectrum of issues ranging from environmental concerns to human rights violations. The growth of these state-like institutions has not gone unnoticed. Global networks are increasingly organizing, responding, and resisting to what are perceived by some as illegitimate institutions.[3] The complexity of these issues leads analysts to question the future functions of the nation-state and the mechanisms that will need to be employed, which serve toward its legitimization.

A further consequence of globalization is the growing heterogeneity of societies around the globe, especially in the industrialized world. While cultural contacts can lead to greater tolerance for otherness, and an appreciation of diverse traditions and values, this new form of multiculturalism has also led to the emergence of strong nationalistic and fundamentalist movements, both in the West and other regions. The escalation of migration and the new forms of transnationalism with which this migration is accompanied today, is also characterized by new forms of inclusion

---

[1] For a nuanced discussion of this topic see Gupta and Sharma (2006). They problematize the state and point out that in order to understand the relationship between the state and globalization, we need to understand that there is no such "unit" as the state. "Such an approach problematizes the unity of the state by looking at different levels, sites, and scales, weighs the enormous amount of cultural work that goes into efforts to represent 'the state,' its legitimacy, and its authority, and finally, by considering the interplay between political economy, social structure, institutional design, and everyday practices and representations, allows for a nuanced appreciation of continuities across seemingly historic transformations." (p. 281).

[2] Giddens includes himself in this second perspective.

[3] See the discussion later on about the "un-democratic" nature of these institutions.

and exclusion based on economic inequalities as well as markers such as race, ethnicity, national origin, and gender. This growing diversity of populations, especially in nation-states that have build their identity around concepts of unity and homogeneity, poses unique challenges in the future.

8.1 The Role of the Nation-State with Respect to Its Citizens

The contemporary concept of the nation-state stems from the seventeenth century and is also linked to the philosophical concept of "reason," a remnant of the French Revolution. Primary to the concept of nation was the recognition that "each state was the sole political authority with exclusive possession of a defined territory" (Hirst and Thompson 1996, p. 171 in Carrington 2002, p. 88). The French Revolution passed on to contemporary times the notion that "creating and defending the unity of the nation, [is] identified with the universal principles of reason, liberty and equality, against all its internal and external enemies" (Tourraine 1990, p. 124 in Carrington 2002, p. 88). The roots of contemporary capitalism are also associated with this period in history, which explains the popular association between capitalism, the nation-state, and rationality. However, universal social changes have rendered these conceptualizations as untenable in the contemporary context. States are no longer able to remain independent, with respect to either economic issues or the affiliations of their citizenry, in the same manner as they were historically. Clarke (2005) explains

> So, where concepts of the nation-state assumed a unity of people, place and culture which were embodied in a sovereign political system, such assumptions now appear less plausible in the face of spatial, scalar and social dislocations. First, the territorial character of nations no longer seems quite so secure as boundaries become more permeable, more contested and even more mobile. Nations seem less solid than they once did. Secondly, the authority, power and effectivity of the nation state appears to be threatened or undermined by the shift towards multi-tier or multi-level governance implied in processes of globalization, regionalization, Europeanization and localization…Finally, the social character of the Nation is put into question by changing ways of life, forms of work, patterns of household formation and processes of migration and mobility. (p. 407)

This new conceptualization of the place of the nation-state amidst globalizing forces raises the question of how states will create a unified national identity with which to mobilize their people (Carrington 2002).[4] We are, thus, faced with a contemporary dilemma that places the role of the nation-state at odds with processes that are constantly pulling its citizenry, and its primary institutions, such as the economy and governmental functions, into an international sphere where it exercises less control and loses some of its legitimacy. On a societal level, the nation-state is faced with fundamental changes with respect to family life, work

---

[4] See Carrington (2002) for her informative treatise on this topic, as well as a psychoanalytic analysis of the relationship between states, normative concepts of family and globalizing forces.

patterns, needs for services and issues around multiculturalism. For example, Rattansi and Westwood (1994) points out,

> Globalization means, among other things, that the cultural boundaries of nation-states are breached in myriad ways, creating opportunities for cultural cosmopolitanisms of various kinds, but also generating anxieties which are experienced in different ways by locales and their populations, and managed and mobilized through a range of strategies by local and national state agencies, political parties. (p. 27 quoted in Carrington 2002, p. 85)

Nation-states are faced with the dilemma of responding adequately to forces that pull them simultaneously outwards, and inwards. As will be seen, however, the situation is even more complex than this brief discussion indicates. The role of the nation-state is viewed very differently depending on global location. What we find again is that globalization is an uneven process at each systemic level of the social order, and individuals in the same society and between societies are affected in a multitude of ways. There is a constant articulation of local culture with plural global influences. This actually points to the continuing role of nation-states. While their influence may be declining, or at least changing, the continuing importance of locality cannot be disputed (Baars 2006). Contemporary nation-states are influenced, to varying degrees, by international or global concerns, organizations, and citizens and communities. Nation-states also exercise power with respect to integrating their economies, and thereby their citizens, to a certain extent, into the global market place.[5] They continue to be involved in setting policies and boundaries that encourage or discourage this form of participation. As the global arena evolves, so do the responses and actions that are taken by nation-states, as well as their inhabitants. However, George and Wilding (2002) also suggest that,

> [National policies] will fail unless complemented and underpinned by parallel policies at the global level. When national welfare states came into being and flourished in the 1940s, 1950s and 1960s there were few social problems that had ramifications beyond the reach of individual nation-states. States could be sovereign in their social policies. Half a century later, national self-sufficiency in social policy is no longer a realistic option. In an increasing number of areas, action at the national level has to be complemented and supplemented by action at a supranational level. (p. 187)

This suggests that nation-states will increasingly have to work in conjunction with transnational entities to effect and enforce programs and policies that serve their populations.

Before we continue onto an analysis of some of these processes, I wish to turn to a conceptual problem in the discourse itself. Analysts of social policy almost uniformly equate welfare, nation, and state with the same entity. Thus, it is difficult to find incidents or examples that do not mention nation-states and welfare-states within the same discussion. Clarke (2005) explains that welfare was associated with states because it was "delivered by the state, in pursuit of the national interest, for the purposes of reproducing, maintaining and developing the Nation." (p. 408). In the contemporary context, it may be useful to decouple some of these concepts, which would lead to

---

[5] The word citizen is used here to stand for individual or resident. It does not imply legal status in this context.

more dynamic discussions on the processes that are at work within and between nations. As Clarke (2005) states, "What we might look for in comparative studies are the (contested) projects to remake and resettle the nation (as space and as people); the state (as a site of condensation of social forces, as a locus of shared sovereignty, and as a system of governance); and welfare (as the policies and practices that produce the normative regulation and development of a particular people)." (p. 414).

Teasing apart these concepts would allow us to gain better insight into how these processes function, not just in the industrialized world, but also in the developing world.

As pressures on nation-states increasingly become global rather than national, nation-states are becoming interrelated at an accelerating pace, in complex interactions that are not easily understood or detangled (Dannefer 2003). Castells (2004) suggests that the "instrumental capacity of the nation-state is decisively undermined by the globalization of core economic activities, by the globalization of crime, by the globalization of social protest, and by the globalization of insurgency in the form of transborder terrorism" (p. 304). Increasingly, nation-states seem to be not able to regulate some of the most fundamental processes that take place within their borders. Yet, Hirst and Thompson (1996) clarify that "Nation states are now simply one class of powers and political agencies in a complex system of power from world to local levels, but they have a centrality because of their relationships to territory and population. Populations remain territorial and subject to the citizenship of a national state." (p. 190).

The last several decades have witnessed the emergence and growing power of various international entities that are today significant players in the globalization spectrum. The most notable ones include the WB, the World Bank, the IMF, the International Monetary Fund and the WTO, the World Trade Organization. Baars (2006) raises the interesting point that despite the claims of democratic processes in much of the industrialized world, these organizations have arisen and are governed through nondemocratic structures. In this transnational arena, policies are developed that the weakened nation state can draw on to legitimize actions that may otherwise not be particularly popular with their citizenry. However, these policies and programs are created and, often implemented, through the will of a few, and often without input from those that will ultimately be held accountable for their implementation.

In this discussion, it is important to note that while nation-states seem to be losing some of their historically ascribed power, they are not losing their influence. Instead, nation-states are in the process of reformulating themselves. From an organizational perspective, nation-states can best be understood as participating in the global arena, as one of the multiple players.

8.2 The Role of States and Global Financial Flows

While, as we have seen, globalization is a highly disputed term that is connected with multiple phenomena, many analysts, today, link globalization, or at least its power, to the movement of capital on a global basis. Appadurai (1999) suggests

"What is new about this era clearly has a lot to do with the workings of global capital, but we do not yet know very much about how capital really works globally" (p. 230). Others highlight that global capitalism implies that finance has moved to a different plane, one that is more ephemeral and one that is increasingly tied to information technologies (Carrington 2002). With this realization comes the recognition that as the speed and impact of technology increases, so do the consequences of globalizing capitalism. For example, while in the past, capital was tied to production, in today's global marketplace, value is determined, in part, by access to credit rather than production capabilities, physical wealth, or fixed assets.

Currently, economic interdependency and international interactions are increasingly perceived as the primary challenge to states' sovereignty. The beginning of this "new" period is primarily linked to the political and economic events of the late 1960s and the early 1970s. During this time, developing world nations moved away from government controlled closed trading structures to open structures, setting the stage for incorporation into the global economy. These forces are thought to have accelerated after the end of the Cold War. Some analysts even argue that due to the lack of an international security agenda, this was the time when capitalism was allowed to flourish without much oversight (Carrington 2002). It is important to note, however, that the end of the Cold War also coincided with the increasing power of information and communication technologies, leading to a compression of time and space, unlike anything that was witnessed beforehand. We, thus, have at this point the basis for a new world order, the effects of which we are only now beginning to identify and understand.

Pyle and Ward (2003) have identified multiple trends as capitalist processes and ideologies have spread to different parts of the world, beginning in the late 1960s and early 1970s. During this period, many nations increased the role of markets in their economies, simultaneously reducing the centrality of government. This move is attributed to the spread of neoliberalism, a market based orientation towards economies that advocates for restricted involvement by nation-states. A range of countries engaged in this process, including the formerly socialist countries of Eastern Europe, Southeast Asia, and China, countries in the developing world, and industrialized countries including the United States and the United Kingdom (beginning in the early 1980s). Many developing countries and formerly socialist countries shifted from production for their own countries' needs to an export-oriented development strategy that focused on production for foreign trade. Concurrently during this time, organizations in the financial, manufacturing, and service sectors became multinational. They heightened their presence in the global economy by shifting their activities to new tiers of countries, and by setting up wide networks of subcontractors. Simultaneously, international oversight organizations such as the World Bank and the IMF began to gain influence in the global arena. These international entities instituted wide-ranging policies, some of which have had long term detrimental effects on, particularly, developing economies. For example, the World Bank, and the IMF, stipulated Structural Adjustment Policies (SAPs), as a requirement for lending. These SAPs mandated that governments increasingly open their economies to financial flows and trade, often challenging native sustainable development and creating financial volatility. A further notable trend is that as market oriented institutions such as the IMF or the WTO gained in importance, organizations focused on human rights and social conditions, for example, some of the United Nations agencies, and nongovernmental agencies, lost some of their significance and power (Pyle and Ward 2003).

These profound economic changes have had global effects. Pyle and Ward (2003) point out that while this global restructuring employs the language of "liberalization" and "free markets," it also has propagated the idea that competitive markets lead to economic outcomes.

> This perpetuates the myth that subsequent economic outcomes result from competitive markets, where everyone has similar opportunities, and governments have minimal involvement in their economies....These forms of global restructuring have resulted from *deliberate* interventions by governments pressured by institutions such as MNCs, (Multi National Corporations) the IMF, (International Monetary Fund) or the World trade Organization (WTO) and are not 'free market' strategies. The misappropriation of language obscures the realities that these institutions, fundamentally concerned with profits or payment of loans, dominate countries' economies *and* formulate the mandates to 'open' and 'liberalize' and economy. (Pyle and Ward 2003, p. 464)

8.3   Restructuring and Gender Effects

Strategies promulgated by organizations such as the IMF and the World Bank, such as SAPs, have had unforeseen and unintended consequences on a social level. Pyle (2005) highlights the fact that particularly women have been affected by many of these economic changes, specifically in developing countries. In particular, SAPs, have led to an increase in the number of women working in the informal sector of their economies. This has occurred because in order to generate the revenues needed to repay loans, government expenditures need to be reduced. Organizations such as the IMF, promote policies that minimize government expenditures, which usually translate into cuts in employment in the governments themselves (jobs that are often occupied by women) and reduce social programs (housing, food subsidies, health allowances, and the like).[6] These effects are primarily felt by women as they try to assist their families by taking on part time work in the informal sector, to generate extra income, and more household work, to make up for the cuts in services (Pyle 2005). Thus, one effect of globalization is that in certain regions and at specific times, women are forced to take on part time or low-wage work in order to assist their families. As Kingfisher (2002) explains, "The basic contradiction is that globalization and restructuring entail a simultaneous increase in, dependence

---

[6] Structural adjustment policies included other provisions, as well, including devaluation of currencies, shrinking the private sector, "realigning" domestic prices to the global market, privatizing state enterprises and regularizing land titles. See Eisenstein (2005) for a more detailed discussion.

on, and yet devalorization of female-typed labor *and* a twined decrease in state support and therefore increase of pressure on women's reproductive labor." (p. 47). The women most affected by restructuring policies are also most frequently the ones who then take on work as domestics, caregivers, home wage work, and the like. These are also the women who today make up such large percentage of migrants seeking work either in their own societies or internationally, in search of employment that will assist their families to survive.

With respect to the role of the nation-state, Pyle (2005) points out that particularly in developing countries, many national governments actually support policies and strategies that favor the role of women working in export-processing industries, domestics and caregivers abroad, and as home-based workers in multilevel subcontracting networks. Pyle (2005) attributes this phenomenon to the desire of governments to attract multinationals to their locations (which brings revenues), the focus on developing tourism (which is often accompanied by a sex industry), and the exportation of surplus labor to other nation (resulting in the migration of significant numbers of women to other places as domestics, caregivers, and sex workers). Policies are developed as a response to the need in their societies for employment and income and to satisfy the interests of more powerful entities. The fact that these policies often have unintended and detrimental consequences, in particular for women, is largely ignored. For the most part, governments do not intervene in the conditions that often accompany subcontracted work or migration. A desire to encourage multinational corporations to base their activities in their countries, coupled with the need for remittances that flow particularly to the poorest sectors of society, leads to the very circumstances that female employees may be trying to resist against – with little or no assistance from – their governments. In fact, it is often primarily the governments that have vested interests in preserving the status quo, since the resulting effects, primarily cash flow, work to their advantage. The money that is brought in through these work activities serves an ulterior function as well. It is perceived as a means to stem social unrest that can, potentially, result from extreme poverty and unemployment. For nation-states, working in conjunction with international entities such as the IMF or the WTO, can provide a means for them to legitimize actions, that would otherwise, potentially, be very unpopular with their populace.

With respect to the progression of globalizing capitalism, nation-states continue to participate in the process, albeit to the extent that they can, to their own advantage. Nation-states play a critical role in creating and enabling the conditions that allow global capitalism to flourish. For many, to encourage globalization is to their advantage. As they reconfigure themselves, they draw on new images of the citizenry, of families, and of identity. As Carrington (2002) suggests, "Rather than disappearing, the nation-state is in the process of reconfiguring itself spatially. At present, this spatial reconfiguration refers more to the socio-cultural and racial space of the nation rather than to physical territory. As security and economic activities have altered in the wake of the end of the Cold War and the decline of U.S. hegemony, the need for a particular type of citizen, a particular type of family unit and a particular ethnic/racial shaping of the citizenry has also altered.

The principles of normativity which formerly acted to maintain the socio-cultural space of the nation (and which were linked directly to the security and economic agendas of each state) have ceased to be as vital as they once were." (p. 89).

What is missing from so many perspectives on globalizing capitalism is the implication for individual's lives (Carrington 2002). We know little about the effects of globalizing capitalism on representations of citizens, workers, families, and identities. Scholars such as Pyle and Ward (2003) are beginning to initiate a dialogue around the implications of globalizing capitalism specifically for women's lives. However, we need to delve into the complex topic of the relationship between globalization, nation-states, and the social order with much greater rigor and insight. For example, at this point, we know very little about the lives of men and how they are affected by these processes, and the lives of individuals who are at the very bottom of the socioeconomic ladder in both developing and industrialized countries. We need to learn more about their day-to-day existence, struggles, and needs as states become ever more enmeshed in the global arena. Only through increased insight will we then be able to develop policies and programming that can truly assist vulnerable and disadvantaged individuals and families.

8.4   Debates About the Role of the Welfare State and Globalization

Much of the political and economic discourse on globalization has focused on the relationship between globalization and the role of the welfare state. Brady et al. (2007) point to three trends in these discussions: first, those who are convinced that globalization has brought about positive improvements in welfare states, second, those who believe that globalization leads to negative effects on welfare states, and third, those who postulate that globalization leads to a curvilinear effect with respect to the role of welfare states in citizens' lives. Those that are positively inclined toward globalization, which is sometimes also referred to as the "compensation thesis," deem that globalization creates volatility and uncertainty in individual's lives. Governments respond to the insecurities of their populations by expanding social policies that will stabilize the economy and satisfy them politically. In other words, states legitimize themselves by providing security to their citizens through an expansion of welfare type reforms and services. The second group views the relationship between globalization and welfare states from a much more negative angle.[7] They ascribe to what is also referred to as the "efficiency thesis," which postulates that globalization forces governments to cut back on social welfare programs to make them more competitive and lean. Governments trim these programs as a response to the economic and political pressures that stem from being integrated into

---

[7] Primarily social scientists, and especially sociologists, ascribe to this interpretation of the relationship between globalization and the welfare state. See Brady et al. (2007) for a thorough overview of these debates.

a more global community. The curvilinear thesis holds that globalization causes initial expansion of policies and programs, but then, ultimately, governments cannot sustain these policies and programs, which leads to cutbacks. Vigorous debate and research has led to a growing consensus that globalization has limited effects on welfare efforts. Various political scientists, economists, and sociologists have pointed out, for example, that as aging populations increase in so many industrialized societies, many dimensions of welfare states that would support this group, have neither decreased nor increased proportionally. Interestingly Brady et al. (2007) suggest that "globalization's effects on the welfare state might be better understood as a socially constructed discursive device that legitimates calls for efficiency and undermines calls for egalitarianism. That is, globalization may matter more within the political discourse surrounding welfare states." (p. 319).

This analysis of globalization and its concomitant effects on the role of the welfare state have been called into question by scholars concerned with the role of welfare states in the developing world (e.g., Sharma and Gupta 2006; Rudra 2008). They point out that discussions about these issues focus almost exclusively on Western industrialized nation-states, and either ignore states in the developing world all together, or lump them together as a collective of individualized entities, which are at such different stages of development, that it is not useful to include them in any kind of analysis of these issues. Rudra (2008) suggests that excluding nations in the developing world leads to false conclusions being drawn about the role of globalization in nation-states. She points out that the interrelationship, complexity and scale of contemporary global financial, commodity, and market operation create unknown threats and doubts for the citizens of all nations. While lesser-developed nations are certainly most at risk in this kind of an environment, the spread of certain ideals and rights, such as the right to vote, create an environment where citizens express their views on issues such as market expansion and neoliberal policies. Thus, governments in those countries are not able to act purely in their own interest. Precisely due to globalizing influences, they are more accountable to their citizens than is often portrayed in the prevailing discourse.

This raises the question of exactly what kind of entity the welfare state is. Esping-Andersen (1990) suggests that in order to understand welfare-states, one needs to focus on their involvement in their economies. While in the evolution of the European case, proletarianization was a fundamental problem for societies; this is not the issue in lesser developed countries today. Their citizens have not moved in a sequential fashion, out of the agricultural sector, into manufacturing, and then commerce and service industries. In developing countries, the focus is less on reducing internal class inequalities, and more on decreasing the differences between themselves and wealthier nations. In other words, these states are concerned with increasing wage labor and moving to the level of industrialized countries (Rudra 2008). However, what makes the situation different and more complex for developing nations today is that laborers need greater skills in order to be employable in the contemporary marketplace. This places the state in the position of having to provide more services, to make its workers more competitive in the global workforce. What we can deduce from this discussion is that the pressures on the nation-state in the industrialized world versus those in the developing countries are both different and similar. In each scenario, the nation-state is pressured to provide new or more kinds of services, but with somewhat different goals.

Gupta and Sharma (2006) problematize these type of discussions on neoliberalism and the concept of state "reform." They point out that change at the national level may not necessarily be reflected at the state or local levels. Their analysis illustrates that neoliberalism affects various levels of bureaucracies differently and "thus marks the specificity of global neo-liberal processes" (p. 291). They highlight the critical point that state reform has been analyzed predominantly from a Western liberal democratic state model. They point out that arguments that equate neoliberalism with cutbacks in welfare provisions and services have little meaning in contexts where states have never been welfare states. A transnational perspective such as theirs highlights the fact that one has to look beyond official policies and institutions, and instead, contextualize the multiple ways in which these policies and institutions are legitimized, instituted, and challenged.

8.5   Welfare States and Families

World War II brought about a new world order that included the decolonization of countries in the developing world, and the redrawing of nation-state boundaries. This period also stabilized basic assumptions about the role of states with respect to meeting the social needs and challenges of their societies in the industrialized world. During this period (our previously discussed "golden years of the family"), the following assumptions prevailed in much of the industrialized world: that families would be relatively stable and able to survive on the earnings of the male breadwinner and that families (men) would be the main provider for women, children and the disabled. This assumption was based on the fact that during this period most men, even those with relatively low-skills, were able to find paid, stable employment. The postwar model focused on old age as the area that needed the greatest amount of government intervention. The other arenas, labor markets and families were assumed to be stable. Esping-Andersen (2000) suggests that what has occurred in many welfare states, at least in the Western context, is that the elderly are relatively secure today, while family instability and unemployment have refocused risk on the young. Only a few countries in the Northern Europe have prioritized the needs of young families by redirecting resources and expanding public programs such as parental leave. As social needs have changed because of phenomena such as the world wide increase in single-parent families and longer life expectancies, we have moved to a period when there is actually a greater need for social services and carework. However, it is exactly at this point in time that many welfare-states are moving away from providing these needed state services, specifically for matters pertaining to social reproduction. Instead of redesigning their welfare programs, nation-states are maintaining and modifying their policies despite new economic and social challenges.

It is instructive in this matter to consider briefly the examples of Mexico and the United States. As a prime example of the economic restructuring that was described before, Mexico in the last several decades moved from a statist, centralized economy toward a free market, neoliberal economy founded primarily on export production. This transformation occurred because of changes in the economies of countries in the industrialized world, and was assisted by policies of transnational institutions such as the IMF. This has resulted in economic declines for many Mexican workers who saw their incomes fall as much as 60% because of inflation and the loss of state subsidies and employment. These state legitimized changes have spurred a crisis of social reproduction, forcing many Mexicans to seek employment opportunities in the neighboring U.S., either through legal or illegal migration (Mattingly 2001).

Concurrently, the United States has also been affected by market pressures, leading to a lack of support for policies that encourage and support social reproduction. The U.S. global hegemony that prevailed for the initial period after the end of the war has declined somewhat as multinational corporations have moved their operations to less developed areas of the world. This highly controversial phenomenon has served to reduce the expenses and increase the profit margins of multinationals, and has also opened up new markets to them. However, these economic changes have been accompanied in the United States by a philosophical shift with respect to the welfare state ideology of the mid twentieth century. As redistributive programs such as Aid to Families with Dependent Children (AFDC) have lost favor, they have not been replaced by other welfare oriented programs. It is noteworthy to mention that the U.S. has deviated from other welfare states (specifically the European states) with respect to the fact that with the exception of Social Security for all elders, its welfare programs that deal with issues of care are means based and only available to those who are identified as living in great poverty.

Despite significant social changes with respect to family roles, such as the large number of women who have entered the paid labor force, there have not been any concomitant efforts to subsidize or alleviate the issue of care work. In fact, we have seen a dramatic reduction in social service programs, and a shift of federal responsibility to state and local governments, as well as nonprofit and faith based organizations. Cuts in programs have also had other repercussions, including the more recent movement to link citizenship with benefits. Despite this move, citizens have witnessed an erosion in available resources, which has had the concomitant result of noncitizens becoming even more vulnerable – many are not able to access any resources anymore (Mattingly 2001). Through this process, the state has been able to address two issues at once: it has reduced the benefits provided by the state, and it has partially legitimized this move by focusing on "citizenship" as a means for building "unity" and "nationality."

The neoliberal ideology that has become so popular over the last several decades promotes the concept of a minimalist state. Basically, anything that stems market forces is perceived as detrimental. However, this kind of a philosophical or market orientation can result in vast to problems when applied "on the ground" so, to speak. As Mittleman and Tambe (2000) state so succinctly, "Central to the chain of relationships are the varied ways in which economic globalization marginalizes large numbers of people by reducing public spending on social services and de-links economic reform from social policy. This type of marginalization manifests a gendered dimension inasmuch as women constitute those principally affected by it." (p. 88 in Estes 2006, p. 93).

I would add to this interpretation, that not only are women affected, but all vulnerable populations including predominantly, immigrant workers. Current immigration policies, virtually in every nation that allow migrants to come in, usually favor the employers and make employees vulnerable to deportation. These workers who are often accorded short-term contracts, lack political rights, are not allowed to vote, and in certain countries, they are even forbidden from forming political associations. This raises problematic questions for industrialized states with respect to the application of democratic ideals and to what extent they pertain to foreign workers. It also raises serious questions about neoliberal assumptions about the supposedly benevolent relationship in contemporary capitalism, between globalizing forces, democratic ideals, and the observance of human rights (Parrenas 2005).

As ideologies of globalization collide with local conditions, vulnerable populations such as low-income workers and poor women are affected disproportionately. This phenomenon can be traced back to the global spread of a neoliberal ideology that assumes that healthy individuals, supported by a minimalist nonintervening state, work to maximize results through a free exchange of goods and services in a free market capitalist economy (Kingfisher 2002). However, this perspective has several glaring omissions. In particular, the position of vulnerable populations and the role of reproductive labor are kept out of view. For instance, a neoliberal perspective ignores the implications of this kind of a market system for poor and vulnerable women who must take on employment in the paid labor force while caring for their children and elderly. This assumption also ignores the actual conditions that are often created for those individuals at the bottom end of the employment ladder: the work that is primarily underpaid, temporary, and, at times, exploitative and dangerous.

Inequalities can be exacerbated, and as the state shifts away from the provision of social services, it is primarily women who take on extra responsibilities and burdens. Welfare support in many nations has not addressed the new burdens that have arisen through the increase of women in the paid labor force vis a vis family responsibilities. In fact, reproductive labor is increasingly hidden from view, as gender neutral policies become institutionalized (Kingfisher 2002). Nowhere is this more apparent in the industrialized world, than in the United States, which has the fewest welfare provisions for families, and especially for poor women and children. There is no universal health care, and most individuals are not eligible for paid maternity or family leave, government-subsidized childcare or any form of family caregiving subsidies (Parrenas 2005).[8] While other countries in Europe provide better benefits for families than does the United States, critics still point out that

---

[8] With the exception of California which is the first state to have a small paid leave.

these benefits are constructed around conservative conceptualizations of families. For example, elder care is still primarily relegated to women in families, without residential care provisions (Parrenas 2005). The Scandinavian countries are the only nations that provide benefits such as parental leave on a gender neutral basis, and that administer universal entitlements such as direct services and subsidies to the elderly and single-parent households. It is, thus, instructive to examine a specific aspect of reproductive labor, fertility or child-bearing, in the context of policies of industrialized welfare-states.

8.6 Women's Fertility and the Future of Industrialized Nation-States

Previously, it was noted that the implications of fertility decline must be understood in conjunction with the aging of populations around the globe. Castles (2003) points out that even countries that maintain a fertility rate of 1.70 (above the current 1.56 average in most industrialized countries) will still experience a 50% population decline in 100 years (with the exception of the United States). Countries such as Germany, Austria, and Italy have seen their populations drop over the last 20 years, without any indication of any reverse trends. This significant drop in population in so many industrialized countries has serious implications for the role of nation-states. As populations shrink, the labor force and national product begin to decline. This process eventually leads to a labor market contraction and negative rates of economic growth. In order to stem the economic tide and to cope with the public expenditure effects of the elderly, it seems that governments will have to promote the migration of individuals whose skills are needed in their societies. In particular, southern and western Europe, as well as northeast Asia, will be facing this situation in the relatively near future.

However, sizeable migrations, such as those that are needed to sustain the labor force in these regions of the world, bode poorly for the future. As the current situation in the U.S. and Europe reveals, significant immigration also gives rise to strong nationalist tendencies and anti-immigrant political movements. In fact, it is most often the immigrants who are blamed for a society's economic circumstances, despite the fact, that they are the ones who have usually been recruited to fill certain types of jobs. It is predicted that the decline in populations will also change the global, political, and economic power balance between nation-states. Several countries, such as Germany and Japan, will lose their current economic might because of the shortage of an adequate labor force. Of further concern is the great inequality between industrialized nations and the developing world, coupled with the high fertility of these poorer societies. For example, European and Asian countries are bordered by poorer countries with growing populations. Castles (2003) provocatively questions what the relationships between some of these poorer and richer countries will look like in the future, as extremely large populations with declining living standards live under extreme hardship next to more prosperous neighbors. He and others postulate an even larger "brain drain" Westward (primarily to the United States), also raising questions about the future of societies in the developing world.

Interestingly, these highly political issues seem to be primarily linked to women's fertility decisions. While conventional thinking until recently implied that as women become gainfully employed, they limit their fertility, the most recent analyses show a contradictory trend. Women seem to be more likely to have children in those places where they are also able to easily combine work and family. The older cultural imperative with respect to this issue that employment and child-bearing and child-rearing are mutually exclusive, does not hold up in the European context. Analyses indicate that the countries that have had the greatest success in raising their fertility levels also provide the most support for employed mothers and mothers-to-be.[9] This finding has significant policy implications. If governments in industrialized countries desire to maintain their populations, and sustain and improve their economic situations, they must bring fertility issues to the forefront. This requires expenditures and policies that are family friendly and that, in particular, address the concerns of working women who are trying to balance motherhood with their jobs. Along this line of thinking, one can also infer that one of the primary reasons that the U.S. lags behind other countries in the industrialized world, with respect to implementing family friendly work policies, is the fact that fertility decline is not an issue that the society currently faces.[10]

As women become progressively more incorporated into the paid labor force, their fertility decisions seem to be closely related to the extent to which they can combine paid employment with motherhood. This situation increasingly holds true for both women from industrialized and developing countries. While professional women in the developing world are able to access relatively cheap domestic labor, poorer working women face the dilemma of caring for their children. Women, especially those who migrate abroad, have to make choices about the size of their families, and may opt out of having children. Increasingly, governments are going to become involved in this issue with respect to creating policies that alleviate the domestic situations of these women. As the labor force participation of women continues to grow (and, thus, their economic importance), nation-states will need to institute policies that assist women in balancing both arenas of their lives. Research indicates that some of the most supportive measures that support women and families are high quality, low cost child care, adequate maternity and parental leave, flexible job hours, and legal reentry into jobs after childbirth Castles (2003).

This brief discussion of the relationship between nation-state policies, globalizing forces, and women's fertility and employment decisions, highlights the importance and implications of individual and familial choices in the global arena. What happens at the microlevel matters and has implications for macroprocesses.

---

[9] See Castles (2003) for his numerical analyses.

[10] The U.S. presents a somewhat different case from Europe and the industrialized countries in Asia. U.S. fertility levels are predicted to remain relatively constant due to massive immigration, and the fact, that a group, immigrant women bear more children than what is required to sustain population levels.

We cannot speak of the importance of economic growth in our contemporary context without incorporating some insight into the role of human agency into the process. But in order to arrive at greater understandings of how social forces operate at the macrolevel to shape the microlevel of everyday experiences, we also need to investigate the legitimizing ideologies that are enacted on at that microlevel. In interactions between nation-states, global forces and the population, power inequities are always at play. Larger institutional patterns, however, are occasionally resisted in unexpected ways, pointing to the importance of dynamic and multitiered understandings of phenomena (Baars et al. 2006). As Rosenau (2003) suggests,

> The presumption that people and collectivities shape each other highlights a central problem: while some analysts might agree that the flow between the two levels is central to how collectivities sustain themselves through time and how people shape and are shaped by macro structures, the interactions across the levels have been largely taken for granted and … assessed to be beyond systematic comprehension…..We do not have any viable … theory that anticipates how individuals will vary in response to varying macro inputs or how the structures and policies of macro collectivities might be undermined, redirected, sustained, or otherwise affected by new patterns at the micro level. (p. 23)

As nation-states enact and attempt to respond to national and global dynamics, they are themselves transformed in the process through responses and actions at every level. However, this is not a uniform process. Local conditions intersect with national and international agendas and pressures, resulting at times in great inequalities for those who live within and between nation-states. The looming question on the horizon is if nation-states and the transnational institutions that interact with them will actually implement wide reaching mechanisms to stem these growing inequalities – or if, conversely, local, national, and global resistance movements will be able to quell and redirect the activities of the nation-state to care for its most vulnerable populations.

8.7   Growing Inequalities and the Role of the Nation-State

As we have seen, a growing group of analysts interrelate the restructuring of welfare states to the globalization of production and investments. In fact, Castells (2004) states that,

> In an economy whose core markets for capital, goods and services are increasingly integrated on a global scale, there seems to be little room for vastly different welfare states, with relatively similar levels of labor productivity and production quality. Only a global social contract (reducing the gap without necessarily equalizing social and working conditions), linked to international tariff agreements, could avoid the demise of the most generous welfare states. Yet because in the newly liberalized, networked, global economy such a far-reaching social contract is unlikely, welfare states are being downsized to the lowest common denominator… (p. 314)

Some scholars even predict that nothing is currently preventing our global society from moving into what they refer to as a three tier social structure which is composed of the following levels:

The first tier is made of some 30–40% of the population in core countries and less in peripheral countries, those who hold 'tenured' employment in the global economy and are able to maintain, and even expand, their consumption. The second tier, some 30% in the core and 20–30% in the periphery, form a growing army of 'casualized' workers who face chronic insecurity in the conditions of their employment and the absence of any collective insurance against risk previously secured by the welfare state. The third tier, some 30% of the population in the core capitalist countries, and some 50% or more in peripheral countries, represent those structurally excluded from productive activity and completely unprotected with the dismantling of welfare and developmental states, the 'superfluous' populations of global capitalism, (Hoogvelt 1997 in Polivka 2001).[11]

What we find is that despite the growing poverty and inequality among and within certain countries and populations in the world, the dominance of the global economy has not generated much substantive action to circumvent negative effects of neoliberal globalization.[12] In particular, the poorest developing countries have often been ignored or treated with condescension, with little regard for the socio-historical and political and economic factors that have contributed to their current condition.[13] Given these circumstances, it is not surprising that critics of neoliberalism have, most often, come themselves from developing countries. They point out that there has been little discussion about implementing mechanisms of state intervention and less ideologically driven approaches to privatization and minimalization of the private sector (Polivka 2001). Even though there is some interest in regulating the global movement of finance capital, and lessening the extreme poverty of developing countries, we still have a situation of mounting inequalities.[14] If the welfare state is declining, as is argued by many, then what we need is a new vision for an innovative path forward, for nation-states both in the industrial and developing world. Despite its flaws, the welfare-state provides a fundamental safety net for its citizens, and, especially, its most vulnerable populations. In the context of growing inequalities, the concern arises about the kind of measures that would provide at least some security for our world's most susceptible inhabitants.

Pyle and Ward (2003), however, question the whole notion that governments seek to protect the rights of all of its citizens by focusing on the issue of women's employment in the developing world. They ask if it is really feasible to create

---

[11] Polivka (2001) cites a Human Development Report (1999) that points out that the world's top three billionaires together have assets that are greater than the GNP of *all* least developed countries and their combined 600 million inhabitants. The same report also states that by the late 1990s, the poorest fifth of the global population had 1% of the world GDP in comparison to the top fifth, which had 86%.

[12] There is much debate in the academic literature on this topic, specifically among sociologists. However, this debate has had marginal effects on actual social policies. That becomes particularly obvious around issues such as reproductive labor or the rights of migrating noncitizens.

[13] It is striking the extent to which discussions about colonialism and its after-effects have been relegated completely to the sidelines in mainstream discourse at this point.

[14] Under growing pressure, the IMF and World Bank have begun to institute measures to raise the standard of living for citizens of the poorest of the developing countries. However many of these initiatives are criticized due to their over reliance on Western ideas, which may actually have detrimental effects in local contexts. See Kingfisher (2002) for a wide ranging set of examples.

gender blind economic and social policies when states adhere to a firmly entrenched neoliberal agenda. Instead, in the developing world, governments seek to maximize favorable conditions that attract multinationals and their subcontracting networks. For the most part, governments have not concerned themselves with issues such as women's reproductive labor, or the increasing role of women in production, domestic and sex work, since the money that flows from these channels provides an important source of revenue for some of the poorest sectors of their societies. I would add to this analysis from a gendered perspective, that as this is women's work and thus subsumed under a "less" important category, it is most likely not seen as a "critical" issue to be dealt with. What we find is a situation where "… given the international political economy, the very institution women might seek assistance from in combating the problems of work in these sectors (i.e., their own government) has vested interests in the existence of these industries." (Pyle and Ward 2003, p. 478).

In our current situation, women and other vulnerable populations are caught between the interests of the nation-state and multinationals, each of which is trying to maximize its profits through the labor and exploitation of the least advantaged in their sphere of influence. The degrees to which this occurs differ within and between societies; however, the trend seems to be clear. While individuals *and* nation-states negotiate, resist, and cooperate with globalizing forces, depending on their particular set of circumstances, the upwards spiraling trend of growing inequalities raises immense concerns about the position of individuals and families in the current context, as well as in future.

8.8   Agency and the Contemporary Nation-State

Before concluding this discussion, it is instructive to examine one more aspect of neoliberalism and its relationship to the policies and strategies of nation-states. Nation-states are not homogenous entities that respond in the same manner to global conditions. Nation-states, themselves, exercise a certain agency based on both internal and external conditions. Thus, when we speak of neoliberalism and the nation-state, we need to clarify exactly which entity we are speaking about and at what level.

Gupta and Sharma (2006) raise the point that the legitimacy and authority of states are dependent on an enormous amount of cultural work devoted to creating a coherent unified picture of who and what a state is. Much of this work is done through the everyday practices of state bureaucracies. Through this work, the state becomes an integral and legitimized force in its citizens' lives (Gupta and Sharma 2006). From a different perspective, the state is a multilayered and conflicted entity. What constitutes a policy agenda at the national level may be understood and implemented quite differently at the local level. By viewing states as multileveled and multi-sited, it becomes easier to understand their contemporary transnational nature.

Throughout history, national policies and programs have resulted from the convergence of transnational ideologies and agendas. Gupta and Sharma (2006) point out, for example, that contemporary programs in India that stress empowerment are the direct result of global concerns with feminism and the role of women. What we find is an articulation of the spread of a global ideology with practical applications on the ground, so to speak. However, while in the Western case, neoliberalism is perceived as a sequential process, neoliberal policies replace welfare programs; in the case of developing nations, this may not be the case. For example, in India, empowerment initiatives have been accompanied by efforts to assist those who are the neediest in society. This kind of action on behalf of a state can be explained by its need to legitimize itself. As the global economy draws in certain groups of individuals, it also leaves behind large groups of people who do not have the skills or the services that are needed in that environment. Thus, there is pressure on certain governments, such as in India, to intervene on behalf of those who are left behind. These kinds of welfare-like programs serve to legitimize the government. While neoliberal ideology supports cutting back on government programs, in the Indian case, neoliberalism has been accompanied by an expansion of certain types of services, specifically for women. The Indian case serves as an example that we cannot conjecture about universal outcomes based on models that are only focused on the Western or industrialized world. Ideologies may span the globe, but they are articulated in local places in specific fashions.

8.9 What Should be Next Steps?

While the growing recognition that current nation-state policies have significant impacts on the worldwide spread of the poverty of households, and specifically women, children, and other vulnerable populations, disentangling the multilevel effects of macropolicy changes is complex work (Marcus et al. 2002). For example, the large-scale statistics and procedures that are often employed to test the impacts and outcomes of certain initiatives may actually produce conflicting results. Numerical outputs may not accurately reflect lived circumstances. What is often not measured in human development research is the actual effect, for example, of household poverty on various members of the same family. Men, women, boys, and girls may suffer very different consequences from poverty within the same family, but these disparities are usually lost through aggregate statistics. Variations within, and even between households, depend on a complex array of social, economic, cultural and political factors including the relationship of gender and the labor force, access to credit markets, and legal rights with respect to owning land and inheritance rights, as well as socio-cultural norms and values (Ansell 2005).

As we have seen, macro-nation-state policies can profoundly impact the well-being of citizens and their families. For example, women and children may be faced with an excessive work burden through the restructuring of wages and employment opportunities (Waddington 2004). A further, often unaccounted for consequence, is the impact of work on care roles and care work. Women struggle in both industrialized and developing countries with balancing their domestic and labor force responsibilities. The contexts may be very different, but to a certain extent, the tasks are not.[15] Families are also affected by market forces through changes in the prices of goods and services. In particular, nutritional, educational, and health care needs of family members may suffer through inflation or the devaluing of wages. And as we have discussed, nation-state and transnational policies can result in severe cuts of social services. The consequences for families can be devastating and can lead to even further work strain, as low-income women, in particular, attempt to make up for these shortfalls.

For the contemporary nation-state in both the industrialized as well as the developing world, the most pressing social problems revolve around the fact that as technological change weakens the role of low-skilled workers, the poor and the young become the most vulnerable members of the workforce. Further, for virtually every country, population aging is about to change the traditional balance between generations. As fertility continues to decline in many industrialized countries, and workers are forced to delay entry into the workforce as well as enter into early retirement, low overall employment is leading to a whole host of economic and labor force issues (Esping-Andersen 2000). These changes in the labor force are coupled with a decline in state support for economic and health provision for the citizens of most nation-states (Estes 2006). We currently have a situation wherein globalizing influences that became increasingly pervasive throughout the 1990s and 2000s have exacerbated inequalities across geographic, gender, class, and generational lines.

In order to begin to tackle the problems promulgated by globalizing forces in conjunction with nation-states, Pyle (2005) suggests some useful next steps for policymakers and scholars: one, we need critical analyses of market ideology and discourse, and we need to illustrate that market processes are shaped by large powerful institutions which base much of their policy on the desire for profit; two, we need development policies that encourage indigenous development that employs both men and women rather than encouraging just export oriented development, and we need to recognize and find solutions for the fact that these are gendered processes; three, we need to force multinationals and their subcontracting networks to institute policies and procedures that protect workers' rights; and four, we need to strengthen international organizations that are concerned with human-based development. By implementing this multilevel strategy, we will be able to initiate a new and different dialogue and bring actual, positive change into individuals' lives.

In certain sectors, the ethical implications of the growing inequality between industrialized and developing countries are beginning to be taken more seriously.

---

[15] I do not mean to imply here that women in the industrialized and developing world have the "same" tasks or circumstances, only that women in both regions are still principally responsible for the care domain of their households, be it child or elder care.

Those analysts concerned with issues of global social justice suggest taking a Rawlsian perspective that individuals rather than nations or peoples or families should be considered as the crucial unit. From this point of view, a social justice approach, rather than a neoliberal perspective, creates the foundation for relationships between societies (Polivka 2001). This suggestion has even been extended to suggest that tolerance should only be given to societies that do not violate basic human rights and that live in peace with their neighbors. Of course, that raises a whole other spectrum of issues, too complex to be dealt with in this discussion, but at least it does provide one model or vision for a path forward in our ever accelerating and interconnected world. Polivka (2001) recommends that in order to reduce global inequalities, we need to include "commitments for long-term aid and development, extensive debt relief and greater involvement of developing countries in the governance of international agencies in exchange for enforceable labor rights and environmental standards in all countries" (p. 162).

From a somewhat different vantage point, Esping-Andersen (2000) suggests a wider implementation of the Scandinavian welfare model. In particular, Esping-Andersen encourages universalizing the dual-earner household, which in the Scandinavian context has translated into a reduction in poverty while raising families' consumption of services. Universalizing the dual-earner household creates jobs and provides services and financial incentives for working women to have children. It also moves us away from the patriarchal breadwinner/homemaker model of the family that undergirds social policy in both the industrialized and developing world. From this perspective, the costs of domestic services come out of a public budget instead of a household budget, creating long-term safety nets for families and, thus, decreasing social vulnerability and risk. It is important to note here that the Scandinavian countries are the only societies without the alarming rates of female-headed households in poverty that are on the rise everywhere else. Esping-Andersen (2000) also raises an important point that is not always dealt with in utopian notions of socially just societies: he points out that the notion of egalitarian wages and labor market regulation are not really universally applicable. Since egalitarian wages have not taken hold in the industrialized world, and he predicts, will probably never really be instituted in most societies, then maybe inequality needs to be reframed in a new manner.

> One way to think of a win-win strategy is to recall Schumpeter's famous analogy of the autobus: always full of people, but always different people. Low wages, unpleasant work, and even poverty are not necessarily diswelfare if there is a guarantee against entrapment. If people are mobile and exit at the next bus stop, low-end jobs will have no consequences for overall life chances. The welfare state as we know it assumed that the labor market would provide well-paid (but not necessarily enjoyable) jobs for all. It put its faith in simple human capital theory and delegated the responsibility of life chances to basic education and to the labor market. This assumption is anachronistic in a postindustrial labor market that is subject to very rapid technological change and can promise full employment only if we accept a mass of low-end (and low-productivity) service jobs. (Esping-Andersen 2000, p. 10)

To build on this analogy, if unequal jobs and pay are combined with training and educational opportunities, then we would have a situation where low-wage labor can actually lead to opportunities. If nation-states were to institute policies that have a stronger social justice underpinning, we would begin to see some of the rampant inequalities that are currently characterizing so many societies around the world, begin to be controlled. In the long run, controlling run-away inequality would lead to more peaceful conditions within and between societies. Technological change offers us the opportunity to build on those ideas. Technology, today, can be harnessed in previously unimagined ways, to link individuals and opportunities. Nation-states and the transnational institutions they interact with could play an instrumental role in furthering some of these ideas.

Chapter 9
Debates Around Globalization, Poverty, and Inequality

Poverty and inequality lie at the heart of the controversy around globalization. Specifically, global economic integration is often perceived as widening the divide between poorer and richer countries, families, and individuals. Sen (2002) suggests that the main intent of the "anti-globalization" movement, which is itself a highly global form of organizing, is not globalization per se, but the perceived growing economic disparities that seem to stem from globalizing processes. While there is immense debate over poverty measurement and the actual number of individuals and families that live below certain standards, there is no disputing that poverty and inequality continue to impact the lives of millions around the globe. Moreover, in today's world, visual images of poverty *and* wealth spread more easily and faster than ever before. This influences assessments of the material and ideological circumstances of external observers, as well as by the individuals of concern themselves.

It is difficult to draw conclusions about the actual effects of globalization on poverty and inequality, because the process itself is not just based on unbiased market forces or technological advancements. Instead, globalization occurs in specific contexts and is influenced by national and transnational policies. Nissanke and Thorbecke (2005) argue that, "despite the utmost importance of understanding the globalization-poverty nexus, the precise nature of the various mechanisms, whereby the on-going process of globalization has altered the pattern of income distribution, and the conditions facing the world's poor are yet to be carefully analyzed. This is because the globalization-poverty relationship is complex and heterogeneous, involving multifaceted channels. It is highly probable that globalization-poverty relationships may be nonlinear in many aspects, involving several threshold effects" (p. 3). Ravallion (2003) also calls attention to the fact that the "starting point" for many countries differs with respect to their initial level of economic development, making it difficult to generalize across countries and regions.

The controversial and intense nature of globalization-poverty debates have not gone unnoticed. In fact, some analysts such as Aisbett (2007)) suggest that interpretations of facts and figures are actually more indicative of personal value systems, with respect to globalization, than anything else. Ravallion (2003) even points out that some of the most popular and opinionated books on the relationship between globalization and poverty do not have any empirical proof that "would

B.S. Trask, *Globalization and Families*: *Accelerated Systemic Social Change*,
DOI 10.1007/978-0-387-88285-7_9, © Springer Science+Business Media, LLC 2010

allow one to identify the roles played by greater openness to external trade (as one aspect of globalization) in the distributional changes observed, as against other factors such as rising agricultural productivity, demographic factors, changes in the distribution and returns to education, and internal policy reforms" (p. 749).

9.1 What and How is Poverty Determined?

In order to lay out the parameters of the debate, it is essential to clarify what is meant by poverty. Without entering in detail into the disagreements about exact definitions of poverty, for the purpose of this discussion, it is sufficient to delineate poverty as the context within which an individual cannot attain adequate living standards to meet his or her needs (Santarelli and Figini 2002). A minimal living standard refers to consumption, the lowest possible income necessary for basic consumption and service needs, or the value of the household's own production. In contrast to poverty, inequality is a relational concept positing disparities in living levels between individuals or groups.

Poverty is the outcome of a diverse set of economic, political, social, and environmental conditions that differ greatly from place to place. Because of the complexity of the concept, most poverty debates focus primarily on income and/or consumption levels to determine who is poor. Income is thought to represent a dependable proxy for determining sufficient levels of consumption, particularly in between nation comparisons. Within country, poverty is primarily understood to stem from the average level of income combined with the degree of inequality in its distribution (Santarelli and Figini 2002). In order to make their case that globalization has either contributed to growing poverty and inequality around the world, or, conversely, that globalization is a positive force in the lives of most of the world's citizens, both sides of this contentious debate have relied on "their favorite poverty numbers" (Ravallion 2003, p. 749). Complicating the assessment of poverty is the fact that, almost universally, poverty is measured through the delineation of a poverty line. A relative poverty line is determined by computing the average income of a population annually, while an absolute poverty line refers to the amount of money that is necessary to access a certain set of goods and services.[1]

Once the poverty line has been determined, data are gathered to approximate how many individuals live below this standard. Over the last two decades, expanded information gathering techniques and surveys are increasingly being employed that measure income and consumption at the household level. These surveys now provide the data for global calculations of poverty. Nonetheless, the determination of poverty is still riddled with methodological issues. Ravallion (2003) points out that there are multiple concerns with an over reliance on these surveys. For example, some surveys focus on income to measure poverty status, and others emphasize

---

[1] The value of goods and services are updated every year to take into account changes in cost.

consumption, making the data not comparable. Moreover, even in well designed, nationally representative surveys, household inequalities and the potential for risk to individual's livelihoods are usually not measured.[2] Santarelli and Figini (2002) also suggest that the wealthiest individuals and households in many countries under-report their incomes in surveys, leading to an underestimation of income inequalities and relative poverty.

Complicating the issue of measurement techniques is the fact that there are vast differences in how the poverty line is determined, within countries, as well as between countries. For example, wealthier countries often have higher poverty lines as they base what is deemed as "acceptable" on the level of income and standard of living that is the norm in their particular region at a specific point of time. As that level shifts upward, so does the poverty line. In poorer countries, absolute consumption is usually considered the primary standard. Thus, the poverty line shifts with consumption (Ravallion 2003.

A country's poverty line is thought to equal the least amount of income or consumption that is needed to meet basic living requirements. The World Bank has estimated poverty lines at $1 and $2 a day for the lowest income countries.[3] These measures are used as a comparative point between countries in order to determine policies. However, the World Bank's application of the $1 per day and $2 per day poverty lines are often criticized as random and inaccurate measures of worldwide poverty. For example, analysis of these measures indicates that since 1981 the number of individuals living below $1 has fallen by about 400 million. This represents an approximate reduction in poverty by about 50%. With respect to the world population, these figures translate into a drop in poverty from 33% down to 18%. However, these calculations are less impressive when the total number of individuals is revealed: between 1981 and 2001 the number of poor individuals dropped from 1.5 billion in 1981 to 1.1 billion (Chen and Ravallion 2004). During the same period, between 1981 and 2001, the amount of individuals surviving on $1 to $2 per day escalated from about 1 billion to 1.6 billion. We are, thus, looking at a combined total of 2.7 *billion* individuals around the world who are surviving on less than $2 per day. These are the people who become most vulnerable in times of economic crisis.

These poverty figures have led to two major arguments: one, should poverty be determined by measuring the percentage of individuals who are poor (also known as the incidence) or, the actual number of individuals who are poor; and two, which poverty line, relative or absolute, should be applied in calculating poverty. In terms of the first issue, with respect to measurement, the numerical figures indicate that over the last two decades the incidence of poverty (the proportion) has declined. However, when one factors in the second determinant, in terms of which poverty line is assigned, the absolute number of individuals in poverty has risen.

---

[2] Ravallion (2003) suggests that national datasets are often inaccurate because the rich under-report their incomes.

[3] The $1 a day figure actually translates into $1.08 and $2 equals $2.16 in 1993 purchasing power parity dollars. See Harrison (2007) for a more extensive explanation.

This is witnessed in the numbers presented above, that the number of people surviving on less than a dollar per day declined over the 1980s and 1990s; however, the number of people living on a dollar, or between a dollar and two dollars, has not (Harrison 2007).

Another compounding factor in the controversies around measurement is the role that the growing economies of China and India play in the globalization arena. For example, Wade (2004) suggests that it is possible that the global proportion of individuals living in poverty has fallen due to increases in the standards of living in China and India, in combination with growth in the world wide population. In response to various analyses of World Bank figures, he argues that "the magnitude of world population increase over the past 20 years is so large that the [World] Bank's poverty numbers would have to be *huge* underestimates for the world poverty rate not to have fallen. Any more precise statement about the absolute number of the world's people living in extreme poverty and the change over time currently rests on quicksand" (Wade 2004, p. 574). Chen and Ravallion's analyses concur, illustrating that the determination of poverty numbers is dependent not just on aggregate calculations, but on region as well. For example, they point out that when China is removed from the calculations, the number of individuals living in poverty (defined at $1 per day) remains virtually the same as 20 years ago, or may even be a bit higher (2004). Moreover, they illustrate that while the number of individuals living in poverty in Asia is declining, the number of poor in Africa is rising steadily. Also troubling, is the fact that poverty in Africa is markedly deeper than in other parts of the world, highlighting the fact that poverty is the outcome of a series of interrelated complex factors.

9.2 Inequality Between and Within Societies

While progress toward worldwide poverty reduction has been uneven, analyses indicate that, at least extreme poverty may have declined somewhat globally, over the last 25 years. This finding is accompanied by compelling evidence that the benefits of globalization have been distributed unevenly among various players. As poverty and measurement are disputed and redefined, inequality and the overall distribution of income are increasingly viewed as equally important elements in these analyses. However, different measures of globalization are also connected to different understandings of poverty and inequality. To determine if globalization is good or bad for the poor, it is now understood that that depends on what qualities of globalization are measured. For example, proglobalization analysts and policymakers highlight foreign investment and measures of export activity, while critics of globalization point to the removal of market protections as exacerbating poverty (Harrison 2007). In order to bolster their case, critics of globalization may also incorporate the absolute number of people in poverty into their argument, while the proglobalizationists rely, instead, on the percentage of individuals in poverty. Much of this argumentation is connected to questions around the spread of neoliberal economic ideologies and philosophies, and the value orientations of analysts and policymakers.

According to neoliberalist perspectives, we are increasingly moving into a world characterized by greater equal income distribution and declining poverty. From this view point, economic integration between countries has led to a better utilization of resources on a global level, as countries specialize and produce those items that they are in a particularly advantageous position to generate. They argue that the breakdown of the Bretton Woods monetary system in the early 1970s, coupled with the processes of globalization since then, have worked to improve the standard of living for most of the world's population. In order to assist those remaining less developed countries that have not been able to keep up, especially countries in Africa, greater integration into the world economy through increased trade deregulation and more open financial markets will reverse their financial situation (Wade 2004). According to neoliberal economists, as markets open up, their societies prosper, and this experience leads to a greater progress. From this perspective, we are in the midst of a greater leveling out of economic inequalities between developing and industrialized countries than ever before. Proglobalizationists suggest that the World Trade Organization, the International Monetary Fund, and other such transnational economic organizations are intermediaries in creating a more equitable arena, unfettered by nation–state controls on markets. Subscribers to the neoliberal perspective are also the "major" players in this arena, and include the U.S., the U.K., the World Bank, the International Monetary Fund and a group of prominent economists.

Critics of neoliberalism and globalization favor a different interpretation of current events. They advocate that the most powerful and wealthiest countries and individuals have little, if any, interest in reducing global poverty and inequality. This group suggests that global poverty, despair, and inequalities are mounting rapidly due to the forces of globalization. They advocate greater restrictions on markets and the intervention of nation–states. Aisbett (2007) explains that critics of globalization are not against globalization per se, but instead are concerned with the current process and the direction that globalization is taking, particularly in certain instances. These critics of globalization argue that by giving nation–states some leeway, governments will, on their own, implement social and environmental policies that are particularly appropriate to their local circumstances.[4]

Ravallion (2004) suggests that all of these different perspectives on poverty and inequality relate to varied value systems. Thus, globalization advocates focus on aggregate statistics while globalization critics focus more on what he terms "vertical inequality" (p. 4). Meanwhile, Basu (2006) points out that while both sides of the debate may be correct, the staggering inequality between countries and

---

[4] Aisbett (2007) summarizes the consensus between globalization advocates and critics. She points out that there is agreement that trade is equated with growth; that growth tends assist the poor; that government policies can buffer negative effects; that poverty should be correlated with education and health, in addition to income; and that political reform is key to positive development.

individuals is obvious and does not need to be disputed. He highlights the great disparity, even with purchasing power parity corrections, between the richest (in terms of per capita) country Norway (at $43,400) when compared to the poorest one, a tie held between Burundi and Ethiopia (at $90.00). On the basis of these figures, an individual living in Norway may be 60 times wealthier than one living in Burundi. Of course, these broad statistical representations gloss over within country inequalities; however, they still reveal the enormous inequities between regions and people. They also raise, from a purely humane and moral perspective, the question of how we can allow this situation to exist, and as some argue, to worsen.

Any discussion of inequality is, however, again skewed by the incorporation of the poverty statistics from China and India. China and India currently account for about 38% of the global population. The statistical inclusion of their rapid economic growth has contributed to several large scale analyses and conclusions that world poverty and inequality have been declining over the last couple of decades.[5] However, complicating these assessments is that while Chinese and Indian growth statistics counteract a reduction in global income inequality, growing inequality *within* their societies is not accounted for in these appraisals (Wade 2004).[6] It is significant to note that the industrialized countries of the West have also witnessed a growth in income inequality. For example, in the U.S., during the period between 1979 and 1997, the income of the uppermost tier of families, in the top percentile, grew almost 160%. These statistics point to economic processes tied to uneven redistribution schemas. We may not be measuring the phenomena accurately, but we do know that there are individuals and families who are much worse off than others within the same society, and that the same stark differences exist between regions.

9.3   What are the Linkages Between Globalization, Poverty, and Inequality?

An examination of poverty and inequality figures raises complicated issues with respect to globalization. In particular, it begs the question if disparities between individuals, families, and societies are really indicative of forces associated with globalization, or might they reflect other interrelated factors. For many, this discussion is so contentious that it serves as a judgment on globalization itself. However, Basu (2006) suggests, it is useless to attempt to simplistically explain the effects of a complex phenomenon such as globalization. He points out that from a more long term perspective inequality between regions has grown over the last 500 years. In the past, richer countries were better off than poorer places by a proportion of 1.8. Today, in contrast, the wealthiest regions have a per capita income that is about 20

---

[5] See Wade (2004) for a discussion of the various factors that make global statistical comparisons exceedingly inaccurate.

[6] Wade (2004) points out that income inequality in China is greater today than before the Communists took over in 1949.

times that of less well off places. The growth in inequality can, thus, be argued to be part of a long term historical trend that is not necessarily tied to globalization processes. However, what is new and different in the current phase of the evolution of our global society is that developing countries are becoming economically and socially integrated with industrialized countries. This integration is occurring, in part, through technological advances in information, communication, and transport technologies, as well as policy changes. The most distinctive aspect of recent globalizing processes has been the move on the part of some developing nations in Latin America, South Asia, and Sub-Saharan Africa to shift from inward-focused development strategies to more outward oriented processes (Dollar 2005). It is precisely this shift which is under dispute, as it is unclear if local populations have gained or lost in the process. Moreover, particularly controversial are the circumstances under which these transformations have taken place (i.e., their voluntary or coerced nature). Questions abound around what kind of policies and programs allow for an integration of local economies and individuals into the global marketplace, with minimal disruption and maximal gains.

While without a doubt, certain areas of the world have grown and profited economically through current processes, it is more debatable if this growth has been distributed in an equitable manner (Rudra 2008). Moreover, even though policies that promote economic growth are often highlighted as the solution to reducing poverty, Ravallion (2003) points out that economic growth is often accompanied by within country inequality leading to localized concerns and problems. Nissanke and Thorbecke (2005) explain that while it is possible that poor individuals will ultimately profit from growth conditions, poverty reduction relies on the extent to which growth affects income allocation. As they suggest, "Inequality is the filter between growth and poverty reduction." (p. 4). Growth, on its own, does not necessarily imply that equality or parity will be achieved within or between countries. Consequently, when inequality rises, poor individuals, families, and countries do not benefit or can even be harmed by the growth process.

Nissanke and Thorbecke (2005) examine the proposition that when developing countries with a large unskilled labor force, move into export production, they experience a decline in income inequality through an increased demand for unskilled labor. This proposition is usually accompanied by the assumption that the wages of unskilled labor in industrialized countries become less equivalent in the process. Data indicates, however, that wage disparities between skilled and unskilled labor are growing throughout most developing countries, specifically in Latin America and Africa (Nissanke & Thorbecke 2005). The explanation for this phenomenon can again be found in the very processes of globalization. As technological innovations advance, production necessitates skilled labor, which if often in undersupply in developing nations. Conversely, technological developments often emerge as a replacement for unskilled labor, adding to inequalities in both developed and developing countries. This phenomenon coupled with the migration of skilled individuals *out* of the developing world, and to industrialized countries, leads to the possibility of greater income equality in those societies, while contributing to greater inequality in poorer areas.

Increasing inequality and/or poverty raise a range of moral and social concerns. When one group or region is considerably worse off than another, what are the implications of these circumstances and do they affect the larger social fabric? Wade (2004) forcibly argues that, "Higher income inequality within countries goes with: (1) higher poverty (using World Bank data and the number of people below the Bank's international poverty line); (2) slower economic growth, especially in large countries such as China, because it constrains the growth of mass demand; (3) higher unemployment; and (4) higher crime. The link to higher crime comes through the inability of unskilled men in high inequality societies to play traditional male economic and social roles, including a plausible contribution to family income. But higher crime and violence is only the tip of a distribution of social relationships skewed toward the aggressive end of the spectrum, with low average levels of trust and social capital. In short, inequality at the national level should certainly be a target of public policy, even if just for the sake of the prosperous" (p. 582).

Wade also points out that in a globalized world, income inequalities within countries affect world demand between countries, creating a "vicious circle of rising world inequality and slower world growth" (p. 582). In other words, inequality within and between countries prejudices poorer citizens to become resentful toward their elites and wealthier countries. These sentiments tend to be accompanied by social unrest, ultimately leading to deteriorating living conditions for all citizens.

9.4 Local Responses to Globalizing Conditions

In the current global scenario, as between country inequalities rise, they are also accompanied by rising foreign exchange costs for imports and debt repayment. This, in turn, strains the economies of nation–states and leads to reductions in public services and a poorer quality of life for the populace. These cycles fuel internal changes such as migration patterns, as those lesser off individuals seek better financial and educational opportunities in more well-to-do regions and societies. For nation–states in the developing world, this process takes place at the two ends of the social spectrum: highly educated individuals attempt to migrate to those places where they will find better opportunities, and unskilled laborers either move to urban areas or attempt to gain admittance to more well-to-do countries, even if this entails illegal measures. Mass rural-urban migrations and the loss of highly skilled labor represent enormous internal pressures and, potentially, the loss of social capital for developing nations. Currently, in industrialized and developing societies, individuals living in urban areas often benefit from economic growth policies, while those in rural regions may not. This process leads to widening regional disparities and over time, results in increasingly detrimental conditions for the poor.

Ethnographic evidence from China underlines the importance of family strategies in response to growing rural-urban disparities. Contemporary circumstances now encourage men from rural areas to seek wage employment in nonagricultural sectors in urban or coastal regions, leaving women with children, middle aged women, and the elderly to tend to agricultural work. As officials set achievement levels in compliance with national and transnational regulations and recommendations, rural laborers are forced to work harder and yet often are not able to meet these levels. Moreover, much of this work occurs in increasingly hazardous environments. As their air and water becomes polluted and their land suffers massive land erosion, these conditions take a toll on workers' health. In another unanticipated consequence of globalization, these same workers now must ask for permission to move out of their hazardous environments, not just from Chinese government officials, but also from the transnational organizations and developers who have set the new work and poverty standards (Ping 2001). As this situation illustrates, family responses intersect with economic conditions and transnational policies with unexpected, and at times, deleterious, outcomes.

The Chinese example highlights the complexity of establishing programs and policies that rely on multiple sources of authority. For instance, the effects of globalization can be particularly detrimental to the rural poor, when developers and government officials institute "universal" levels, such as the dollar a day minimum poverty line without knowledge about local conditions. As Robinson (1998) explains, "As globalization erodes the linkages among territoriality, production, classes, and state power, the tendency for self-reproduction in the international division of labor is increasingly counterbalanced and undermined by diverse economic, political, and social globalizing dynamics. We can expect sustained class polarization and also continued uneven accumulation between regions or areas characterized by hierarchies and divisions of labor in which some zones are selected for global production activities, others assigned 'feeder' rows (e.g., labor or raw materials reserves), and still others marginalized entirely from the global economy (the so-called fourth world). But, there is no theoretical reason to posit any necessary affinity between continued uneven development and the nation–state as the particular territorial expression of uneven development. Witness, for example, seas of poverty and islands of wealth, and the breakdown of social infra-structure in any Northern city increasingly approximate to any Third World metropolis" (p. 580).

In other words, we cannot blame any single process or entity for evolving global conditions. It is incumbent on all involved parties to continue to explore which factors alleviate and benefit individuals, families and nation–states, and which ones become potentially harmful in local contexts. Moreover, nation–states need to take on new roles in order to regulate growing inequality and maintain stable social conditions and harmony among citizens (Rudra 2008).

9.5 What Can be Done?

The relationship between globalization and poverty is complex and not easily dissected or understood. Poverty and inequality are not just related to the trade or financial aspects of globalization, as is so often supposed, but instead are associated with the interaction of multiple elements in local environments (Harrison 2007). For instance, Rudra (2008) argues that in many developing nations, domestic institutions have historically not protected the poor, and the introduction of globalization has not necessarily changed this situation. While globalization may lead to the improvement of the lives of certain segments of a population, local conditions play an equivalently significant role.

Cross-cultural evidence indicates that the impacts of globalization are very context specific with respect to poverty. For instance, during periods of financial downturns, such as the devaluation of real wages after currency crises in Indonesia and Mexico, the poorest segments of society become most vulnerable (Harrison 2007). However, globalization can also be accompanied by new shared understandings that can be implemented in local environments. Insights into the underlying reasons why some areas of the world have profited from globalization, while other areas have not, need to be incorporated into policies that take local conditions into account, and build on the inherent strengths of specific populations and their environments.

The persistence of extensive poverty and growing global inequality has initiated much discussion about potential next steps and strategies. On the most fundamental analytical level, Robinson (1998) has suggested that "development and underdevelopment should be reconceived in terms of global social groups and not nations, in which core-periphery designates social position rather than geographic location" (p. 580). Other observers, such Rudra (2008), point to the continuing significant role of nation–states, and insist instead, that the key to poverty reduction is sound domestic policies. She makes the case that when nation–state policies have included investments in human capital and infrastructure, as well as a focus on mechanisms that encourage economic stabilization, the outcome has been more likely to lead to growth conditions and the reduction of poverty. Empirical studies indicate that a combination of transnational economic policies, in combination with carefully constructed national measures best constrain the harmful effects of globalization, while capitalizing on its advantages (Harrison 2007). For instance, the effects of globalization can be particularly hurtful to small, local farmers who cannot compete with powerful large scale agricultural enterprises or competition from imported goods. These agriculturalists would be protected from the potentially exploitative practices of large marketing chains, through a national and transnational coordination of legal rules and institutional arrangements.

Adding to the complexity of the situation, Nissanke and Thorbecke (2005) explain that it may disadvantage the poor when one country institutes environmental regulations while a competitor doesn't, leading to price differentials in production costs. This is the kind of predicament that if coordinated with foresight could harness globalization processes for the benefit of these vulnerable populations. For example, the coordination of environmental policies across regions would allow for safer working and living conditions, while not giving any group an unfair advantage. In a similar vein, when restrictions on exports from a developing country are imposed, poverty conditions in that region actually rise. In order for developing countries to profit from globalizing processes that encourage export production, transnational policies need to coordinate access for developing countries to the markets of developed countries. Some evidence indicates that poverty has been somewhat reduced in Mexico, India, Poland, and Colombia through the combination of exports and transnational and domestic policies (Harrison 2007).

Critics of globalization point out that poverty is a complex phenomenon, not just measurable by income (Aisbett 2007). Instead, access to health care and education, as well as illiteracy, sickness, absence of basic service provision, empowerment, participation, and vulnerability to economic shocks need to be considered as aspects of the poverty spectrum. As individuals experience differential access to social services, their opportunities may be enhanced or constrained. For individuals living in poverty, policies that allow them to attain better education and training, as well as basic service provision, alleviate the conditions in which they are mired (Harrison 2007). These types of policies can encourage and assist even the most vulnerable citizens to capitalize on the opportunities that are created through globalizing economic reforms. "Redressing the antecedent inequalities of opportunity within developing countries as they open up to external trade is crucial to realizing the poverty reducing *potential* of globalization" (Ravallion 2003, p. 753).

A less tangible outcome of globalization is that in contemporary studies of the poor, many more individuals feel vulnerable and worse off than in the past. This phenomenon has been explained through today's pervasive spread of images of wealth and lifestyles, not attainable to multitudes of individuals. Globalization has been accompanied by lifestyles and representation of standards of living that affect the perception of the poor and nearly poor about their own condition. Graham (2005) emphasizes that today it is not enough to measure poverty through income measures. Many individuals have new reference points about what is attainable, and may, thus, become more aware of the vulnerability and risk characteristic of their own lives. To circumvent such collective feelings of insecurity, she suggests that nation–states need to invest in social insurance for their most vulnerable citizens otherwise large cohorts will be harmed by globalization processes. The greatest protection for individuals would be the establishment of welfare state based on universalism. In these types of welfare states, every citizen has access to basic necessities and services to sustain a minimal living standard. However, Rudra (2008) suggests that there is no evidence that developing societies with large populations living in poverty are anywhere close to moving toward increasing welfare models. Moreover, even in those places where policies such as worker's insurance or forms of social security are instituted, certain groups continue to remain marginalized. The truly vulnerable populations remain the least beneficiaries of global processes and, in fact, may become the ones most at risk to suffer from downturns.

Chapter 10
Social Change, New Paradigms, and Implications for Families

Accelerated systemic social change is closely associated with globalization. I have argued throughout this work that conventional narratives that approach families, nation-states, or economies as limited static entities, no longer capture the rapid macro–micro interactions that are the fundamental basis of this change. Instead, valuable insight into contemporary social phenomena requires a transnational, dynamic approach that depicts the nature, consequences, and policy implications of these processes. As Robinson (1998) explains, "Social science should be less concerned with static snapshots of the momentary than with the dialect of historic *movement*, with capturing the central *dynamics* and *tendencies* in historic processes. The central dynamic of our epoch is globalization, and the central tendency is the *ascendance* of transnational capital, which brings with it the transnationalization of classes in general......Determinancy on the structural side is shifting to new transnational space that is eroding, subsuming, and superseding national space as the locus of social life, even though this social life is still 'filtered through' nation-state institutions. This situation underscores the *highly contradictory* nature of transnational relations as well as the *indeterminancy* of emergent transnational social structure." (p. 581). Robinson's observations draw attention to the need for new paradigms that allow us to capture the decentralization of power, the transnational nature of phenomena, and the rapidity and movement that are inherent features of contemporary social life.

The need for new approaches and paradigms is particularly acute for understanding contemporary social change with respect to families. As our world becomes increasingly interconnected through economic integration, technological and communication advances, and political transformations, the sphere of the family is a primary arena where globalizing processes are realized. Nonetheless, as has been discussed, observers and analysts of globalization, and of family life, have neglected this critical juncture for investigating contemporary social change. Despite a general acknowledgement of the complexities and social significance inherent in globalization, most analyses remain top-down, focused on the global economy, corporate strategies, and political streams. This limited perspective on globalization has had profound implications for understanding social life and social transformation.

B.S. Trask, *Globalization and Families*: *Accelerated Systemic Social Change*,
DOI 10.1007/978-0-387-88285-7_10, © Springer Science+Business Media, LLC 2010

The impact of globalization on gender ideologies, work-family relationships, conceptualizations of children, youth, and the elderly have been virtually absent in mainstream approaches, creating false impressions that dichotomize globalization as a separate process from the social order. Moreover, most approaches to globalization and social phenomena emphasize the Western experience. These perspectives assume that other parts of the world are probably undergoing similar processes and that ideologies tied to the valuing of individualistic behaviors and Western style family transformations, will soon be dominant around the world.[1] These unsubstantiated assumptions have profound implications for families, and for the globalization process itself. Any presumptions of trends and changes that are not empirically substantiated will lead to false conclusions and policy decisions. In order to create and implement programs and policies that can harness globalization for the good of mankind, and to reverse some of the deleterious effects that we have witnessed, especially with respect to the world's most vulnerable populations, we need to pay closer attention to the dynamic relationship between globalization and families. We also need to refocus our attention to the *global* arena, which implies that non-Western parts of the world play an important role in the globalization phenomenon.

10.1 The Realization of Globalization in the Family Domain

At a primary level, global and local forces are realized in the family domain. Virtually all individuals, in every part of the world, still make decisions in the context of relationships with close others, primarily those they consider family. They may reflect on choices and constraints privately, but the conclusion to move forward very rarely occurs in complete solitude. Instead, it is through debate, negotiation, and at times conflict that decisions are arrived at. Families serve as a mediating structure between globalizing forces and choices, and individual inclinations (Edgar 2004). For instance, Coontz (2000) suggests, "Understanding the specificity of social location and the importance of context does not necessarily produce the relativism that has been associated with some versions of 'postmodernist' theorizing. Rather, it directs our attention to the tension between the institutional or historical constraints under which people operate and the toolkit of personal, cultural, and social resources they use to make choices about how to adapt to or resist those constraints, along with the complex interactions that produce unanticipated outcomes to such choices." (p. 294).

From this perspective, globalization can be understood as having different meanings, consequences and challenges for families depending on their particular context.

---

[1] Interestingly, these are the same arguments that were put forward in a more explicit manner through modernization theory. Despite the fact that this type of evolutionary approach has been discounted in much of the academic literature, it reappears at times in new forms in the globalization literature with respect to social life.

According to Kellner (2002) "Consequently, it is important to present globalization as a strange amalgam of both homogenizing forces of sameness and uniformity *and* heterogeneity, difference, and hybridity, as well as a contradictory mixture of democratizing and antidemocratizing tendencies. On the one hand, globalization unfolds a process of standardization in which a globalized mass culture circulates the globe, creating sameness and homogeneity everywhere. On the other hand, globalized culture makes possible unique appropriations and development everywhere, thus encouraging hybridity, difference and heterogeneity to proliferate. Every local context involves its own appropriation and reworking of global products and signifiers, thus encouraging difference, otherness, diversity, and variety" (pp. 292–293). This standpoint allows us to understand why globalization has varied implications for families, and that the resources and constraints that arise through the process are mediated in the family context.

At the family level, choices and strategies are enacted that are concurrently governed by globalizing processes *and*, conversely, impact them. This construction of a particular version of global space and the role of families therein, allows us to understand globalization not just as an economic, political or social force. Instead, it highlights the fact that globalization is socially constructed. It is not an inevitable material process, but a multifaceted phenomenon both located in the local and superceding it (Nagar et al. 2002).

This vantage point emphasizes the role of agency in the process. As actors make choices, globalization, itself, is impacted and transformed. Moreover, a critical aspect of this process is that it is futuristic, determined by the constant acceleration of its effects. Castells (2000) has termed this time of globalization as a "technological revolution, centred around information, transform[ing] the way we think, we produce, we consume, we trade, we manage, we communicate, we live, we die, we make war, we make love…..Space and time, the material foundations of human experience, have been transformed, as the space of flows dominates the space of places" (p. 1).

10.2 Problematizing Static Concepts

Appadurai (1990) terms the dynamic perspective on the relationship between globalization and the social order as "scapes."[2] Scapes are associated with fluidity and global cultural flows, and the movement away from fixed locales or territories. Globalization is accompanied by a whole new way of perceiving social life, which highlights the need to create new ways of understanding the accelerated nature of social change. In the same vein, Albrow (1997), suggests that concepts of self,

---

[2] Appadurai (1990) identifies five different dimensions: ethnoscapes, the movement of individuals around the globe for reasons of leisure, work, and politics; mediascapes, the flow of media information, and technology; technoscapes, the flow of technology across borders; finanscapes, the flow of global capital; and ideoscapes, the flow of various political ideologies.

community, and culture are no longer clearly defined nor understood. While these concepts constituted an integral aspect of post-World War II social scientific thought, they are no longer valid due to the changes brought on by globalization. In today's context, communities, regions, and citizenship are redefined and fluid, not necessarily tied to fixed space or territory.

Traditionally, in the social sciences, community has been inextricably linked to locale. However Albrow (1997) and Carrington (2001) point out that a crucial recent change brought on by globalization is the shift from geographically defined communities with clearly demarcated borders and values, to abstract, imagined communities. For instance, until relatively recently, transnational migration primarily referred to the permanent move of individuals, families, and groups from one place to another. However, in the contemporary context, migration has morphed into a new phenomenon. Increasingly, individuals move to multiple locations for varying amounts of time and, yet, manage to retain ties to their community of origin, and the various places they may have settled in (Appadurai 1990; Castells 2000). This situation becomes magnified in family contexts as second generation children from a particular ethnic group may be connected in complex ways to the home country of their parents. Their multiple identities as citizens of the host country, as second generation immigrants from a certain society, and their parallel existence with non-immigrants of their same generation, are fashioned and negotiated in great part, across space through communication technologies. Carrington (2001) refers to these relationships as "imagined communities."

Imagined communities are centered around specific, constructed identities, rather than geographical location. From this perspective, homogenous static communities become an inadequate concept for understanding social life. Instead, the social order needs to be reconceptualized as consisting of individuals who participate simultaneously in multiple parallel communities that are in constant flux. This standpoint emphasizes the fluid and dynamic nature of social life, as individuals move across spatial, temporal, and cultural boundaries. Even individuals who adhere, or are forced to adhere to place-bound communities, may experience this dislocation as family members become involved in this form of movement. The fluidity of social life has even been extended to include individuals who travel from locale to locale or "globotourists" who, through their movements, become part of the globalization process (Carrington 2001).

This constant movement, or flow, problematizes static concepts of community and citizenship, and is accompanied by significant implications for conceptualizations of family. Dynamic reconceptualizations of the social order imply that families are not immune from this process. Instead, families themselves are a constantly renegotiated arrangement. As they move through their life cycles and their members make personal, economic, and social decisions, they are inextricably bound to the larger fluid processes in which they are embedded. Globalization provides an accelerated pace and new contexts within which families must make decisions and persevere. Nevertheless, it is again important to highlight that this globalizing context accompanied by constant movement does not imply a uniform evolutionary progression that affects families in a systematic manner, but instead, these developments influence families in a multitude of complex ways. As Robertson (1995) explains, "this is not a question of either homogenization or heterogenization, but rather of the ways in which both of these two tendencies have become features of life" (p. 27). Families are part of the social order *and* it is within their domain that the social order is, in part, created. Globalization plays an intrinsic role in this dynamic.

10.3   Globalization and Family Change

A comprehensive dynamic perspective on globalization allows us to conceptualize the world and its actors in a new manner. Nowhere is this more relevant than with respect to the microcosm of families. Whatever its configuration, for most individuals, families still remains a strategic arrangement that meet certain social, emotional, and economic needs. It is within families that decisions about work, care, movement, and identity are negotiated, contested, and resolved. Globalization has profound implications for how families assess choices and challenges. While social change is an inherent feature of social organization, globalization speeds up the process in an unprecedented manner. Globalizing forces spread opportunities, constraints and images pertaining to families, to increasing parts of the world. Thus, for instance in certain places in the industrialized *and* developing world, families are becoming less patriarchal, as more egalitarian and empowering gender ideologies spread through new communication and information technologies. These ideologies and representations have been accompanied by fundamental changes in the economies of contemporary nation-states, resulting in a worldwide infusion of women into the formal and informal labor force. This process, however, has not been a smooth transition, nor has it always been a particularly advantageous one for women or their families. Depending on their socioeconomic context, families may be faced with serious dilemmas around care work, employment, fertility, the dependency of children and/or elderly, and migration choices. Decisions around these issues are tied not only to economic concerns but also to gender ideologies and conceptualizations of family roles, duties, and obligations, which differ based on culture and context.

Some of the most dramatic globalizing effects within the family sphere revolve around household economics. For example, among the poor in industrialized and developing societies, the choice for women and children to work for pay outside of the home is best understood as a strategy for collective survival rather than as a path for individual advancement (Fernández-Kelly 1997). When economic times worsen, it is imperative that as many members of the household contribute to the family economy as is possible. Interestingly, from a structural perspective, this can result in greater family cohesion rather than fragmentation (Creed 2000). Individuals come together in family contexts in order to better their lot economically. In the contemporary situation, multiple streams of income, collected in the family domain, are often perceived as the most crucial strategy to ensure individual wellbeing. This element of family dynamics is usually not understood by Western scholarly approaches that view family processes through individualistic perspectives. By stressing the agency of individuals rather than collective decision making within a family context, some of the most important and complex aspects of the dynamics between globalization and social life are lost.

An unexpected outcome of the restructuring of economies in the industrialized and developing world has been the feminization of the labor force. In part, changes in the labor force have also resulted in more flexible, part-time, and informal types of work, which have been concurrently accompanied by a decline in full-time, permanent wage labor. These trends are associated with higher rates of women undertaking paid employment, lower rates of men in the labor force, lower real wages, and higher rates of unemployment (Safa 2002). Across the globe, economic pressures coupled with new ideologies about gender roles and relationships are increasingly accompanied by, at times, dramatic rearrangements of roles and relationships within families and societies The economic restructuring that is such an intrinsic aspect of globalization is slowly eroding the traditional gendered division of labor, that, at least ideologically, has been a fundamental aspect of family life, for so many societies around the globe. For example, Safa (2002) highlights the fact that in Japan, 70% of the 2.5 million individuals who have entered the paid, part-time labor force since 1995 are female. Today, 25% of these women are the main breadwinners in their families.

As more women take responsibility for the household budget, new questions arise around the viability of family models built on the dependency of women on men. There is much empirical evidence from around the world that as economic relationships between men and women change, so do marital bonds. Increasingly, these marital bonds are weakened, resulting in marital dissolution, and the rise of female-headed households (Safa 2002). Moreover, as women become economically independent and ideologically empowered to take care of themselves, traditional forms of marriage are becoming less appealing. In the West we see this, for example, in the increase in cohabitation and out-of-wedlock births. In other parts of the world, this trend is reflected in the rising age of marriage for women and the increasing frequency of divorce. Many women, if they have the opportunity, decide not to choose a life of dependency and obligation to others, such as is implied in the patriarchal family model. Instead, these women are actively trying to create new models of family life and relationships. However, these choices are not equally available to women worldwide. Instead, only women of a certain level of education and economic means are able to enact such personal choices. For millions of women, participation in the formal and informal labor force has not improved their lives. They now carry the double burden of working for pay and maintaining traditional care responsibilities. As Zimmerman et al. (2006) explain, "These same forces are reaching into the realm of gender relations and family life, reinforcing gender divides, and fragmenting families as grandmothers, mothers, wives, aunts, sisters and daughters enter into new and stressful dual roles as breadwinners and caregivers.... The economic growth behind globalization offers as much risk for exploitation as it does opportunity for advancement, especially for vulnerable women from developing countries." (p. 369).

Globalization has also had serious implications for men. As their power base has eroded through the loss of jobs and wages, the illusion that the breadwinner/provider role is inherently masculine, is dissipating. In certain segments of society in industrialized and developing countries, men are increasingly forced to rely on the women in their families for economic support. This has led in some cases to a restructuring of family life, with men assisting more with domestic duties. However, that has not been necessarily the norm. Instead, many men have reacted with hostility and resentment to what they perceive as the erosion of their basic rights. In some areas of the world, such as in some Middle Eastern and Latin American countries, these men are supported in their fears and anger, by growing national calls for a restoration of the "traditional" order. Families and the "appropriate" roles of men and women have become the rallying cry for symbolic representations of the ordered community that provides the "basis" for a stable society. Within these representations, gender roles, and especially the place of women in the family, become a pivotal aspect for reinstating order in an increasingly transformed world. These calls for "restoring" the social order have also found their way into the American mainstream discourse. Various political movements associate themselves with "family values" and recreating the "traditional" family domain, despite general acknowledgement that today's heterogeneous environment does lend itself to returning to this form of family life.

While patriarchal family structures have historically been legitimized through religious communities, governments, and other collective entities, in today's world, competing forces, encouraged and perpetuated through globalization, are counteracting entrenched ideologies with respect to gender roles. These representations and norms are slowly eroding and giving way to more diverse constructions of family. Particularly in the West, these new versions of families are accompanied by less prescriptive family roles that, at least ideologically, no longer relegate women as dependents and also weaken family hierarchies (Yan and Neal 2006). Observers of contemporary families remark that we live in a time when not one normative family arrangement prevails anymore (Stacey 1996). As the family domain grows ever more diverse and includes cohabiters with and without children, dual-earner couples, married couples without children, single-parent families, grandparents raising children, mixed race couples, and same-sex families, individuals are struggling to develop new blueprints for themselves with respect to norms, traditions and values. Nowhere is that more the case, than in the United States, where the growth in diverse family forms has also been accompanied by nostalgia for a mythical time when families were not faced with as much choice and variability.

In the contemporary globalized context, family members are taking on new or revised roles, as men lose their traditional provider position and children are increasingly encouraged to extend their period of dependency. As the patriarchal family model very slowly fades, children's voices become ever more significant in family decisions, with respect to their own lives and consumer behaviors. This situation, however, does not pertain to children the world over. Instead, for many children in the industrial and developing world, survival at any cost is their fate. For these children, the opportunities afforded through education, play, and consumerism that are so often the focus of child pedagogies and global legal movements, are irrelevant and unattainable. Their lives are subject to risk, and social and economic vulnerability.

The lives and positions of the elderly, too, are changing as individuals are living longer and are increasingly incorporated into the global order. Again, the differences are stark between those elderly whose resources allow them to enjoy a significant, enjoyable period of time at the end of the lifespan, and those who are faced with poverty and the lack of care. Globalization is inextricably tied to all of these processes as economic restructuring and nation-state policies become coupled with the pervasive spread of representations of varied lifestyles throughout the globe.

Whatever their social position, for many individuals across the globe, the exposure to a multitude of cultural models and normative experiences, is accompanied by stress and conflict, resulting at times in fractured relationships. Around the world, many contemporary families are different from the families in which individuals were raised. Without clear cultural blueprints and with an explosion of alternatives, many people lack certitude about which choices and paths will be optimal for them. While most family diversity, with respect to sexuality and living arrangements, remains confined to the West, representations of these new lifestyles and family forms are rapidly spreading to other parts of the world. And even in areas far removed from Western influence, women's market participation and family immigration decisions are creating new transnational family arrangements, often unprecedented in those communities and societies.

The increasing emergence of transnational mothering, for instance indicates that families are fundamentally adept at transforming themselves and adapting to new conditions. While, women who "mother" across distances, have to defend their choices in environments that advocate intensive mothering and close physical proximity to children, they nevertheless undertake the decision to seek employment in other places for the collective good of their families (Hondagneu-Sotelo 1997). Transnational mothering contradicts family models that assume that a basic aspect of families is a mother's relative physical proximity to her children. Instead, transnational mothers are attempting to provide the best possible opportunities for their children and their families through their economic contributions. Transnational mothering is just one of countless other examples that illustrate that social change is always closely related to economic and technological opportunities and innovations. In today's globalizing context, this same phenomenon continues to hold true with respect to family processes and relationships.

Globalization, thus, touches every individual and every family, albeit in a very diversified manner. The collective forces of globalization are the determinants of this process, which underscores the significance of holistic analyses. New phenomena are constantly arising that, at times, create virtually instantaneous social change. An illustrative example is provided by the unrecognized and pervasive problem of sexual harassment in the Middle East. While repressive regimes are attempting to maintain control through the enforcement of traditional values and norms, new technologies combined with spreading contradictory gender ideologies, are taking hold and being applied in an unprecedented manner. As blogging becomes an increasingly important forum through which young people can express concerns about their lives to each other and the rest of the world, the issue of sexual harassment, long ignored and minimized in Middle Eastern societies, is being exposed through social networking sites and other information technologies. This exposure is leading to public and legal social change, as men are increasingly arrested and punished for these forms of behavior.[3] Here we see the various forces of globalization coming together and resulting in significant social improvement for an oppressed group (women) that in the past has had great difficulty attaining a public voice. As individuals throughout the world continue to interact with each other in an unprecedented informational exchange, this global communication has great potential to address significant social concerns.

10.4 Gender, Globalization, and the Market

An investigation of the intersection of globalization with families brings to the forefront the complex and contentious social phenomenon of changing ideologies with respect to gender ideologies, norms and roles. Specifically, the spread of concepts of gender equality coupled with women's employment has resulted in unforeseen consequences. From a Western feminist perspective, as women work for pay, they may experience heightened decision-making power in their families, they may be able to become more autonomous actors, and they may be in a stronger position to take care of their families when faced with adversity (Ganguly-Scrase 2003). Recent work, however, illustrates that this is not the case for many women in the developing *and* industrialized world. In order for women to experience benefits from participating in the labor force, certain conditions and ideologies need to be in place that support this outcome. There are multiple examples in the scholarly literature (see for example, Gunewardena and Kingsolver 2007) where increased access to financial resources or incorporation into the global market have *not* brought about desired effects. What these divergent studies reveal is that generalizations about the effects of globalization on women, and conversely on men, must be approached cautiously (Beneria 2003).

A major contribution by feminist economists concerned with globalization has been their rendering of links to the market as being "historically different for men and women, with consequences for their preferences, choices, and behavior" (Beneria 2003, p. 74). Women tend to be disproportionally represented in unpaid production with this work only being indirectly linked to markets. Their unpaid and usually unacknowledged activities include agricultural work, especially on family farms, domestic work, child care, and volunteer activities. The continuation of the responsibilities of women for the domestic domain makes them economically vulnerable, and lessens their options with respect to participating in the labor force in the same manner as men. This phenomenon is prevalent, to a greater or lesser extent, across societies and social class.

---

[3] See the New York Times, December 10, 2008 for the story about the relationship between blogging and the eventual arrest of a male sexual harasser, the first such measure against harassment in Egyptian history.

Debate has also ensued on the relationship between export-oriented growth, women's wages and working conditions, and gender equality (Beneria 2003). The optimists contend that gender inequity is improving as wages become more equal, as access to jobs becomes more gender-neutral and educational achievement is on the rise. Those on the other side of the fence argue that as markets grow, gender inequalities remain, and are at times, exacerbated. They point out that economic growth is often fueled by taking advantage of women's cheaper labor, informal participation in the workforce, and their "flexibility." Again, as with all aspects of globalization, both processes seem to be ensuing concurrently.

Globalization has exaggerated the need to produce things at an increasingly more cost-effective or cheaper level. This need has had a profound effect on production, and, consequently, on the women who are involved in this process. Certain market sectors now prefer a female labor force. For example, Fussel (2000) has argued that in order to keep manufacturing costs low, multinational corporations in Tijuana, Mexico are increasingly relying on the low-wage, female work force. Today, gender norms and stereotypes define certain jobs and careers as "appropriate" for women specifically. Beyond the market place, gendered discourses construe women as more docile than men and "better suited" for repetitive tasks. These gender ideologies also legitimize the notion that women are less likely to organize into formidable political entities, and more willing to accept poor working conditions (Marchand and Runyan 2000). These conceptualizations illustrate that the social construction of gender can be utilized to advance market or corporate benefits in a covert manner.

Gender constructions and their accompanying expectations also come into play in circumstances where governments decrease programming and services in order to satisfy the demands of international lending institutions. As basic service provisions are reduced, it is consistently women who are expected to step in and take over these responsibilities. Thus the "feminization of labor" brought about by global restructuring does not just imply that there are large numbers of women working in the formal and informal labor force, but it also points to the "flexibility" of women's labor, which works to keep the costs of production and services down. Today, in both industrialized and developing countries, certain aspects of the labor force continue to be gendered – however, in many places financial responsibility for the maintenance of the family has now shifted from men to both women and men. For many women this has translated into increased work responsibilities in the paid labor force and at home, as they continue to engage in their traditional domestic responsibilities.

In the current situation, globalization has proven to be highly detrimental for certain groups of vulnerable women. Their subordinate gender status draws them into gendered types of employment where they are underpaid and at risk for exploitation. For many of these women, their work burden has increased. While these women used to combine subsistence work with reproductive labor due to the proximity of their work to their homes, today many of these women need to make complicated arrangements for their families while they work in the production sectors of their economies. Moreover, a new dimension has been added to these circumstances: in certain developing countries the expectation is growing that women will go abroad and send remittances back home. For low-skilled and poorer women, migration has become the vehicle to lift them and their families into a more stable financial future. This has translated specifically into a historically unprecedented international female migration.

In this discussion, it is critical to realize that globalization has been accompanied by constraints as well as by a multitude of opportunities for women. There are increasingly greater chances for education and training for women the world over. In the West, middle class women in particular, have benefited from the combination of access to education and employment combined with ideologies emphasizing the equality of the sexes with respect to opportunities. In less developed countries, transnational organization and some nation-states are increasingly concerned with the opportunity structure for girls and women and, thus, are instituting programs and policy changes that will allow them to attend school while taking domestic responsibilities into account. These change are not uniform, nor do the reach every disadvantaged population. However, their very presence promises that under appropriate conditions and through the mobilization of resources, positive transformation can be brought about specifically through globalizing forces.

While the relationship between gender, economics, and markets is quite well documented at this point, less well understood are the implications of women's participation in the formal and informal labor force with new conceptualizations of gender roles. As Beneria (2003) eloquently suggests "A nonessentialist view of gender differences implies that economic and social change are likely to influence gender (re)constructions and gender roles. As women become direct participants in the market, their motives and aspirations will be shaped by the ways in which they respond to it, probably adopting patterns of behavior traditionally observed more frequently among men …. However, there are areas of ambiguity, tensions and contradictions in the answer to these questions" (p. 84). By participating in a global market, gender ideologies are negotiated, recreated, and transformed. However, current insight into this topic is inconclusive. We know little about the construction of femininities and masculinities under changing market conditions. An understanding of the adaptable nature of gender representations and experiences are crucial for gaining insight into the transformation of families, and the emergence of new forms of the global social order.

As women and men are exposed to new images and forced to take on changed roles, traditional values and ways of doing things are questioned and reworked. In some places, and for some families, patriarchal assumptions and practices are slowly dissipating and being replaced by a form of gender convergence. This can result in the freeing up women from the double burden imposed by domestic and paid work. However, for other women, incorporation into markets and the exposure to globalized gender images, may lead to exploitation and gender-based practices. These contradictions can, ultimately, be explained by differential access to power and resources.

In order to gain greater insight into the complicated dynamics of these processes, we need critical analyses of market ideology and gender discourse. We also need to investigate how market processes are shaped by large powerful institutions and the extent to which these are gendered processes (Pyle 2005). However, in agreement with Sen (1995), I would argue that it is critical that analyses of the linkages between globalization and gender do not just portray women as "passive victims of cultural oppression and material forces, but instead emphasize, that however dispossessed and marginalized they may be, working-class and peasant women have a history of organizing themselves to combat violence and marginalization in creative and strategic ways……[it]is essential to enable women-especially those who own few resources other than their labor and who today are increasingly and miraculously surviving in greater numbers into old age-to grow old with pride and not simply be viewed as victims of cultural oppression" (p. 39). While so many contemporary approaches present women as "victims," constantly exploited by ever more greedy industries, a minority discourse reveals that complex, and, often contradictory factors are involved in understanding women's relationships to the global market place. For instance, under appropriate conditions, women's participation in the labor force in the industrial and developing world can open up a series of opportunities for them. However, it is impossible to generalize about this issue as it is primarily determined by context, and women's unique personal circumstances.

Crucial to understanding the relationship between globalization, gender, and the market domain, is the often neglected issue of paid and unpaid care work. As women the world over, enter into various forms of employment, care work, primarily relegated to the family sphere, becomes an increasingly complex and contentious issue. Care work transcends personal and political boundaries of government policy, family and the labor market (Browne and Braun 2008). As women, the world over, increasingly are incorporated into the market domain, the issues associated with care also take on a global nature. For example, Ehrenreich and Hochschild (2003) have suggested that as more affluent women in the industrialized world become increasingly integrated into the paid labor force, they respond to their double set of responsibilities by replacing their domestic labor through the bought services of women from less well-off societies. One critic of the current crisis in care, Parrenas (2003) has termed the contemporary condition as an international transfer of caretaking. She describes current care arrangements as a specific form of a transnational division of labor that connects women in an interdependent relationship.

Critics such as Hochschild, Ehrenreich, and Parrenas argue that this arrangement does not put enough pressure on men to change their contribution in the domestic domain. This argument, however, ignores contemporary realities where men themselves are struggling to make sense of an employment field in which they have become increasingly vulnerable and disposable. As families restructure themselves due to employment decisions and constraints combined with changes in roles, issues of reproductive care move to the foreground for both women and men. It may be useful to rethink the domestic domain and its responsibilities by not only emphasizing more equal responsibilities between partners, but also by recognizing that under certain conditions, services do need to be "bought." However, the provision of domestic services as paid employment, needs to occur under humane conditions. Nussbaum (2002) points out that "care must be supplied to those who need it, without exploiting the givers of care… at present in all nations of the world, this difficult social problem has not been solved" (p. 39, in Browne and Braun).

From a broader perspective, we need to consistently acknowledge that while some women and men have benefited from globalization, others have less control over their own lives and, few, if any, choices. For instance, gender-based discussions on equality, often ignore other parts of the world where women are often severely disadvantaged in their position vis a vis men. Particularly poor women do not have the same power to negotiate their relationships with their husbands – a right that so many contemporary Western women consider a fundamental aspect of being female. Nothing highlights this more so, than the current situation with respect to HIV/AIDS (UNICEF 2008). In Western countries, HIV/AIDS is primarily associated as a male disease, due to the greater acceptance of male homosexuality. However, in Africa and some parts of Asia, due to myths around the benefits of sex with virgins, as well as the prevalence of rape, prostitution, and the lack of governmental interference, HIV/AIDS is spreading primarily to women. For instance, in South Africa 24.8% of women have been contaminated versus 11.3% men and in Botswana, the figures are a staggering 34.3% for women and 15.8% for men (Edgar 2004). Global HIV/AIDS statistics are just one indicator of the highly vulnerable position of many girls and women around the globe. When HIV/AIDS statistics are combined with issues around exploitative work situations, and patriarchal family arrangements, gender issues rise to the forefront of significant social concerns in a globalized world.

Scholars also need to examine the relationship between women's and children's rights more closely. It is important to understand under what conditions do women and children rights coincide, and at what points should they be treated separately. Current debates treat women and children and their relationships to family conditions separately. However, in many areas of the world, both women and children share common interests and situations. We need to find new ways of supporting the most vulnerable members of every society, instead of characterizing certain groups as worthy of attention and others as not.

10.5 Harnessing the Forces of Globalization

Globalizing forces channeled in an appropriate manner, may provide tools for vulnerable individuals, to negotiate their circumstances and come together collectively to enact change. The first step in this process is to expose underlying concerns and issues, and emphasize the significance of power relationships. By utilizing Bourdieu's concept of an economy of practice, we need to recognize that all human activity is tied to social power, and that different sets of practice have different values depending on the social field (Bourdieu 1991). Every social field is constructed and reconstructed in relation to its own evolution through time and space, and in relation to the actors who function within these domains. Institutions and individuals relate to one another according to relative accumulations of capital, by attempting to maximize and strategically employ their power and control within their arenas. By making power and an economy of practice central to the social analyses of globalization processes, we can begin to understand the complicated and fluid processes through which various forms of femininities and masculinities are socially and culturally constructed, and the extent to which markets and economics are interrelated with family decisions (Chow 2003). As Folbre (2001) emphasizes "Markets cannot function effectively outside the framework of families and communities built on values of love, obligation, and reciprocity." (p. vii).

The recent focus on gender and market participation highlights the debate around channeling the impacts of globalization. Currently, the primary controversy, with respect to globalization, is not that our ability to communicate with each other at a rapid pace has improved, or that we can travel with ease between countries, or that economic changes have accelerated. Instead for many, the primary concern is that the gains made through globalization are distributed inequitably between nation-states, and between the individuals and families who reside in these places. We are currently faced with a situation where there are protections in place for the flow of capital, but that same concern has not been accorded to those individuals who actually perform the labor (Heymann 2006). In fact, in order to compete and profit in the global marketplace, some countries are offering their labor at the cheapest possible price. This competitive edge stems through the provision of extremely low salaries, few, if any, safeguards for workers, and the lack of opportunities to unionize (Heymann 2006). Globalization, in and of itself, is not inherently a negative process. However, it is the disregard for its interaction with social conditions that has led to a sense of disarray, discontent, and, at times, extreme human cost.

Issues of poverty and inequalities, within and between societies, will continue to sharply influence societal instability, migration flows and labor force demands. This suggests that power relations and the access to resources remain the foundational elements in understanding significant aspects of globalization. As we all become increasingly incorporated into a globalized system, awareness grows about the disparities between groups. Even just this consciousness about perceived inequities, is a critical factor for social unrest. This context, in combination with a fundamental human social morality, highlights the need for measures that would provide some security for the world's most vulnerable individuals. While there is selected interest in regulating the global movement of finance capital, and lessening the extreme poverty of developing countries, we are still faced with mounting disparities between groups.[4] If the post-World War II welfare-state is not as functional anymore, as is argued by many, then what is needed is a new vision for an innovative path forward, both in the industrialized and developing world. Despite its flaws, the welfare-state provides a fundamental safety net for its citizens, and, especially, its most vulnerable populations. Moreover, nation-states still retain power

---

[4] Under growing pressure, the IMF and World Bank have begun to institute measures to raise the standard of living for citizens of the poorest of the developing countries. However many of these initiatives are criticized due to their over reliance on Western ideas, which may actually have detrimental effects in local contexts. See Kingfisher (2002) for a wide ranging set of examples.

with respect to domestic policies, even in a globalizing world. They are the entity that is able to institute provisions that alleviate social conditions, and they act as a broker between transnational entities and their citizens. Nation-states are also in the position to ensure that work that is carried out in their purview complies with basic standards of humanity. They retain the power to, concurrently, encourage the oversight of policies that restructure work places. Reconceptualizing aspects of nation-states may provide a primary vehicle to mediate social conditions that affect families in the global order.

It is imperative to realize that the same forces that are producing a globalized economy, can also be harnessed to put in place standards that guarantee the humane treatment of individuals, at their places of work, as well as in their home lives.

As we move forward, it is time to reexamine the basic principles on which we are building our societies. We should be asking ourselves if *all* individuals should not have the right to earn a decent living wage, access parental leave, be able to take care of sick and disabled family members, work under safe conditions and within a set amount of hours, and access proper nutrition and medical care. This is not to imply that all wealth needs to redistributed or that individuals should not be rewarded for exhibiting talent or productivity. Instead, as a *global* community we need to advocate setting a minimal standard or foundation which guarantees a basic safety net for all. Some of this work is already underway. A number of transnational entities, as well as private charitable organizations have undertaken initiatives to improve the wellbeing of the world's most vulnerable populations. Globalization, in all its dimensions, allows us to explore and to expand global solutions to global problems.

10.6   The Continued Significance of Families

Despite arguments to the contrary, a multilevel analysis of globalization indicates that we are not living in a "runaway" world, nor are families disappearing or decaying. Our global social order may be in the process of transformation, but history indicates that this is a significant aspect of the human condition. Globalization highlights the worldwide nature of social changes due to the ease with which information is relayed in contemporary times. Moreover, a critical often unrecognized aspect of contemporary discourse that focuses on family change, is its emphasis on individualism. This is a unique Western point of view, deriving much of its legitimacy from psychology. For much of the world, and even for most Western individuals, decisions are made in family contexts. The decisions to partner, to have children, to take up employment, to move, and to care for the young, the elderly, and the disabled, are usually arrived at in a social context between intimate individuals. Moreover, macro-social conditions such as poverty and racial or ethnic discrimination mitigate personal agency. For many individuals, families provide a refuge where they can come together to find emotional, social, and / or economic support. It is often within the family domain that individuals are able to negotiate strategies that allow them to cope with external circumstances.

Empirical evidence from around the globe indicates that families continue to be a primary resource for acquiring social and economic capital. Approaches to families that assume that decision-making and the acquisition of social capital are purely individualistic, discount the social nature of human life. For instance, in the West, the family that a child is born into continues to be a significant determinant for young people's future prospects, as they navigate ever more choices with respect to education, employment, travel, and partnerships. Families also continue to be a central domain for childhood socialization, for social integration, and for providing resources and social capital. In fact, some scholars argue that Western families are actually gaining in importance with respect to children's future chances. This perspective deems the socio-economic status of a child's parents as a critical indicator of his or her future success (Lareau 2003; Edgar 2004). In other regions of the world, families continue to play a critical role for almost every type of choice and behavior that individuals engage in. Life chances are at times virtually completely determined by family positioning, and by larger forces such as religion, politics, gender ideologies, economic circumstances, and the legal system. Under those conditions, individual actors may still exercise some agency, albeit in a very limited manner. Moreover, in certain societies cultural traditions dictate that significant personal decisions need to be arrived at in a collectivistic familial environment that is very difficult for those who were not raised within those contexts to comprehend.

The decisions that are made in a familial context have enormous significance for macro-processes. For instance, national fertility rates and labor force participation are dependent in great part on internal family dynamics. Women and men decide to have children and to join the labor force not just based on personal inclination, but most often weigh their choices against a number of factors that will affect the group as a whole. As we have seen, evidence from various countries in Europe, for example, indicates that a woman's fertility is directly related to her opportunities for maintaining lucrative employment while bearing and raising a child. This decision, made at the familial level, has had marked outcomes for nation-states facing an impending increase in the number of elderly, and an insufficient number of individuals in the labor force. This is not to suggest that there are not times when individuals do not pursue choices that primarily advantage themselves, nor to downplay the reality that conflicting power dynamics may be at work in domestic scenarios. However, neither should we assume that individual decisions are arrived at in a social and ideological vacuum, and that most individuals, even in the contemporary Western context, make choices just based on free will. Instead, choices, decisions, and negotiations occur at the family level and take into account a spectrum of material, emotional and ideological factors. From this perspective, that which occurs on the familial level is in a constant dynamic relationship with those processes that are often deemed as superceding social life.

10.7   Concluding Thoughts

Globalization has had highly differential impacts. As information travels at an ever accelerating pace, and an increasing number of individuals migrate across the globe, new ideas and multicultural configurations are increasingly becoming the norm. These varied ideological representations and lived experiences, are not occurring effortlessly, however. Instead, in every society, traditional assumptions about family relationships, gender roles, and issues around identity, ethnicity, and belonging are being questioned and renegotiated. For some families, globalization has resulted in greater access to resources and opportunities and has led to progress in their lives. For example, for more affluent groups in industrialized and develop- ing countries, globalization has translated into new opportunities for lifestyles, business, travel, contact with others, access to information, and communication technologies, and opportunities to draw on new ideas, beliefs, and traditions. Globalization has allowed individuals to reshape their identities and to link with like-minded individuals in wider social networks. Globalization has also sensitized individuals, families, and communities to the importance of understanding other peoples' and culture's points of view. However for others, globalization has had deleterious effects. Globalization has been translated into greater poverty, disloca- tion and marginalization. It has separated family members, drawn individuals in and out of the workforce, and transformed critical care relationships. In this work, I have illustrated that it is not globalization, per se that is to "blame." Instead, glo- balization interacts with local forces and conditions, and across localities.

As we attempt to comprehend the relationship between globalization, families, and social transformation, it is critical that we remain aware that changes are not unidirectional, that they occur in fits and starts, and that they often involve uneven negotiations. The outcome of most globalizing processes is not clear due to the con- stantly accelerating nature of the progression, and the accompanying transformations. While, as has been argued, globalization privileges some, it also constrains others. On the one hand, globalization is associated with the power of the large, the dominant, and the influential. Nonetheless, inherent in these same processes is the potential to empower those individuals, families, and groups that are marginalized, ignored, and forgotten. They are now able to circulate their ideas, complaints, and suggestions in a global arena, not bound by territory, citizenship, gender, ethnicity, race or other such defining criteria. It is this power of global communication and organizing that will determine much of what happens in the future, with respect to social change. As Kellner (2002) eloquently suggests, "Thus, rather than just denouncing globalization or engaging in celebration and legitimation, a critical theory of globalization reproaches those aspects that are oppressive while seizing opportunities to fight domi- nation and exploitation and to promote democratization, justice, and a progressive reconstruction of the polity, society, and culture." (p. 294).

Globalization is accompanied by an unprecedented means to undertake globalized collective action. While many analysts view globalization with suspicion, that perspective disregards the *potential* of globalization to be harnessed for the good of mankind. For instance, political organizing over the Internet has forced major multinationals such as Nike to reexamine its production and employment practices. Environmental issues and human rights have also been the subject of similar forms of cooperative clashes and associations. These trends portend new forms of organizing and influential effects on the social order. Significantly, they transform the context in which families and their members make decisions that affect their lives.

Globalization and the global financial system with which the process is so often associated are created by individuals. These activities are set into motion based on a series of choices, and do not just posit an inevitable last stage in social evolution. Instead, many of the social phenomena that accompany globalization can be alleviated through informed public policy choices. This is a critical point because historical precedent illustrates that when one group becomes subordinated to another, transformations eventually lead to unexpected social change. As Coontz elucidates, the conditions that "constantly transform the institution, idea or relationship that originally gave them birth.....In families as well as in social formations, the same processes that are essential to maintain a particular relationship or institution simultaneously create oppositions that eventually transform, undermine, or even destroy it." (p. 291).

As this book has illustrated, families continue to reformulate and redefine themselves and their activities in innovative, and, at times, controversial ways. It is within families that the social processes and transformations associated with globalization are realized and acted upon. These transformations do not portend as has been argued by some social observers, that families are disappearing or that we are experiencing the final postmodern stage of social evolution. Instead, the significance of family arrangements for so many individuals *around* the globe, indicate that the idiom and lived experience of family within a globalized world, continues to be strong, adaptable, and of primary significance for individuals. Most people still choose to maintain close relationships by living in small bonded units, bound by ties of affection and / or economics. These groups may dissolve at times or be reconceptualized depending on context and inclination and yet, individuals continue to pursue some form of close attachment to others. We may be in the midst of a profound transformation, but as history has taught us human beings and the social institutions they create are constantly evolving. Families, however they are delineated, are part of this progression. Globalization promises to lead us into a new future that may look quite different from that which we currently imagine.

References

Ackroyd, J., & Pilkington, A. (1999). Childhood and the construction of ethnic identities in a global age: A dramatic encounter. *Childhood, 6* (4), 443–454.

Afshar, H., & Barrientos, S. (1999). *Women, globalization and fragmentation in the developing world*. London: Macmillan.

Aisbett, E. (2007). Why are the critics so convinced that globalization is bad for the poor? In A. Harrison (Ed.), *Globalization and poverty* (pp. 33–85). Chicago: University of Chicago Press.

Aitken, S. (2001). Global crises of childhood: Rights, justice and the unchildlike child. *Area, 33*, 119–127.

Aitken, S., Estrada, S. L., Jennings, J., & Aguirre, L. (2006). Reproducing life and labor: Global processes and working children in Tijuana, Mexico. *Childhood, 13*, 365–387.

Alanen, L. (2003). Childhoods: The generational ordering of social relations. In B. Mayall & H. Zeiher (Eds.), *Children in generational perspective* (pp. 27–45). London: Institute of Education.

Albrow, M. (1997). Traveling beyond local cultures: Socioscapes in a global city. In J. Eade (Ed.), *Living the global city: Globalization as local process* (pp. 37–55). London: Routledge.

Ambert, A. (1994). An international perspective on parenting: Social change and social constructs. *Journal of Marriage and the Family, 56*, 529–543.

Ansell, N. (2005). *Children, youth and development*. New York: Routledge.

Appadurai, A. (1990). Disjuncture and difference in the global cultural economy. In M. Featherstone (Ed.), *Global culture: Nationalism, globalization and modernity*. London: Sage.

Appadurai, A. (1999). Globalization and the research imagination. *International Social Science Journal., 51*, 229–238.

Archard, D. (1993). *Children: Rights and childhood*. New York: Routledge.

Aries, P. (1962). *Centuries of childhood: A social history of family life*. New York: Alfred A. Knopf.

Arnett, J. J. (2002). The psychology of globalization. *American Psychologist, 57*, 774–783.

Arno, P. (2006). *The economic value of informal caregiving*. Paper presented at the Veterans Association Conference on Care Coordination, Bethesda, 25 January.

Asis, M., Huang, S., & Yeo, B. (2004). When the light of the home is abroad: Unskilled female migration and the Filipino family. *Singapore Journal of Tropical Geography, 25*, 198–215.

Baars, J. (2006). Beyond neomodernism, antimodernism, and postmodernism: Basic categories for contemporary critical gerontology. In J. Baars, D. Dannefer, C. Phillipson & A. Walker (Eds.), *Aging, globalization and inequality: The new critical gerontology* (pp. 17–42). Amityville, NY: Baywood Publishing.

Baars, J., Dannefer, D., Phillipson, C., & Walker, A. (2006). Introduction: Critical perspectives in social gerontology. In J. Baars, D. Dannefer, C. Phillipson & A. Walker (Eds.), *Aging, globalization and inequality: The new critical gerontology* (pp. 1–16). Amityville, NY: Baywood Publishing.

Baca Zinn, M. (2000). Feminism and family studies for a new century. *Annals of the American Academy of Political Science Society, 571*, 42–56.

Bacallao, M., & Smokowski, P. (2007). The costs of getting ahead: Mexican family system changes after immigration. *Family Relations, 56*, 52–66.

Barnett, R. C., & Hyde, J. S. (2001). Women, men, work, and family: An expansionist theory. *American Psychologist, 56*, 781–796.

Barnett, R. C., & Garesi, K. C. (2002). Full-time and reduced-hours work schedules and marital quality: A study of female physicians with young children. *Work and Occupations, 29*, 364–379.

Basu, K. (2006). Globalization, poverty, and inequality: What is the relationship? What can e done? *World Development, 34*, 1361–1373.

Becker, G. (1976). *The economic approach to human behavior*. Chicago: The University of Chicago Press.

Becker, G. (1985). Human capital, effort, and the sexual division of labor. *Journal of Labor Economics, 3*, 33–58.

Becker, G. (1993). *Human capital* (3rd ed.). Chicago: The University of Chicago Press.

Becker, S. (2000). Young careers. In M. Davies & M. Davies (Eds.), *The Blackwell encyclopedia of social work* (p. 378). Oxford: Blackwell.

Becker, S., & Silburn, R. (1999). *We're in this together: Conversations with families in caring relationships*. London: Carers National Association.

Becker, S. (2007). Global perspectives on children's unpaid caregiving in the family: Research and policy on 'young carers' in the UK, Australia, the USA and Sub-Saharan Africa. *Global Social Policy, 7*, 23–50.

Beneria, L. (2003). *Gender, development and globalization: Economics as if all people mattered*. London: Routledge.

Bernal, B. (1994). Gender, culture, and capitalism: Women and the remaking of Islamic 'tradition' in a Sudanese village. *Comparative Studies in Society and History, 36*, 36–67.

Berger, B. (2002). *The family in the modern age: More than a lifestyle choice*. New Brunswick, NJ: Transaction Publishers.

Berkowitz, S. D., & Wellman, B. (2003). *Social structures: A network approach*. Toronto: Canadian Scholars' Press.

Bernhardt, E., Goldscheider, C., Goldscheider, F., & Bjeren, G. (2007). *Immigration, gender and family transitions to adulthood in Sweden*. Boulder, CO: University Press of America.

Bhagwati, J. (2004). *In defense of globalization*. New York: Oxford.

Bianchi, S. Milkie, M. A., Sayer, L.C. (2000). Is anyone doing the housework–trends in the gender division of household labor. *Social Forces*, 79:1 191–228

Bianchi, S., Robinson, J., & Mikie, M. (2007). *Changing rhythms of American family life*. New York: Russell Sage Foundation.

Blossfeld, M., & Hofmeister, H. (2005). *Globalife: Lifecourses in the globalization process*. Bamberg: University of Bamberg Press.

Bogenschneider, K., & Corbett, T. (2004). Building enduring family policies in the 21st century: The past as prologue? In M. Coleman & L. Ganong (Eds.), *Handbook of contemporary families: Considering the past, contemplating the future* (pp. 41–468). Thousand Oaks, CA: Sage Publications.

Booth, A., Crouter, A., & Landale, N. (eds). (1997). *Immigration and the family: Research and policy on U.S. immigrants*. Mahwah, NJ: Lawrence Erlbaum.

Boss, P. G., Dougherty, W. J., LaRossa, R., Schumm, W. R., & Steinmetz, S. K. (1993). Family theories and methods: A contextual approach. In P. G. Boss, W. J. Dougherty, R. LaRossa, W. R. Schumm & S. K. Steinmetz (Eds.), *Sourcebook of family theories and methods: A contextual approach* (pp. 3–30). New York: Plenum Press.

Bouis, H., Palabrica-Costello, M., Solon, O., Westbrook, D., & Limbo, A. (1998). *Gender equality and investments in adolescents in the rural Philippines*. Research Report 108, International Food Policy Research Institute.

Bourdieu, P. (1991). *Language and symbolic power*. J. B. Thompson (Ed.) Trans. M. Adamson. Cambridge: Polity Press.

Bourdieu, P., & Coleman, J. (1991). *Social theory for a changing society*. Boulder, CO: Westview Press.

Bowes, J. M. (2004). *Children, families, and communities: Contexts and consequences*. Melbourne: Oxford University Press.

Boyden, J. (1990). Childhood and the policy makers. A comparative perspective on the globalization of childhood. In Constructing and reconstructing childhood: Contemporary issues in he sociological study of childhood. Ed. A. James and A. Prout. Pp. 190–230. Routledge

Boyden, J. (1997). Childhood and the policy makers: A comparative perspective on the globalization of childhood. In A. James & A. Proust (Eds.), *Constructing and re-constructing childhood* (pp. 184–216). Basingstoke: Falmer Press.

Brady, D., Beckfield, J., & Zhao, W. (2007). The consequences of economic globalization for affluent democracies. *Annual Review of Sociology, 33*, 313–334.

Browne, C., & Braun, K. (2008). Globalization, women's migration, and the long-term-care workforce. *The Gerontologist, 48*, 16–24.

Brecher, J., Costello, T., & Smith, B. (2000). *Globalization from below: The power of solidarity*. Boston: South End Press.

Brenner, S. (1995). Why women rule the roost: Rethinking Javanese ideologies of gender and self-control. In A. Ong & M. Peletz (Eds.), *Bewitching women, pious men: Gender and body politics in Southeast Asia* (pp. 19–50). Berkeley: University of California Press.

Bruce, J., & Chong, E. (2006). The diverse universe of adolescents, and the girls and boys left behind: A note on research, program and policy priorities. Background paper to the report. *Public Choices, Private Decisions: Sexual and Reproductive Health and the Millennium Development Goals*. New York: UN Millennium Project.

Bryceson, D., & Vuorela, U. (2002). Transnational families in the twenty-first century. In D. Bryceson & U. Vuorela (Eds.), *The transnational family: New European frontiers and global networks* (pp. 3–30). New York: Oxford.

Bulato, R. A. (2001). Introduction. In R. A. Bulato & J. B. Casterline (Eds.), *Global fertility transition* (pp. 1–14). New York: Population Council.

Burr, R. (2002). Global and local approaches to children's rights in Vietnam. *Childhood, 9*, 49–61.

Carrington, V. (2001). Globalization, family and nation-state: Reframing 'family' in new times. *Discourse: Studies in the Cultural Politics of Education, 22*, 185–196.

Carrington, V. (2002). *New times: New families*. London: Kluwer Publishers.

Cassels, D., Hanen, M., Barber, A., & Chumir, S. (2002). *Community values in an age of globalization*. Calgary: Sheldon M. Chumir Foundation for Ethics in Leadership.

Castles, F. G. (2003). The world turned upside down: Below replacement fertility, changing preference and family-friendly public policy in 21 OECS countries. *Journal of European Social Policy, 13*, 209–228.

Castles, S., & Miller, M. (2003). *The age of migration: International population movements in the modern world*. New York: Guilford.

Castells, M. (1997). *The power of identity*. Oxford: Blackwell.

Castells, M. (2000). *The end of millennium*. Malden, MA: Blackwell.

Castells, M. (2004). *The power of identity* (2nd ed.). Oxford: Blackwell.

Cerny, P. G., & Evans, M. (2004). Globalization and public policy under new labour. *Policy Studies, 25*, 51–65.

Chang, G. (2006). Disposable domestics: Immigrant women workers in the global economy. In M. Zimmerman, J. Litt & C. Bose (Eds.), *Global dimensions of gender and carework* (pp. 39–47). Stanford: Stanford University Press.

Chant, S. (1991). *Women and survival in Mexican cities: Perspectives on gender, labour markets, and low-income households*. New York: Manchester University Press.

Chant, S. (2000). Men in crisis? Reflection on masculinities, work and family in north-west Costa Rica. *The European Journal of Development Research, 12*, 199–218.

Chen, S., & Ravallion, M. (2004). How have the world's poorest fared since the early 1980s? *The World Bank Research Observer, 19*, 141–169.

Chow, E. (2003). Gender matters: Studying globalization and social change in the 21st century. *International Sociology, 18*:3, 443–460

Chugani, H. T., Phelps, M. E., & Mazziota, J. C. (1987). Positron emission tomography study of human brain function development. *Annals of Neurology, 22*, 487–497.

Cigno, A., Rosati, F., & Guarcello, L. (2002). Does globalization increase child labor? *World Development, 30*, 1579–1589.

Clarke, J. (2005). Welfare states as nation states: Some conceptual reflections. *Social Policy and Society, 4*, 407–415.

Cole, J., & Durham, D. (2006). Introduction: Age, regeneration and the intimate politics of globalization. In J. Cole & D. Durham (Eds.), *Generations and globalization: Youth, age, and family in the new world economy* (pp. 1–28). Bloomington, IL: Indiana University Press.

Collier, J., Rosaldo, M., & Yanagisako, S. (1992). Is there a family? New anthropological views. In B. Thorne & M. Yalom (Eds.), *Rethinking the family: Some feminist questions* (pp. 25–39). New York: Longman.

Collins, P. H. (1990). *Black feminist thought: Knowledge, consciousness, and the politics of empowerment*. Boston: Unwin Hyman

Coltrane, S. (2000). Research on Household Labor: Modeling and Measuring the Social Embeddedness of Routine Family Work. *Journal of Marriage and Family, 62*, 4 1208–1233

Comacchio, C. (2003). Family History in *International Encyclopedia of Marriage and Family* (pp. 555–559). New York: Thompson Gale.

Connell, R. W. (2005). Change among the gatekeepers: Men, masculinities, and gender equality in the global arena. *Signs, 30*, 1801–1825.

Coontz, S. (1992). *The way we never were: American families and the nostalgia trap*. New York: Basic Books.

Coontz, S. (1997). *The way we really are: Coming to terms with America's changing families*. New York: Basic Books.

Coontz, S. (2000). Historical perspectives on family studies. *Journal of Marriage and Family, 62*, 283–297.

Cree, V. (2008). Confronting sex trafficking: Lessons from history. *International Social Work, 51*, 763–776.

Creed, G. (2000). "Family values" and domestic economies. *Annual Review of Anthropology, 29*, 329–355.

Crittenden, A. (2001). *The price of motherhood: Why the most important job in the world is the least valued*. New York: Macmillan.

Crompton, R., lewis, S., & C. Lyonette. (2007). *Women, men, work and family in Europe*. Palgrave: Macmillan

Cunningham, H. (1995). *Children in Western society since 1500*. London: Longman.

Cvetkovich, A., & Kellner, D. (1997). Thinking global and local. In A. Cvetkovich & D. Kellner (Eds.), *Articulating the global and the local: Globalization and cultural studies, 5* (pp. 1–32). Boulder, CO: Westview Press.

Daly, K. (2003). Family theory versus the theories families live by. *Journal of Marriage and Family, 65*, 771–784.

Dannefer, D. (2000). Bringing risk back in: The regulation of the self in the postmodern state. In K. W. Schaie & J. Hendricks (Eds.), *The evolution of the aging self: The societal impact on the aging process* (pp. 269–280). New York: Springer Publishing.

Dannefer, D. (2003). Cumulative advantage/disadvantage and the life course: Cross-fertilizing age and social science theory. *Journal of Gerontology, 58*, S327–S337.

Davis, S. G. (1997). *Space jam: Family values in the entertainment city*. Paper presented at the American Studies Annual Meeting. Washington, DC.

De Carvalho, M. (2001). *Rethinking family–school relations: A critique of parental involvement in schooling*. Mahwah, NJ: Lawrence Erlbaum.

Dehesa, G. (2007). *What do we know about globalization? Issues of poverty and income distribution*. Oxford: Blackwell Publishing.

Dion, K., & Dion, K. (2001). Gender and cultural adaptation in immigrant families. *Journal of Social Issues, 57*, 51–521.

Dollar, D. (2005). Globalization, poverty and inequality since 1980. *The World Bank Research Observer, 20*, 146–175.

Dollar, D., & Gatti, R. (1999). Gender inequality, income, and growth: Are good times good for women? *Policy Research Group on Gender and Development, Working Paper Series, no. 1.* Washington, DC: The World Bank.

Drago, R., & Golden, L. (2005). The role of economics in work–family research. In M. Pit-Catsouphes, E. Kossek & S. Sweet (Eds.), *The work and family handbook: Multi-disciplinary perspectives, methods and approaches* (pp. 267–282). Mahwah, NJ: Lawrence Erlbaum.

Drucker, P. F. (1993). *Post-capitalist society.* Oxford: Butterworth-Heineman.

Easterlin, R. (2000). The globalization of human development. *Annals of the American Academy of Political and Social Science, 570,* 32–48.

Edgar, D. (2004). Globalization and Western bias in family sociology. In J. Scott, J. Treas & M. Richards (Eds.), *The Blackwell companion to the sociology of families* (pp. 3–16). Malden, MA: Oxford University Press.

Ehrenreich, B., & Hochschild, A. (eds). (2003). *Global woman: Nannies, maids and sex workers in the new economy.* New York: Metropolitan Books.

Eisenstein, H. (2005). A dangerous liaison? Feminism and corporate globalization. *Science and Society, 69,* 487–518.

Elder, G. (1999). *Children of the great depression: Social change in life experiences.* Boulder, CO: Westview Press.

Ennew, J., & Morrow, V. (2002). Releasing the energy: Celebrating the inspiration of Sharon Stephens. *Childhood, 9,* 5–17.

Erikson, E. (1963). *Childhood and society.* New York: W.W. Norton.

Erickson, R. (2005). Why emotion work matters: Sex, gender and the division of household labor. *Journal of Marriage and Family, 67,* 337–351.

Esping-Andersen, G. (1990). *The three worlds of welfare capitalism.* Cambridge: Polity.

Esping-Andersen, G. (2000). The sustainability of welfare states into the twenty-first century. *International Journal of Health Services, 30,* 1–12.

Espiritu, Y. (1997). *Asian American women and men: Labor, laws, and love.* Sage: Thousand Oaks, CA.

Estes, C. (2006). Critical feminist perspectives, aging and social policy. In I. J. Baars, D. Dannefer, C. Phillipson & A. Walker (Eds.), *Aging, globalization and inequality: The new critical ger-ontology* (pp. 81–102). Amityville, NY: Baywood Publishing.

Evans, J. L., Myers, R. G., & Ilfeld, E. M. (2000). *Early childhood counts: A programming guide on early childhood care for development.* WBI Learning Resources Series. Washington, DC: World Bank.

Evans-Pritchard, E. E. (1940). *Some aspects of marriage and the family among the Nuer.* Rhodes-Livingstone Institute: Papers. 11.

Everard, J. (2000). *Virtual states: The Internet and the boundaries of the nation-state.* London: New York.

Fass, P. (2003). Children and globalization. *Journal of Social History, 36,* 963–977.

Fass, P. (2005). Children in global migration. *Journal of social history, 38.* 937–953

Ferree, M. (1991). The gender division of labor in two-earner marriages. *Journal of Family Issues, 12,* 158–180.

Fernández-Kelly M.P., (1997). Maquiladoras: the view from the inside. In Nalini Visvanathan, Lynn Duggan, Laurie Nisonoff & Nan Wiegersman (Eds.), *The women, gender and develop-ment reader* (pp. 203–250). London, England: Zed Books.

Flax, J. (1990). *Thinking fragments: Psychoanalysis, feminism, and postmodernism in the contem-porary West.* Berkeley: University of California Press.

Folbre, N. (2001). *The invisible heart: Economics and family values.* New York: The New Press.

Forna, J. (1995). *Cultural theory and late modernity.* Thousand Oaks, CA: Sage Publishers.

Forrest, M., & Alexander, K. (2004). The influence of population demographicsL What does it mean for teachers and teacher education? *Journal of family and consumer sciences education, 22*(2), 67–73.

Fountain, J. (2001). *Building the virtual state: Information technology and institutional change.* Washington, DC: Brookings Institution Press.

Fouron, G., & Glick Schiller, N. (2001). All in the family: Gender, transnational migration, and the nation-state. *Identities: Global Studies in Culture and Power, 7*, 539–582.

Freeman, C. (2001). Is local: Global as feminine: Masculine? Rethinking the gender of globalization. *Signs, 26*, 1007–1037.

Freeman, R. (1996). The new inequality. Boston: *Boston Review*. December/January.

Freeman, R. (2006). People flows in globalization. *The Journal of Economic Perspectives, 20*, 145–170.

French, J. L., & Woktuch, R. E. (2005). Child workers, globalization, and international business ethics: A case study in Brazil's export-oriented shoe industry. *Business Ethics Quarterly, 15*, 615–640.

Frones, I. (1994). Dimensions of childhood. In J. Qvortrup, M. Bardy, G. Sgritta & M. Wintersberger (Eds.), *Childhood matters: Social theory, practice and politics* (pp. 145–164). Avebury Press: Aldershot.

Fussel, M. E. (2000). Making labor flexible: The recomposition of Tijuana's macquiladora female labor force. *Feminist Economics, 6*, 59–80.

Fyfe, A. (1993). *Child labor: A guide to project design*. Geneva: ILO.

Galinsky, E. (1999). *Ask the children: What America's children really thing about working parents*. New York: William Morrow.

Ganguly-Scrase, R. (2003). Paradoxes of globalization, liberalization, and gender equality. The worldviews of the lower middle class in West Bengal, India. *Gender & Society, 17*, 544–566.

George, V., & Wilding, P. (2002). *Globalization and human welfare*. London: Palgrave.

Geertz, C. (1973). *The interpretation of cultures*. New York: Basic Books.

Gibson, C. B., & Cohen, S. G. (2003). *Virtual teams that work creating conditions for virtual team effectiveness*. In Jossey-Bass Business and Management Series (p. 464). Jossey-Bass.

Giddens, A. (1990). *The consequences of modernity*. Stanford: Stanford University Press.

Giddens, A. (1991). *Modernity and self-identity*. Cambridge: Polity Press.

Giddens, A. (2003). *Runaway world: How globalization is reshaping our lives*. New York: Routledge.

Gilligan, C. (1982). *In a different voice: Psychological theory and women's development*. Cambridge: Harvard University Press.

Giovannetti, E., Kagami, M., & Tsuji, M. (2003). *The internet revolution: A global perspective*. Cambridge: Cambridge University Press.

Glatzer, M., & Rueschemeyer, D. (2005). *Globalization and the future of the welfare state*. Pittsburgh: University of Pittsburgh Press.

Glewwe, P. (1999). *The economics of school quality investments in developing countries: An empirical study of Ghana*. London: Macmillan.

Goode, W. (1982). *The theoretical importance of the family. The Family Pp. 1–14*. Englewood Cliffs, NF.: Prentice Hall

Goody, J. (1972). Evolution of the family. In P. Laslett & R. Wall (Eds.), *Household and family in past time: Comparative studies in the size and structure of the domestic group over the last three centuries in England, France, Serbia, Japan, and colonial North America* (pp. 103–124). Cambridge: Cambridge University Press.

Graham, C. (2005). *Globalization, poverty, inequality and insecurity: Some insights from the economics of happiness*. WIDER Research Paper no. 2005/33.

Gramsci, A. (1985). *Selections from cultural writings*. D. Forgacs & G. Nowell-Smith (Eds.) Trans. W. Boelhower. Cambridge: Harvard University Press.

Grew, R. (2005). On seeking global history's inner child. *Journal of Social History, 38*, 849–858.

Guillen, M. F. (2001). Is globalization civilizing, destructive, or feeble? A critique of five key debates in the social science literature. *Annual Review of Sociology, 27*, 235–260.

Gupta, A., & Ferguson, J. (1997). *Culture, power, place: Explorations in critical anthropology*. Durham, NC: Duke University Press.

Gupta, A., & Sharma, A. (2006). Globalization and postcolonial states. *Current Anthropology, 47*:2 277–307

Gunewardena, N., & Kingsolver, A. E. (2007). *The gender of globalization: Women navigating cultural and economic marginalities.* New York: School for Advanced Research Press.

Hadi, A. (1999). Overseas migration and the well-being of those left behind in rural communities of Bangladesh. *Asia-Pacific Population Journal, 14,* 43–58.

Hareven, T. (1974). The family as process: The historical study of the family cycle. *Journal of Social History, 7,* 322–329.

Hareven, T. (2000). The history of the family and the complexity of social change. In T. Hareven (Ed.), *Families, history, and social change: Life-course and cross-cultural perspectives* (pp. 3–30). Boulder, CO: Westview Press.

Harrison, A. (2007). *Globalization and poverty.* Chicago: University of Chicago Press.

Hartmann, H. (1981). The family as the locus of gender, class and political struggle: The example of housework. *Signs, 6,* 366–394.

Hartmann, H. (1987). Changes in women's economic and family roles in post-World War II United States. In L. Beneria & C. Stimpson (Eds.), *Women, households, and the economy* (pp. 33–64). New Brunswick, NJ: Rutgers University Press.

Hattery, A. (2001). *Women, work and family: Balancing and weaving.* London: Sage.

Hecht, T. (1998). *At home in the street: Street children of Northeast Brazil.* Cambridge: Cambridge University Press.

Held, D., & McGrew, A. (2001). The great globalization debate: An introduction. In D. Held & A. McGrew (Eds.), *The global transformation reader* (pp. 1–45). Oxford: Polity Press.

Hengst, H. (1987). The liquidation of childhood – an objective tendency. *International Journal of Sociology, 17,* 58–80.

Heymann, J. (2006). *Forgotten families: Ending the growing crisis confronting children and working parents in the global economy.* Oxford: Oxford University Press.

Hirst, P., & Thompson, G. (1996). *Globalization in question.* Oxford: Polity Press.

Hochschild, A. R. (1989). *The second shift: Working parents and the revolution at home.* New York: Viking.

Hochschild, A. R. (1997). *The time bind: When work becomes home and home becomes work.* New York: Metropolitan Books.

Hochschild, A. R. (2001). Global care chains and emotional surplus value. In A. Giddens & W. Hutton (Eds.), *On the edge: Living with global capitalism* (pp. 130–146). London: Vintage.

Hodge, D. (2008). Sexual trafficking in the United States: A domestic problem with transnational dimensions. *Social Work, 53,* 143–1152.

Hoffman, D. M. (2003). Childhood ideology in the United States: A comparative cultural view. *International Review of Education, 49,* 191–211.

Hoffman, D. M., & Zhao, G. (2007). Global convergence and divergence in childhood ideologies and the marginalization of children. *Education and Society, 25,* 57–75.

Hondagneu-Sotelo, P. (1992). Overcoming patriarchal constraints: The reconstruction of gender relations among Mexican immigrant women. *Gender & Society, 6,* 393–415.

Hondagneu-Sotelo, P. (1994). *Gendered transitions: Mexican experiences of immigration.* Berkeley: University of California Press.

Hondagneu-Sotelo, P. (1997). "I'm here, but I'm there." The meanings of Latina transnational motherhood. *Gender & Society, 11,* 548–571.

Hondagneu-Sotelo, P. (2000). Feminism and migration. *The Annals of the American Academy of Political and Social Science, 571,* 107–120.

Hondagneu-Sotelo, P. (ed). (2003). *Gender and U.S. immigration: Contemporary trends.* Berkeley: University of California Press.

Hoogvelt, A. (1997). *Globalization and the postcolonial world: The new political economy of development.* Baltimore: Johns Hopkins University Press.

Hooyman, N., & Kiyak, A. (2006). *Social gerontology.* Boston: Allyn & Bacon.

Hossfeld, K. J. (1994). Hiring immigrant women: Silicon Valleys 'Simple Formula'. InWomen of color in U.S. society. Eds. Maxine Baca Zinn and Bonnie T.d Dill, Temple University Press. Pp. 65–93

Human Development Report. (1999). In *United Nations Development Programme*. New York: Oxford

ILO (International Labor Organization). (2002). Progressive elimination of child labor at http://www.ilo.org/public/english/standards/relm/ilc/ilc87/rep-i.htm#.

International Organization for Migration. (2005). *World migration 2005: Costs and benefits of international migration, no. 882-22*. Geneva: International Organization for Migration.

IPEC (International Program on the Elimination of Child Labor). (2004). *Investing in every child: An economic study of the costs and benefits of eliminating child labour*. Geneva: International Labor Organization.

Jayakody, R., Thornton, A., & Axinn, W. (2008). Perspectives on international family change. In R. Jayakody, A. Thornton & W. Axinn (Eds.), *International family change: Ideational perspectives* (pp. 1–18). New York: Lawrence Erlbaum Publishers.

Joseph, S. (2005). Teaching rights and responsibilities: Paradoxes of globalization and children's citizenship in Lebanon. *Journal of Social History, 38*, 1007–1026.

Kabeer, N. (2000). *The power to choose: Bangladesh women and labor market decisions in London and Dhaka*. London: Verso.

Katz, C. (1993). Growing girls/closing circles: Limits on the spaces of knowing rural Sudan and US cities. In C. Katz & J. Monk (Eds.), *Full circles: Geographies of women over the life course* (pp. 88–106). New York: Routledge.

Katz, C. (2004). *Growing up global: Economic restructuring and children's everyday lives*. Minneapolis: University of Minneapolis Press.

Kellner, D. (2002). Theorizing globalization. *Sociological Theory, 20*, 285–305.

Kelly, M. (1991). Delicate transactions: Gender, home, and employment among Hispanic women. In F. Ginsburg & A. Tsing (Eds.), *Uncertain terms: Negotiating gender in American culture*. Boston: Beacon Press.

Kelly, R. M. (2001). *Gender, globalization and democratization*. Lanham, MD: Rowman & Littlefield Publishers.

Kibria, N. (1993). *Family tightrope: The changing lives of Vietnamese Americans*. Princeton, NJ: Princeton University Press.

Kim, K., Bengtson, V., Myers, G., & Eun, K. (2000). Aging in East and West at the turn of the century. In V. Bengtson, K. Kim, G. Myers & K. Eun (Eds.), *Aging in East and West: Families, states and the elderly* (pp. 3–16). New York: Springer.

King, M. (1999). *Moral agendas for children's welfare*. New York: Routledge.

King, N., & Calasanti, T. (2006). Empowering the old: Critical gerontology and anti-aging in a global context. In J. Baars, D. Dannefer, C. Phillipson & A. Walker (Eds.), *Aging, globalization and inequality: The new critical gerontology* (pp. 139–158). Amityville, NY: Baywood Publishing.

Kingfisher, C. (2002). *Western welfare in decline: Globalization and women's poverty*. Philadelphia, PA: University of Pennsylvania Press.

Kinsella, K., & Phillips, D. (2005). Global aging: The challenge of success. *Population Bulletin, 60*(1), 1–40.

Kjorholt, A. T. (2002). Small is powerful: Discourses on 'children and participation' in Norway. *Childhood, 9*, 63–82.

Kuznesof, E. (2005). The house, the street, global society: Latin American families and childhood in the twenty-first century. *Journal of Social History, 38*, 859–872.

Lamanna, M. A. (2002). *Emile Durkheim on the family*. Thousand Oaks, CA: Sage Publications.

Lareau, A. (2003). *Unequal childhoods: Class, race and family life*. Berkeley: University of California.

Lee, W. (2001). *Parents must read, 223*, 13–14

Levi-Strauss, C. (1956). The family. In H. Shapiro (Ed.), *Man, culture and society*. New York: Oxford University Press.

Levison, D. (2000). Children as economic agents. *Feminist Economics, 6*, 125–134.

Levitt, T. (1991). *Thinking about management*. Toronto: New York Free Press.

Lieber, R., & Weisberg, R. (2002). Globalization, culture and identities in crisis. *International Journal of Politics, Culture and Society, 16*, 273–296.

Lim, L. (1998). *The sex sector. The economic and social basis of prostitution in South East Asia.* Geneva: ILO.

Lowell, B., Findlay, A. M., & Stewart, E. (2004). *Brain strain: Optimising highly skilled migration from developing countries.* Asylum Working Paper 4, Institute for Public Policy.

Lutz, H. (2002). At your service madam? The globalization of domestic service. *Feminist Review, 70*, 89–104.

Macleod, A. (1993). *Accommodating protest: Working women, the new veiling and change in Cairo.* New York: Columbia University Press.

Mahler, S., & Pessar, P. (2006). Gender matters: Ethnographers bring gender from the periphery toward the core of migration studies. *International Migration Review, 40*, 27–63.

Malkki, L., & Martin, E. (2003). Children and the gendered politics of globalization: In remembrance of Sharon Stephens. *American Ethnologist, 30*, 216–224.

Marchand, M., & Runyan, A. S. (2000). Introduction. Feminist sightings of global restructuring: Conceptualizations and reconceptualizations. In M. Marchand & A. S. Runyan (Eds.), *Gender and global restructuring: Sightings, sites and resistances* (pp. 1–22). London: Routledge.

Marcus, R., Wilkinson, J., & Marshall, J. (2002). Poverty reduction strategy papers (PRSP): Fulfilling their potential for children in poverty? *Journal of International Development, 14*, 1117–1128.

Masnick, G., & Bane, M. J. (1980). *The nation's families.* Boston: Auburn House.

Mattingly, D. (2001). The home and the world: Domestic service and international networks of caring labor. *Annals of the Association of American Geographers, 91*, 370–386.

McGraw, L., & Walker, A. (2004). Gendered family relations: The more things change, the more they stay the same. In M. Coleman & L. Ganong (Eds.), *Handbook of contemporary families: Considering the past, contemplating the future* (pp. 174–191). Thousand Oaks, CA: Sage Publications.

McMichael, P. (1996). Globalization: Myth and realities. *Rural Sociology, 61*, 25–55.

Mensch, B., Ibrahim, B., Lee, S., & El-Gibaly, O. (2000). Socialization to gender roles and marriage among Egyptian adolescents. *Studies in Family Planning, 34*, 8–18.

Mintz, S., & Kellogg, S. (1988). *Domestic revolutions: A social history of American family life.* New York: Free Press.

Mittleman, J. (2002). Globalization: An ascendant paradigm? *International Studies Perspectives , 3*, 1–14.

Mittleman, J. H., & Tambe, A. (2000). Global poverty and gender. In J. H. Mittleman (Ed.), *The globalization syndrome* (pp. 74–89). Princeton: Princeton University Press.

Murdock, G. 1949. Social structure. New York: Macmillan

Moen, P. (1989). *Working parents: Transformation in gender roles and public policies in Sweden.* Madison: Univ. of Wisconsin Press.

Moen, P., & Schorr, A. L. (1987). Families and social policy. In M. B. Sussman & S. K. Steinmetz (Eds.), *Handbook of marriage and the family* (pp. 795–813). New York: Plenum.

Moen, P., & Sweet, S. (2003). Time clocks: Work-hour strategies. In P. Moen (Ed.), *It's about time: Couples and careers.* Ithaca: Cornell University Press.

Moghadam, V. (2003). A political explanation of the gendered division of labor in Japan. In M. Marchand & A. Runyan (Eds.), *Gender and global restructuring: Sightings, sites and resistances* (pp. 99–115). London: Routledge.

Mortgan, K., & Zippel, K. (2003). Paid to care: The origins and effects of care leave policies in Western Europe. *Social Politics: International Studies in Gender, State, and Society, 10*, 49–85.

Murdock, G. (1949). *Social Structure.* New York: Macmillan

Myers, W. E. (2001). The right rights? Child labor in a globalizing world. *The Annals of the American Academy of Political and Social Science, 575*, 38–55.

Nagar, R., Lawson, V., McDowell, L., & Hanson, S. (2002). Locating globalization: Feminist re-readings of the subjects and spaces of globalization. *Economic Geography, 78*, 257–284.

Neal, M., & Hammer, L. (2007). *Working couples caring for children and aging parents. Effects on work and well-being.* Mahwah, NJ: Lawrence Erlbaum.

Nieuwenhuys, O. (1994). *Children's lifeworlds: Gender, welfare and labor in the developing world.* London: Routledge.

Nissanke, M., & Thorbecke, E. (2005). *The impact of globalization on the world's poor: Transmission mechanisms.* Paper presented at the WIDER Jubilee Conference in Helsinki.

NRCIM (National Research Council and Institute of Medicine). (2005). *Growing up global: The changing transitions to adulthood in developing countries.* Washington, DC: National Academies Press.

New York Times. In Booming Gulf, Some Arab Women find freedom in the skies. December 22, 2008 http://www.nytimes.com/2008/12/22/world/middleeast/22abudhabi.html?pagewanted=all.

Nussbaum, M. (2002). Long-term-care and social justice. In World Health Organization (Ed.), *Ethical choices in long-term care: What does justice require?* (pp. 31–66). New York: World Health Organization.

Okin, S. M. (1989). *Justice, gender and the family.* New York: Basic Books.

Oldman, D. (1994). Adult–child relations as class relations. In J. Qvortrup, M. Bardy, G. Sgritta & H. Wintersberger (Eds.), *Childhood matters: Social theory, practice and politics* (pp. 43–58). Aldershot: Avebury Press.

Ong, A. (1999). *Flexible Citizenship: The cultural logics of transnationality.* Durham. Duke University Press.

Ong, A., & Peletz, M. (1995). Introduction. In A. Ong & M. Peletz (Eds.), *Bewitching women, pious men: Gender and body politics in Southeast Asia* (pp. 1–18). Berkeley: University of California Press.

Ong, A. (1987). *Spirits of resistance and capitalist discipline: Factory women in Malaysia.* Albany, NY: State Univ. of New York Press

Orellana, M., Thorne, B., Chee, A., & Lam, W. (2001). Transnational childhoods: The participation of children in processes of family migration. *Social Problems, 48,* 572–591.

Orozco, M. (2002). Globalization and migration: The impact of family remittances in Latin America. *Latin American Politics and Society, 44,* 41–66.

Ortner, S. (1990). Gender hegemonies. *Cultural Critique, 15,* 35–80.

Osmond, M. W., & Thorne, B. (1993). Feminist theories: The social construction of gender in families and society. In P. G. Boss, W. J. Doherty, R. LaRossa, W. R. Schumm & S. K. Steinmetz (Eds.), *Sourcebook of family theories and methods: A contextual approach* (pp. 591–622). New York: Plenum Press.

Oswald, L. (2003). Branding the American family: A strategic study of the culture, composition, and consumer behavior of families in the new millennium. *The Journal of Popular Culture, 37,* 309–335.

Palkovitz, R. J. (2002). *Involved fathering and men's adult development: Provisional balances.* Hillsdale, NJ: Lawrence Erlbaum Press.

Parasuraman, S., & Greenhaus, J. H. (2002). Toward reducing some critical gaps in work–family research. *Human Resource Management Review, 12,* 299–312.

Parkin, R., & Stone, L. (2004). General introduction. In R. Parkin & L. Stone (Eds.), *Kinship and family. An anthropological reader* (pp. 1–24). Malden, MA: Blackwell.

Parrenas, R. S. (2003). The care crisis in the Philippines: Children and transnational families in the new global economy. In B. Ehrenreich & A. R. Hochschild (Eds.), *Global woman: Nannies, maids, and sex workers in the new economy* (pp. 39–55). New York: Metropolitan Books.

Parrenas, R. S. (2001). *Servants of globalization: Women, migration and domestic work.* Palo Alto: Stanford University Press.

Parrenas, R. S. (2005). The international division of reproductive labor: Paid domestic work and globalization. In R. P. Applebaum & W. I. Robinson (Eds.), *Critical globalization studies* (pp. 237–248). New York: Routledge.

Parsons, T. (1943). The contemporary kinship system of the United States. *American Anthropologist, 45,* 22–38.

Parsons, T. (1949). The social structure of the family. In R. Anshen (Ed.), *The family: Its function and destiny* (pp. 173–201). New York: Harper.

Parsons, T., & Bales, R. (1955). *Family, socialization and interaction process.* Glencoe, IL: Free press.

Pearson, R. (2000). Moving the goalposts: Gender and globalization in the twenty-first century. *Gender and Development, 8*, 10–19.

Penn, H. (2002). The World Bank's view of early childhood. *Childhood, 9*, 118–132.

Perry-Jenkins, M., & Folk, K. (1994). Class, couples, and conflict: Effects of the division of labor on assessment of marriage in dual-earner families. *Journal of Marriage and Family, 56*, 165–180.

Perry-Jenkins, M., & Turner, E. (2004). Jobs, marriage, and parenting: Working it out in dual-earner families. In M. Coleman & L. Ganong (Eds.), *Handbook of contemporary families: Considering the past, contemplating the future* (pp. 155–173). Thousand Oaks: Sage Publishers.

Pessar, P.R (1982). The role of households in international migration and the case of U.S. bound migration from the Dominican Republic. *International Migration Review, 16*, 342–364.

Pessar, P. (1999). Engendering migration studies: The case of new immigrants in the United States. *American Behavioral Scientist, 42*, 577–600.

Pessar, P., & Mahler, S. (2003). Transnational migration: Bringing gender in. *International Migration Review, 37*, 812–846.

Peterson, P. (1999). Gray dawn: The global aging crisis. *Foreign Affairs, 78*, 42–55.

Phillipson, C. (2006). Aging and globalization: Issues for critical gerontology and political economy. In J. Baars, D. Dannefer, C. Phillipson & A. Walker (Eds.), *Aging, globalization and inequality: The new critical gerontology* (pp. 43–58). Amityville, NY: Baywood Publishing.

Ping, H. (2001). Talking about gender, globalization and labor in a Chinese context. *Signs: Journal of Women in Culture and Society, 26*, 1278–1281.

Piotrkowski, C. S., Rapoport, R. N., & Rapoport, R. (1987). Families and work. In M. Sussman & S. Steinmetz (Eds.), *Handbook of marriage and the family* (pp. 251–283). New York: Plenum.

Pocock, B. (2003). *The work/life collision*. Sydney: The Federation Press.

Polivka, L. (2001). Globalization, population aging and ethics. *Journal of Aging and Identity, 6*, 147–163.

Popenoe, D. (1993). American family decline, 1960–1990: A review and appraisal. *Journal of Marriage and the Family, 55*, 527–555.

Porter, A. (1996). Global villagers: The rise of transnational communities. *The American Prospect, 2*, 74–77.

Prakash, A., & Hart, J. (2000). Coping with globalization: An introduction. In A. Prakash & J. Hart (Eds.), *Coping with globalization* (pp. 1–26). London: Routledge.

Punch, S. (2004). The impact of primary education on school-to-work transitions for young people in rural Bolivia. *Youth and Society, 36*, 163–182.

Pyle, J., & Ward, K. (2003). Recasting our understanding of gender and work during global restructuring. *International Sociology, 18*, 461–489.

Pyle, J. (2005). Critical globalization and gender studies. In R. Applebaum & W. Robinson (Eds.), *Critical globalization studies* (pp. 249–258). London: Routledge.

Rapoport, R., Lewis, S., Bailyn, L., & Gambles, R. (2005). In S. Poelmans (Ed.), *Work and family: An international research perspective* (pp. 463–484). Mahwah, NJ: Lawrence Erlbaum.

Rattansi, A., & Westwood, S. (eds). (1994). *Racism, modernity, and identity: On the Western front.* Cambridge: Polity Press.

Ravallion, M. (2003). The debate on globalization, poverty and inequality: Why measurement matters. *International Affairs, 79*, 739–753.

Ravallion, M. (2004). Competing concepts of inequality in the globalization debate. *World Bank Policy Research Working Paper 3243*. Washington: World Bank.

Reynolds, P., Nieuwenhuys, O., & Hanson, K. (2006). Refractions of children's rights in development practice: A view from anthropology. *Childhood, 13*, 291–302.

Richards, M. (1998). The meeting of nature and nurture and the development of children: Some conclusions. In C. Panter-Brick (Ed.), *Biosocial perspectives on children, The Biosocial Society Symposium Series 10* (pp. 131–146). Cambridge: Cambridge University Press.

Ritzer, G. (2003). Rethinking globalization: Glocalization/grobalization and something/nothing. *Sociological Theory, 21*, 193–208.

Robertson, R. (1995). Glocalization: Time–space and homogeneity–heterogeneity. In M. Fetherstone, S. Lash & R. Robertson (Eds.), *Global modernities* (pp. 25–44). London: Sage.

Robertson, R., & Khondker, H. H. (1998). Discourses of globalization: Preliminary considerations. *International Sociology, 13*(1), 25–40.

Robinson, W. (1998). Beyond nation-state paradigms: Globalization, sociology, and the challenge of transnational studies. *Sociological Forum, 13*, 561–594.

Robson, E. (2004). Hidden child workers: Young carers in Zimbabwe. *Antipode, 36*, 227–248.

Rodrik, D. (1997). *Has globalization gone too far?*. Washington, DC: Institute for International Economics.

Rollins, J. (1985). *Between women: Domestics and their employers*. Philadelphia: Temple University Press.

Rosenau, J. (2003). *Distant proximities: Dynamics beyond globalization*. Princeton: Princeton University Press.

Rosenau J.N. (1997) The complexities and contradictions of globalization. *Current History*, 360–364

Ruhs, M., & Chang, H. (2004). The ethics of labor immigration policy. *International Organization, 58*, 69–102.

Ruddick, S. (2003). The politics of aging: Globalization and the restructuring of youth and childhood. *Antipode, 35*, 334–362.

Rudra, N. (2008). *Globalization and the race to the bottom in developing countries: Who really gets hurt*. Cambridge: Cambridge University Press.

Rumbaut, R. (1997). Ties that bind: Immigration and immigrant families in the United States. In A. Booth, A. Crouter & N. Landale (Eds.), *Immigration and the family: Research and policy on U.S. immigrants* (pp. 3–46). Mahwah, NJ: Lawrence Erlbaum.

Rumbaut, R. (2006). Ages, life stages, and generational cohorts: Decomposing the immigrant first and second generations in the United States. *International Migration Review, 38*, 1160–1205.

Rust, L. (1993). How to reach children in stores: Marketing tactics grounded in observational research. Part 2. *Journal of Advertising Research, 33*(6), 67–72.

Sacks, K. (1989). Toward a unified theory of class, race, and gender. *American Ethnologist, 16*(3), 534–550.

Safa, H. (2002). Questioning globalization: Gender and export processing in the Dominican Republic. *Journal of Developing Societies, 18*, 11–31.

Santarelli, E., & Figini, P. (2002). Does globalization reduce poverty? Some empirical evidence for the developing countries. *Understanding globalization, employment and poverty reduction*. Working Paper for the International Labour Office (ILO) Project.

Sassen, S. (1994). *Cities in a world economy*. Thousand Oaks, CA: Pine Forge/Sage Press.

Sassen, S. (2002). *Global networks, linked cities*. New York: Routldege.

Sassen, S. (2003). Strategic instantiations of gendering in the global economy. In P. Hondagneu-Sotelo (Ed.), *Gender and U.S. immigration: Contemporary trends* (pp. 43–60). Berkeley: University of California Press.

Sassen, S. (2006). Global cities and survival circuits. In M. Zimmerman, J. Litt & C. Bose (Eds.), *Global dimensions of gender and carework* (pp. 30–38). Stanford: Stanford University Press.

Scholte, J. A. (2000). *Globalization: A critical introduction*. New York: St. Martin's Press.

Scott, J. W. (1989). History in crisis: The others' side of the story. *American Historical Review, 94*, 680–692.

Scott, J. W. (1993). Women's history: New perspectives on historical writing. In L. Kauffman (Ed.), *American feminist thought at century's end* (pp. 234–257). London: Blackwell.

Segalen, M. (1986). *Historical anthropology of the family*. Cambridge: Cambridge University Press.

Seguino, S. (2000). Accounting for gender in Asian economic growth: Adding gender to the equation. *Feminist Economics, 6*, 27–58.

Sen, A. (2002). Globalization, inequality and global protest. *Development, 45*, 11–16.

Sen, K. (1995). Gender, culture and later life: A dilemma for contemporary feminism. *Gender and Development, 3*, 36–42.

Seward, E. (1978). *The American family: A demographic history*. Beverly Hills, CA: Sage.

Sherif, B. (1996). Unveiling the Islamic family: Concepts of family and gender among middle class Muslim Egyptians. Unpublished Dissertation Thesis, University Microfilms.

Sherif, B. (1999). Gender contradictions in families: Official vs. practical representations among upper middle-class Muslim Egyptians. *Anthropology Today, 15*, 9–13.

Sherif-Trask, B. (2006). Families in the Islamic Middle East. In B. Ingoldsby & S. Smith (Eds.), *Families in global and multi-cultural perspective* (pp. 231–246). Thousand Oaks, CA: Sage Publishers.

Smith, J., & Johnston, H. (Eds.). (2002). Globalization and resistance: Transnational dimensions of social movements. Lanham, Maryland.

Smith, D. E. (1993). The standard North American family: SNAF as an ideological code. *Journal of Family Issues, 14*, 50–65.

Smith, R. (2004). Globalization, individualization and childhood: The challenge for social work. *New Global Development, 20*, 71–77.

Spain, D., & Bianchi, M. (1996). *Balancing act: Motherhood, marriage, and employment among American women*. New York: Sage.

Stack, C. (1974). *All our kin*. New York: Harper & Row.

Stacey, J. (1996). *In the name of the family: Rethinking the family in the postmodern age*. Boston: Beacon Press.

Standing, G. (1999). Global feminization through flexible labor: A theme revisited. *World Development, 27*, 583–602.

Stephens, S. (1992). Children and the UN Conference on environment and development: Participants and media symbols'. *Barn/Research on Children in Norway, 2–3*, 44–52.

Stephens, S. (1994). Children and the environment: Local worlds and global connections. *Childhood, 2*, 1–21.

Stephens, S. (1995). Introduction: Children and the politics of culture in 'late capitalism'. In S. Stephens (Ed.), *Children and the politics of culture* (pp. 3–48). Princeton: Princeton University Press.

Stephens, N. D. (1998). Contested childhoods in a changing global order. Approved Mellon Foundation Sawyer seminar proposal. Advanced Study Center of the International Institute, University of Michigan, Ann Arbor, MI.

Stiglitz, J. (2002). *Globalization and its discontents*. New York: W.W. Norton.

Suarez-Orozco, C., & Suarez-Orozco, M. (2001). *Children of immigration*. Cambridge: Harvard.

Sun, J. (2005). *Global connectivity and local transformation: A study of space and culture in post 1980 Shanghai (China)*. Dissertation. University of Illinois at Chicago.

Sullivan, O. (2006). *Changing gender relations, changing families: Tracing the pace of change over time*. New York: Rowman & Littlefield Publishers.

Talbot, M. (2000). The New Counter Culture: Fundamentalist Christians." *New York Times Magazine, 27*, 16.

Talcott, M. (2003). Gendered webs of development and resistance: Women, children and flowers in Bogota. *Signs: Journal of Women in Culture and Society, 29*, 465–489.

Trask, B. S., & Hendriks, S. (2009). Building the foundations. *Because I am a girl. The state of the world's girls, 2009*. London: Plan UK.

Thomas, G. S. (1998). *The United States of suburbia*. Amherst, NY: Prometheus Press.

Thomas, W. I., & Znaniecki, F. (1918–1920). *The polish peasant in Europe and America*, vols. 1–2. Urbana: University of Illinois Press.

Thompson, L., & Walker, A. (1989). Gender in families: Women and men in marriage, work and parenthood. *Journal of Marriage and the Family, 51*, 845–871.

Thorne, B. (1982). Feminist rethinking of the family: An overview. In B. Thorne & M. Yalom (Eds.), *Rethinking the family: Some feminist questions* (pp. 1–24). New York: Longman.

Tomlinson, J. (1999). *Globalization and culture*. Chicago: University of Chicago Press.

Tourraine, A. (1990). The idea of revolution. In M. Featherstone (ed.). *Global culture: Nationalism, globalization and modernity* (pp. 121–142). London: Sage

Townsend, N. (2002). *The package deal: Marriage, work and fatherhood in men's lives.* Philadelphia: Temple University Press.

Townsend, P. (2006). Policies for the aged in the 21st century: More 'structured dependency' or the realization of human rights? *Ageing & Society, 26,* 161–179.

UNICEF. (2008). United for children, united against AIDS. Fact sheet accessed 25 March 2009, http://www.uniteforchildren.org/resources_publications.html.

United Nations. (1999). *1999 Survey on the role of women in development: Globalization, gender and work.* UN Division for the Advancement of Women, New York: Department of Economic and Social Affairs.

Nations, U. (2000). *Female labor force participation.* New York: Department of Economic and Social Affairs.

Nations, U. (2002). *World population ageing: 1950–2050.* New York: Department of Economic and Social Affairs.

Nations, U. (2004). *World economic and social survey, 2004: Part 2. International migration.* New York: Department of Economic and Social Affairs.

United Nations (2008). http://esa.un.org.migration/index.asp?panel=1

United Nations Programme on the Family. (2003). *Families in the process of development: Major trends affecting families world-wide.* New York: Department of Economic and Social Affairs.

United States Census Bureau. (2005). *65+ in the United States: 2005.* Washington, DC: He, W., Sengupta, M., Velkoff, V., & DeBarros, K. Retrieved January 26, 2009 from http://www.census.gov/prod/2006pubs/p23-209.pdf

United States Census Bureau. (2008). *Statistical abstract of the United States: 2008.* Washington, DC: United States Government Printing Office.

Waddington, H. (2004). *Linking economic policy to childhood poverty: A review of the evidence on growth, trade reform and macroeconomic policy.* Chronic Poverty Research Center (CHIP) Report, no. 7, London: Save the Children.

Wade, R. H. (2004). Is globalization reducing poverty and inequality? *World Development, 32*(4), 567–589.

Waldinger, R., & Gilbertson, G. (1994). Immigrants' progress: Ethnic and gender differences among US immigrants in the 1980s. *Sociological Perspectives, 37*(3), 431–444.

Waters, M. (2001). *Globalization.* London: Routledge.

Watts, C., & Zimmerman, C. (2002). Violence against women: Global scope and magnitude. *Lancet, 359,* 1232–1237.

Weedon, C. (1987). *Feminist Practice and Poststructuralist Theory.* Oxford: B. Blackwell

Wellman, B. (1999). *Networks in the global village: Life in contemporary communities.* Boulder, CO: Westview Press.

West, C., & Zimmerman, D. (1987). Doing gender. *Gender & Society, 1,* 125–151.

Wharton, C. (1990). Reflections on poverty. *American Journal of Agricultural Economics, 72*(5), 1131–1138.

White, B. (1996). Globalization and the child labor problem. *Journal of International Development, 8,* 829–839.

White, L., & Rogers, S. (2000). Economic circumstances and family outcomes: A review of the 1990s. *Journal of Marriage and the Family, 62,* 1035–1051.

Woldehanna, T., Jones, N., & Tefera, B. (2008). The invisibility of children's paid and unpaid work: Implications for Ethiopia's national poverty reduction policy. *Childhood, 15,* 177–201.

Wollons, R. (2000). Introduction: On the international diffusion, politics and transformation of the kindergarten. In R. Wollons (Ed.), *Kindergartens and cultures: The global diffusion of an idea* (pp. 1–15). New Haven: Yale University.

Wong, P. L. K., & Ellis, P. (2002). Social ties and partner identification in Sino-Hong Kong international joint ventures. *Journal of International Business Studies, 33,* 267–289.

World Bank. (2000). *World development report, 2000–01: Attacking poverty.* New York: Oxford University Press.

World Bank. (2008). Migration and Remittances Factbook 2008. http://econ.worldbank.org/
WBSITE/EXTERNAL/EXTDEC/EXTDECPROSPECTS/0,,contentMDK:21352016~pageP
K: 64165401~piPK:64165026~thesitePK:476883~is CURL: Y, 00.html

Woronov, T. E. (2007). Chinese children, American education: Globalizing child rearing in contemporary China. In J. Cole & D. Durham (Eds.), *Generations and globalization: Youth, age,
and family in the new world economy* (pp. 29–51). Bloomington: Indiana University Press.

Wright, M. (1997). Crossing the factory frontier: Gender, place and power in the Mexican maquiladora. *Antipode, 29*, 278–302.

Yan, R., & Neal, A. (2006). The impact of globalization on family relations in China. *International
Journal of Sociology of the Family, 32*, 113–125.

Zarembka, J. (2003). America's dirty work: Migrant maids and modern-day slavery. In B.
Ehrenreich & A. Hochschild (Eds.), *Global woman: Nannies, maids and sex workers in the
new economy* (pp. 142–153). New York: Metropolitan Books.

Zimmerman, M., Litt, J., & Bose, C. (2006). Conclusion. In M. Zimmerman, J. Litt & C. Bose
(Eds.), *Global dimensions of gender and carework* (pp. 369–377). Stanford: Stanford
University Press.

Zhan, H., & Montgomery, R. (2003). Gender and elder care in China: The influence of filial piety
and structural constraints. *Gender & Society, 17*(2), 209–229.

Index

CPSIA information can be obtained at www.ICGtesting.com
Printed in the USA
LVOW012131271112

309061LV00002B/6/P